▼ MEDIA STUDIES

**Aquinas College
Learning Resources Centre**

'The material "hits the spot"! It's excellent, at last, to read Media Studies material appropriate for a pre-undergraduate audience.'

Patrick Russell, *George Abbot School*

'In ten years of teaching I haven't come across a Media textbook that comes near this one . . . Highly readable.'

Joanna Bailey, *St Brendan's Sixth Form College, Bristol*

This fully comprehensive and easy-to-use textbook covers all aspects of Media Studies for students at the pre-university level. It is particularly suited for students of the new A Level Media Studies syllabuses.

The authors, who are experienced teachers and examiners, introduce students step by step to the skills of reading media texts, and address key areas such as media technologies, media institutions and media audiences. Individual sections cover:

*   Introduction to Studying the Media * Study Skills * Reading Media Texts * Media Institutions * Media Audiences * Case Studies of News, Advertising and Music * Research and How to Do It * Preparing for Exams * Coursework and Production Guide.

Media Studies: The Essential Introduction will give students the confidence to tackle every part of an introductory media course. Its key features include:

*   Activities and further work * Practical assignments and exam questions * Further reading and a glossary of key terms * Case studies showing how theoretical ideas can be applied in everyday situations

Philip Rayner is a Senior Lecturer in Media Communications at Cheltenham & Gloucester College of Higher Education and Principal Moderator for A Level Media Studies. **Peter Wall** is a Chief Examiner and Principal Moderator for GCSE Media Studies and a Chair of Examiners for Media Studies A Level. **Stephen Kruger** is a Chief Examiner for Media Studies A Level and Head of Media Studies at Holland Park School.

MEDIA STUDIES

THE ESSENTIAL
INTRODUCTION

Philip Rayner, Peter Wall and
Stephen Kruger

London and New York

First published 2001
by Routledge
11 New Fetter Lane, London EC4P 4EE

Simultaneously published in the USA and Canada
by Routledge
29 West 35th Street, New York, NY 10001

Reprinted 2002

Routledge is an imprint of the Taylor & Francis Group

Typeset in Bell Gothic by Keystroke, Jacaranda Lodge, Wolverhampton
Typographic design by Dom Wright
Printed and bound in Great Britain by TJ International Ltd, Padstow, Cornwall

British Library Cataloguing in Publication Data
A catalogue record for this book is available from the British Library

Library of Congress Cataloging in Publication Data
Rayner, Philip, 1947–
    Media Studies: the essential introduction / Philip Rayner, Peter Wall, and Stephen Kruger.
        p. cm.
    Includes bibliographical references and index.
    1. Mass media. I. Wall, Peter. II. Kruger, Stephen, 1951– III. Title.
    P90 .R345 2001
    302.23–dc21   00–068970

ISBN 0–415–23610–X (hbk)
ISBN 0–415–23611–8 (pbk)

▼ CONTENTS

▼ FIGURE ACKNOWLEDGEMENTS

The authors and Routledge thank those who have kindly given permission to reproduce the following illustrations. Every effort has been made to locate copyright-holders of material although in some cases this has not been possible. Any omissions will be corrected in the next edition if the company is contacted.

1	Papuans watching *Grease*, courtesy *The Age*, Melbourne, and photographer Jason South	2
2	'Time spent – average media day' from *Radio Days 2* (1999), copyright Radio Advertising Bureau	8
3	'Which media are under threat and why?', copyright Michael Svennevig, University of Leeds	10
4	Printout of screen page for keyword enquiry on 'Media Studies', courtesy of Google Inc., Mountain View, California	25
5	Tribe advertisement, courtesy of Caroline Rieger, agency for Tribe perfume	31
6	Crossroads sign, courtesy Department of Transport	35
7	Dolce & Gabbana ad, courtesy Dolce & Gabbana	36
8	Protesters and police in Prague at the International Monetary Fund and World Bank meeting September 2000, courtesy Jorge Ordonez	46
9	*The Evil Dead II*, 1987, copyright Palace Pictures, courtesy Kobal Collection	47
10	Newsreader for ITV Evening News, Trevor McDonald, courtesy ITN	48
11	*Citizen Kane* plot segmentation, from *Film Art: An Introduction*, D. Bordwell and K. Thompson (1993), courtesy McGraw-Hill, USA	49
12	*Police Story*, 1985, director Jackie Chan. Copyright Golden Harvest, Hong Kong, Kowloon. Courtesy BFI	53
13	*Goodfellas*, 1990, copyright Paramount, courtesy Kobal Collection	55
14a	*Dixon of Dock Green*, courtesy BBC Picture Archive	60
14b, c	*The Bill*, courtesy Pearson Television Ltd	60
15	*Carry on Loving*, 1970, copyright Rank Corporation, courtesy Kobal Collection	64
16	*Wakefield Express*, 21 April 2000, Huddersfield-Sheffield v. Wildcats. Photo courtesy John Clifton	68

▼ PREFACE

The media have been the subject of academic study for over 70 years. However, it is only in the last decade that Media Studies as a subject has really come into the public's awareness.

Although there have been some ill-informed criticisms of the subject in recent years, Media Studies has proved to be increasingly popular and successful with students in schools and colleges. In the summer of 2000 over 15,000 students sat an A Level in Media Studies. In Higher Education there are approximately 35,000 students studying the media, of whom about 75 per cent, according to the National Graduate Employment Agency, will find media-related employment. Currently one ex-Media Studies student, Michael Jackson, heads Channel 4.

Part of the success and popularity of Media Studies has been due to the enthusiasm and hard work carried out by teachers in schools and colleges as well as the work of individuals at the examining boards. Over the years they have not only helped to establish the academic credibility and worth of the subject but have also worked to inspire students. We ourselves have all been involved in teaching and examining Media Studies for over 20 years.

One of the joys of studying the media is the way in which it can empower students both as consumers and as producers of the media. We hope that this sense of empowerment and our enthusiasm for the worth of Media Studies will be infectious to the readers. We have tried to write a book that is stimulating, accessible and relevant to both our readers' lives and to the new A and AS Level specifications that we have helped to design.

We have arranged the book around three main concepts: Reading the Media, Media Audiences and Media Institutions. At the end of each of these three parts there is an example (title sequences, magazines, cinema) that illustrates how the concepts addressed in each section can be applied to particular examples. We have also included three case studies on particular aspects of the media (News, Advertising and Pop Music) as well as a section on the essential skills we feel students need, such as carrying out research, undertaking production work and preparing for examinations.

Throughout the book there are suggestions for activities, further work and further reading. We hope that these will enable students and teachers to move beyond the written text and to engage with their own particular interests and experiences. Suggestions for further reading are intended to help students and teachers who wish to further develop particular issues and ideas. At the end of the book we have included a glossary of terms and a list of resources.

One of the joys, and one of the dilemmas, of writing about the media is the dynamic nature of the subject and the speed at which changes occur, whether it be in the development of new technology, changes in ownership or the latest 'cult' text. We therefore have a website where we offer further up-to-date information and links to other relevant sites.

We would also welcome readers' comments on both the book itself and the new AS and A Level specifications. You can contact us through our publishers.

Finally we would like to thank those who have helped and supported us in the writing of this book:

our families and partners
colleagues, friends and students
Moira Taylor, Juliane Tschinkel and the rest of the team at Routledge
Francine Koubel and all the other examiners, moderators and subject officers, both past and present
Jessica Dee at *Inside Soap*
Kelly Taylor
our copy editor, Sandra Jones.

Philip Rayner
Peter Wall
Stephen Kruger

▼ INTRODUCTION

It is rather a cliché today to say that the media are an important part of our lives – especially as often it is the media themselves who are saying as much.

It is true, however, that we live in a 'mediated' society (see section on Representation, p. 63) where many of our ideas about the world, knowledge of what is happening and, perhaps most importantly, values come from beyond our individual daily or immediate experience, usually via the media. Our ideas of the world are derived largely from the modern media which produce and 'package' versions of events and issues in their output and which we consume as part of our daily lives and situations. The media therefore have a very strong influence on us both as individuals and as a society.

In this introduction we want to consider why we should study the media and also offer some guidelines on how to study the media. Before we study the media in detail, it is useful to consider two basic questions:

- What do we mean by 'the media'?
- Why are the media important?

The first question is perhaps more easily answered than the second.

WHAT DO WE MEAN BY 'THE MEDIA'?

Although what constitutes the media and their products may change over time, we can identify certain key characteristics that seem to apply to all media products at any time in history. These basic characteristics can be summed up in the following general statements:

- The media reach a large number of people.
- The media, although centrally produced, are usually privately consumed.
- Media products are 'shared'.
- The media are controlled or 'regulated'.
- The media rely on sophisticated technology.
- The media are 'modern'.
- The media are expensive.

Figure 1 *Papuans watching* Grease

Let us now examine each of these in turn.

The media reach a large number of people

What counts as a 'large' number of people will vary depending upon the historical period. *The Times* used to sell about 7,000 copies a day in the early nineteenth century. This was a high circulation when we consider that there were no other major forms of media or mass communication. In July 1985 *Live Aid* was seen by 1.5 billion viewers in over 160 countries. Every day the Internet has a potential 'audience' of millions of people across the world. Most media products today are constructed to be consumed by large numbers of people.

Such large numbers of people, however, will be 'fragmented', divided up into various different groups, depending on the media concerned. They will also 'consume' the media in many different ways. Each media 'text' will nevertheless be aimed at a large number of people, in many cases many millions of people throughout the world. In Part 2 on Media Audiences (p. 109) we look in more detail at how this 'mass' audience is made up.

TEXT Although we usually associate this word with something that is printed or written, in media studies the term is used to refer to all media products. This can include television programmes and/or adverts, photographs, films either on video or in the cinema, newspaper articles (or the newspapers themselves), radio programmes and/or jingles, billboards, video games or web pages.

ACTIVITY . . .

Make a list of all the ways in which you are part of 'an audience'. Go through your list and for each occasion where you are part of an audience think about the setting, other activities that you might be doing at the same time, your companions at the time (if any) and any other factors that you think might be important. Can you identify any particular trends or patterns that might be significant or might influence your patterns of consumption?

Using the list above, consider the different types of text that you consume.

- Are they local or national?
- Who else might be consuming these texts at the same time as you?
- Again, are there any particular patterns or trends that you can identify?

Now carry out a more detailed survey of other people's patterns of consumption. You can design your own questionnaire or you might find the worksheet below of some help in deciding the sort of questions you might ask.

WORKSHEET . . .

WORKSHEET TO DETERMINE MEDIA CONSUMPTION PATTERNS

Newspapers:

- Which daily newspapers (if any) do they read?
- What sections of newspapers do they turn to first, and why?
- What sections do they never read, and why?
- What kinds of stories do they usually read and why?
- Do they, or someone else, buy the newspaper they read?

Magazines:

- What magazines (if any) do they buy regularly? Why?

- What sections of the magazines do they read and not read, and why?

Television:

- Approximately how many hours a week do they spend watching television?
- What times of day do they usually watch television?
- What programmes do they like best and why?
- What programmes do they dislike most and why?
- Do they watch alone or with others?
- If they watch with others, who decides what they will watch?

Radio:

- What stations do they like best and why?
- Approximately how many hours a week do they spend listening to the radio?
- What times of day do they usually listen to the radio?
- What stations do they dislike most and why?
- Do they listen alone or with others?
- Where do they listen to the radio?
- What other activities (if any) do they do whilst listening to the radio?

Cinema:

- What films, if any, have they seen at the cinema in the last month?
- What films have they seen in other places – for example, through video purchase or rental, satellite film channels (free or otherwise) or through video-on-demand?
- Who else watched the films with them?
- Who decided what films to watch?

Internet:

- How often do they access the Internet?
- Where do they access the Internet – at home, at college or school, or at work?
- What are the main sites that they access?
- What are the main reasons for accessing these sites – for example, for information, to make purchases, communicate with friends or for entertainment?
- What other activities (if any) do they do whilst accessing the Internet?

The media, although centrally produced, are usually privately consumed

This may appear to be a paradox, but one of the key characteristics of the media today is that, despite large audiences, consumption is still very much a personal experience. We still talk of 'family viewing'. There may be 18 million people watching a particular episode of *EastEnders*, but the experience will largely be individual and private. We usually watch television in the privacy of our own home with perhaps one or two other people or we may watch it alone in our bedroom whilst elsewhere in the house someone else is also alone, watching the same programme at the same time.

Many millions of people will have seen a film like *Titanic*, yet for each person their experience of the film is usually a personal and intimate one – even if we are part of an audience of 300 people all sitting together in the dark in the cinema.

We often consume the radio as individuals, carrying out other tasks, either at home or perhaps in the privacy of our car – in our own 'personal space'. The *Sun* newspaper may be read by over 12 million people each day, but for each person it is a private act, often carried out in a private and personal space (even in the lavatory!). Some commentators suggest that it is this sense of the media coming into our private worlds, our homes, and 'saturating' our daily lives that makes them so important.

MEDIA SATURATION   A term used to describe the way in which the media today 'saturate' all aspects of our lives and the extent to which our experience of the world is dominated by the media.

Yet we need to remember that media products are constructed like a production line in a factory, whether it is the newspaper, the television show or the Hollywood film. The distribution is also very centralised, whether it is the transmission of a television news bulletin across the whole country at one particular point in time, the fleet of lorries that deliver the newspapers to the newsagents, or the distribution of a film over a period of time to be shown at cinemas, on subscription television and eventually on video.

Media products are 'shared'

The media produce texts that are both popular – hence the high audience figures – and also 'shared' in the sense that they become part of our common culture. Today we are all familiar with the expression 'Phone a friend' – even those who do not regularly watch or have never seen the television show *Who Wants to Be a Millionaire?* will know the phrase, its origin and what it means. The phrase has become part of our daily vocabulary in the way that 'Good morning, have you used Pears Soap?' was in the late nineteenth century (see p. 237). Although the level of our particular knowledge may vary, almost everyone is familiar with the stories of the *EastEnders* characters Ricky and Bianca. Media images can become a common 'language' – across the world millions of people know about Luke Skywalker or Pocahontas or what MTV stands for. Although many commentators suggest that this 'colonisation' of the world's media by predominantly American companies and artefacts is damaging, it is again a sign of the media's power and the universality of its images. See, for example, Figure 1, which depicts some tribesmen in Papua New Guinea wandering around a television store and looking at an extract from the film *Grease*.

We are all very 'media literate' and share a sophisticated understanding of the 'language' of media images that are constantly being shown, repeated and referred to (see the subsection on Semiotics, p. 30).

KEY TERM

SEMIOTICS The study of signs and sign systems.

The media are controlled or 'regulated'

Perhaps because of the large audiences they attract, and the power, reach and popularity of the media, another key characteristic is the way in which the media are seen as being in need of control or regulation. Even in cases of media forms like the Internet, where there is some difficulty in deciding how actually to control and regulate it, there is nevertheless the desire to make rules about who has access and what is shown. (See subsection on Regulation and the BBFC, p. 188.)

Consider the number of dictatorial countries where the media are still largely controlled by the government as a means of 'controlling' the circulation of ideas and criticisms. One of the first things that often happens in a revolution is that the national media and communications centres are taken over, so that the new leaders can 'control' the messages that are transmitted. In this way they use the media to win the 'hearts and minds' of the people.

The media rely on sophisticated technology

Especially to produce and transmit the texts they produce. Even in today's world where media hardware is seemingly becoming smaller and more personalised (i.e. Walkmans, mobile phones or wristwatches with television receivers inside them), the media are still very dependent upon a highly sophisticated technology. We may perhaps take this level of technological sophistication for granted. However, it is important to consider the technology required to make the television programmes that may be seen on a wristwatch, or to download videos from the Internet, or to produce 'blockbuster' films or glossy magazines.

The media are 'modern'

The media are seen as being 'up to date' or 'modern' – or even 'postmodern' (see p. 14). Although we can trace newspapers back to the early 1700s when the *Daily Courant* (the first daily newspaper) was first printed, the media (as we understand the term today) are a very modern phenomenon. Increasingly it is part of any definition of the media that they respond to, and quickly incorporate, the most up-to-date innovations and trends such as the 'convergence' of communications, computing and telephone technologies. Today this means MP3 players, WAP phones, ADSL telephone lines, 200 digital television channels (many of them interactive), or digital radio.

The media are expensive

The media, partly because of the technology required to produce and distribute texts, are expensive and so tend to be owned either by large commercial companies, often multi-nationals (and, increasingly, American), or by state-owned or government organisations. This means that the media tend to be very centralised and a few companies have a lot of power and control in particular industries. (See the section on the Cinema, p. 206.) It also means that it can be very difficult for newcomers to set up and become successful. It is interesting to watch how 'new' media, like the Internet and dot.com companies, are being increasingly taken over by established companies that have already been financially successful in other areas of the media.

(In the section on Production Skills on p. 284, we offer some guidance on how to produce media images without the use of the complex, sophisticated and expensive equipment that most media companies use.)

ACTIVITY

The 'key characteristics' (p. 1) are our own suggestions, and you may disagree with them. You can 'measure' different types of media against this list of key characteristics to see how accurate it is. Can you suggest any other key characteristics that could be applied to all media?

WHY ARE THE MEDIA IMPORTANT?

The second question as to why we should study the media is perhaps more complicated. However, here is a list of some suggestions:

- The media tell us what is going on in the world.
- The media are a central part of our lives.
- The media are influential.
- Domestic media hardware has become an intrinsic part of our homes.
- The media are very profitable.

Let us look in more detail at each of these.

The media tell us what is going on in the world

The media are important because they tell us what's going on both in the world at large (natural disasters, wars, etc.) and at home (political and sporting events, star 'gossip', etc.). Try to imagine what life would have been like before broadcasting. Think about what we would know (or not know) of the world without television, radio, newspapers or the Internet.

The media are a central part of our lives

Think about how much time you spend being 'exposed' to the media's products every day and the different ways in which you 'use' the media. We turn to the media for entertainment, to relax after a hard day working. We use the media for information, whether it is to find out the latest cricket results, the weather tomorrow or what is happening in the rest of the world. Perhaps less willingly, we accept the media as a source of persuasion, most noticeably through advertising but also through campaigns like the 'drink/drive' ones at Christmas or political campaigns during an election.

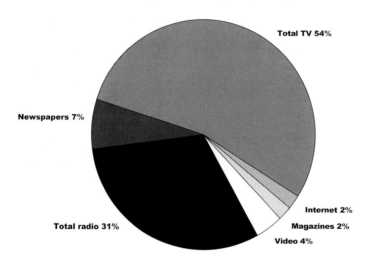

Time spent - average media day

Total TV 54%

Newspapers 7%

Internet 2%

Magazines 2%

Total radio 31%

Video 4%

Based on time spent x all those participating

Source: Radio Days 2.

Figure 2

The media are influential

Because the media are so much a central part of our daily lives, they obviously wield influence: however, it is not always clear what that influence is and whether it is good or bad (it is most probably a mixture of both). Often the media are blamed for many of the problems in today's society: violent films encouraging crime, sexual advice in teen magazines encouraging promiscuity (see p. 152), pin-ups in 'lads' ' magazines encouraging sexist attitudes, or tabloid newspapers running 'name and shame' campaigns, etc. (see section on News, p. 215).

Draw up a list of your own examples to show the influence of the media. Separate your list into negative and positive influences; positive influences could include encouraging healthier lifestyles, anti-drink/drive campaigns, charity promotions, etc.

We need to recognise that, despite the prevalence of the media in our lives, there are other influences that are as strong or even stronger. Family, education, religion, peer groups, all help to shape our ideas, values, beliefs and behaviour, and it is very difficult to isolate one factor and say that this, the media, caused that to happen. (See the page on the James Bulger case.)

Domestic media hardware has become an intrinsic part of our homes

One of the ways to understand the importance of the media in our everyday world is to think about the hardware we have in our homes for receiving the media's products. In Britain 99 per cent of all homes have at least one television set; although many homes nowadays have several, perhaps one in each bedroom as well as a communal one. About 30 per cent of British households are now considered to be 'multi-channel' homes, in other words they can received more than just the five terrestrial television channels. In Britain there are more radios than adults: for every 100 adults there are about 120 radios. In some parts of Africa one radio is shared between, on average, 18 adults and there are no television sets at all (often there is not even a reliable supply of electricity). Think about the rest of the technology that today we take for granted in our homes: VHS and DVD recorders, personal stereos for CDs and mini-discs as well as cassettes, mobile phones, personal computers and MP3 players. It is hard to imagine having a car without at least a radio, probably a cassette-player and, increasingly, a CD player.

Look around you next time you are in a town centre or on public transport and note the extent to which the media, both public and private, are present.

The media are very profitable

Companies and organisations like News International, Time-Warner, Disney, etc., exist to make a profit. They do not make films or produce newspapers because they are nice people who want to help us be entertained and/or better-informed. They make films like *Pocahontas* or print newspapers like the *News of the World* because they know that they will make large amounts of money. (See, for example, the section on Magazines, p. 147.) However, it is also important to realise that media organisations can often make mistakes and actually lose large amounts of money, for example the Kevin Costner film *The Postman*, the film *Honest* made by Dave Stewart and All Saints, or the publisher Dorling Kindersley when its tie-in books of *Star Wars Episode 1* failed to meet sales expectations, thereby bankrupting the company and causing a takeover by Pearson/Penguin.

ACTIVITY . . .

Look through the financial pages of newspapers to see what information is available about media companies. Access the websites of media companies to try to find out about their financial details or the amount of profit that they make.

THE CHANGING MEDIA WORLD

One of the difficulties in studying or writing about the media is that the media world is constantly changing. This change may be fairly superficial, for example in terms of what is this week's most controversial television programme or the current best-selling 'lads' ' magazine. Often, however, these changes are the result of developments in technology, and the rate of these technological changes is speeding up. One of the biggest changes taking place today in the media is the development of the Internet.

Figure 3 *Which media are under threat and why*

	Portability	Demands on attention	Choices available	Interactivity	Cost
Radio	High	Low	Wide	Low	Low
Newspaper	High	Medium	Wide	Low	Medium
Magazine	High	High	Wide	Low	High
Terrestrial TV	Low	Medium	Limited	Low	Low
Cable/satellite	Low	High	Wide	Medium	High
Video recorder (VCR)	Low	High	Wide	High	High
Video on demand (VOD)	Low	High	Wide	High	High
Internet/Web	Low	High	Wide	High	High
Future Internet/ Web	High?	Variable?	Wide?	High?	Low?

Notes: The basic premise is that the greater the difference in attributes between a medium and its rivals, the more likely that medium is to have a loyal audience/user base. Radio on this basis faces its main threat from print rather than from television-based media. In turn, the latter face the threat of the VCR and VOD.
Source: 'A neglected medium? The future role of radio', Michael Svennevig, University of Leeds

The Internet

The Internet has been described as a giant car-boot sale or an enormous feast. It is estimated that there are over 400 million easily accessible web pages available at present, plus several million more 'subscription' pages. In Britain it is estimated that by 2010 nearly 90 per cent of the population will have Internet access either at home, at work or through their schools and colleges.

NOTEBOX

The Internet was developed in America in the 1960s by the military, who wanted to protect the information contained on their computers. They worked with people from universities who soon took over the idea as a means of exchanging ideas and information. The Internet as we know it today came about through a variety of technological events that took place during the 1990s. These included the development of a common 'language' for computers to talk to each other and exchange data, the upgrading of telephone lines (which is still going on in Britain) to enable data to be sent quickly and easily from one computer to another, the availability of cheap, fast, domestic computing systems and software like those of Intel, AppleMac and Microsoft, and the growth of computer-literate people who could understand and use the software. Once the potential of the Internet was understood, large companies like Compuserve in America or Freeserve in Britain became involved and spent millions of pounds developing it as a consumer tool.

Increasingly we can talk of the Internet in the same way that we discuss other media forms – television, radio, newspapers, magazines, etc. The Internet also shares the same issues about who controls it, who owns it and how much it costs to access it.

In fact no one really owns the Internet, which is possibly part of its attraction. However, increasingly companies from the 'old' media are moving in and either setting up their own sites or buying up newly formed companies. For example, one of the earliest web-browsers was Netscape, who were bought by AOL (who merged with Compuserve), one of the biggest ISPs – Internet Service Providers. AOL then merged with Time-Warner, one of the world's largest media companies. It is often the established companies, like Time-Warner, EMAP or News International, who can afford the cost of setting up new websites, especially when they can see the opportunity for 'synergy', where the same or similar products can be sold or cross-marketed in more than one medium. Increasingly 'old' media brands now also have websites.

Radio stations have 'webzines' that complement the stations' output because they recognise that young people may well be listening to the radio while they 'surf' the Net and that both these activities are carried out in the privacy of their bedrooms. Chris Evans's Ginger Media Group owns Virgin Radio, Ginger Television which makes programmes like *TFI Friday* and *The Priory* (with Zoe Ball), in addition to Ginger Online which broadcasts output from Virgin Radio as well as offering news, music and e-commerce. In January 2000 Chris Evans sold the Ginger Media Group for £225 million to the Scottish Media Group, which owns newspapers and terrestrial television services in Scotland.

There have been opportunities for new companies to be established through the Internet. There has been a lot of publicity about dot.com companies such as lastminute.com or the company www.Revise.it, founded by two 20-year-olds, that 'publishes' GCSE revision guides. The company is said to be worth millions of pounds, but access to the site is free. Like many websites they make their money by charging advertisers who want to target their particular group of 'surfers', in this case 15-year-olds.

Issues about control are in many ways similar to the 'old media' issues: for example, how do you 'measure' the effects of material on the Internet and separate it from other influences? The main problem in terms of control is that the Internet is spread across the world and different countries have different laws. In France, for example, it is illegal to buy Nazi memorabilia, but in America there are sites that claim under the US 'Freedom of Information' Act the right to sell such merchandise. Is a French citizen who accesses an American site to buy this memorabilia breaking the law? There has also been a lot of debate regarding the downloading of music from websites like Napster using MP3 players.

Cases like Gary Glitter's have also highlighted the way in which the Internet can be used by members of subversive or illegal groups such as paedophiles. It is certainly true that the Internet is used by extreme right-wing groups as much as it is by left-wing groups or anti-GM protesters. We may agree with one group and not the other, and this may affect our view as to whether the Internet is a 'good thing' or not. The McLibel case is a good example of a small group of people who used the Internet to 'subvert' the power of a large American multinational. Although they lost the legal case and McDonald's were awarded damages, the 'McLibel 2' are considered to have 'defeated' McDonald's by publishing their evidence against McDonald's on the Internet and so winning the public relations battle and gaining many supporters worldwide (see www.mcspotlight.org). Increasingly, governments are trying to introduce laws that allow them to 'access' private email accounts in the same way that they might 'tap' telephone lines or intercept ordinary mail. Some countries like China and Saudi Arabia have tried to make accessing the Internet illegal but with limited success. In China the government has traditionally been able to control what news is available to the Chinese people. However, the Internet allows 'unauthorised' sites to distribute 'reactionary' information. Websites in China now have to be licensed by the government, which has closed down 'illegal' websites, but then these move to other countries where the Chinese government has no jurisdiction over them (see, for example, www.hrichina.org).

The Internet is still very new, and it is a little difficult to anticipate how it is going to grow or what effect it will have on our lives over the next 10 or 15 years. One of the biggest developments will be the 'convergence' of computer technology, telephone communications and television. Already it is possible to access the Internet through your digital television and mobile phone. Soon the computer will stop being a piece of office furniture and move into the living room. Eventually we may have one piece of hardware, 'an information appliance' that will provide voice telephone, email, fax, video and audio 'webcasts' and web surfing as well as the 'traditional' television channels. Some people now refer to the telephone as a 'portable data apparatus'. As the technology improves and Internet connection speeds increase, the quality of the images we can download will improve. There is speculation that soon we will be able to download films from the Internet, place them on recordable DVD (Digital Video Disc) and then play them on portable DVD players wherever and whenever we want. The 'in-flight' movie could be the one that we decided to bring along instead of relying on the airline's selection.

Many of these new forms of communication will be two-way or interactive as the telephone line will allow us, at home, to send signals back to the producers of these products. This is already happening to a limited extent through 'video-on-demand' experiments, and through television channels where we can select different camera angles, additional pieces of information or, in the case of *Sky News*, select which news story we want to watch.

It is hard to speculate on the extent to which this interactivity will affect the ways in which we consume the media. However, the new TiVo player/recorder is said to offer the potential for each 'viewer' to organise and select his own particular menu of entertainment. Instead of 'broadcasting' it will mean 'narrowcasting', in effect the 'old' mass audiences will become even more fragmented (see Media Audiences, p. 109).

TiVo is one of the newest set-top gadgets. It contains a computer hard-drive that stores up to 30 hours of television digitally and when played back it can skip advert breaks. Like a VCR it can record live or pre-programmed television and will also suggest particular programmes based on the owner's viewing habits. It is connected to the telephone so can send viewing information back to marketing firms (see pp. 197–8).

KEY TERM

Much of this 'technological revolution' is driven by companies who see it as an opportunity to sell us consumer products – games consoles, online services (both for goods and for services), 'edutainment' software on CD-ROM or DVD, and interactive and subscription services that we may be willing to pay extra for – as well as the hardware necessary to access them. 'TiVo' player/recorders will cost around £400 to buy, and viewers will also have to pay around £10 per month subscription plus possible extra 'pay-per-view' charges. The companies will be targeting those who can most easily afford to buy these new products. Those who cannot afford the new hardware or subscription charges will perhaps be excluded, and we will develop a 'digital underclass' or 'information rich–information poor' societies.

Currently most countries in the world have some kind of Internet activity, but it is only used regularly by about 5 per cent of the world's population – those who live in affluent, developed societies – and most of these users are white, male professionals.

The science of estimating how many are online throughout the world is an inexact one at best. Surveys abound, using all sorts of measurement parameters. However, from observing many of the published surveys over the last two years, here is an 'educated guess' as to how many are online worldwide as of December 2000. And the number is 407.1 million.

World total	407.10 million
Africa	3.11 million
Asia/Pacific	104.88 million
Europe	113.14 million
Middle East	2.40 million
Canada and US	167.12 million
Latin America	16.45 million

Source: Various
Compiled: Nua Internet Surveys, © Nua Ltd

Postmodernism

This is a term that is used a lot, although there is still some debate and uncertainty about what exactly 'postmodern' means, the value of the term and the extent to which we are living in a postmodern society (see, for instance, the essay 'Postmodernism and popular culture' by Dominic Strinati, 1995).

According to most art historians, 'modernism' was a movement that started in the late nineteenth century and ended around the 1960s. So 'postmodernism' is a term that is used to characterise the type of society and culture that has developed in western societies since the 1970s and into the beginning of the twenty-first century.

POSTMODERNISM refers to the social, political and cultural attitudes and images of the late twentieth and early twenty-first century.

The idea of postmodernism is partly based on a particular view of contemporary life – a high-tech, post-industrial society dominated by the 'flow' of media images and information around the world. It is claimed that we are increasingly living in a 'world time' where news, financial trading or sporting events are all transmitted 'live' around the world. It is possible to be at home in Birmingham on a Sunday morning and watch 'live' a Formula 1 car race as it takes place in Malaysia. We can trade money and shares around the world 24 hours a day. Enormous amounts of information and imagery can be distributed around the globe almost instantaneously and accessed by large numbers of

14

people in a way that would not have been possible 20 years ago. Increasingly we 'borrow' from other cultures for our music, furnishings, food, clothes, etc. What Marshall McLuhan called the 'global village' is increasingly becoming a reality.

Postmodernism is also said to reflect modern society's insecurities and uncertainties concerning identity, history, progress and truth, and the break-up of those traditional agencies like religion, the family or, perhaps to a lesser extent, class, which helped identify and shape who we are and our place in the world. Artists like Madonna, Michael Jackson and David Bowie are all cited as examples of postmodernism in the ways in which they have created or re-created different identities for themselves.

According to some theorists, our identity is now defined by our lifestyle and what we consume rather than by what we produce or by our background.

Jean-François Lyotard in *The Postmodern Condition* (1979) suggests that what he called 'meta-narratives' or grand theories like religion, Marxism, capitalism or science, no longer have the same importance in our lives. The concept of progress – the certainty that the developments of the arts, technology, medicine and knowledge would be moving inevitably towards a 'greater good' – is now seen to be questionable. Progress is seen by some as a way of controlling people and, using examples like CCTV or the government's reading of private emails, as 'spying' on ordinary citizens.

One of the films often cited as 'postmodern' is Ridley Scott's *Blade Runner* (1982), in which science, technology and progress are all questioned and shown in some way to have 'failed'. The world in *Blade Runner* is polluted by industry and overcrowding; only the rich escape to the 'off-worlds'. One of the key themes of the film is the 'blurring' of the differences between the real and the artificial, between the humans and the replicants. Increasingly it is no longer possible to be clear about what it means to be 'human'.

Another media text described as postmodern is David Lynch's television programme *Twin Peaks* (1990). A characteristic of postmodernism is the way in which 'high' art and popular culture are mixed together, and in *Twin Peaks* we can see an example of popular culture (the television 'whodunnit'/soap-opera) mixed with 'high art' (the work of film director David Lynch that includes films such as *Eraserhead* (1977), *The Elephant Man* (1980) and *Blue Velvet* (1986)). *Twin Peaks* also 'blurs' the distinction between various genres of television programme by being in part cop-show, part comedy and part Gothic horror, amongst others.

SIMULACRA Simulations or copies that are replacing the 'real' artefacts.

KEY TERM

Another key idea of postmodernism is that of 'simulacra', a term introduced by Jean Baudrillard who used it to explain the way in which simulations or copies are replacing the 'real' artefacts. Examples might include theme parks, 'fake' Irish or Australian pubs or American-style coffee-houses where the 'pretend' version seems as real, if not more real, than the actual thing they are copying. This idea can be extended to include much of television's output where for example we, as 'armchair travellers', can visit countries all over the world, see exotic sights and perhaps feel that we have 'experienced' or understood these different places. 'Confessional' shows like *Jerry Springer* can also be seen as false copies that 'pretend' to offer solutions to personal problems but are actually only there to entertain the viewer. In the postmodern world, style is 'celebrated' at the expense of substance and content, while the fake and the artificial increasingly replace the real.

BRICOLAGE The way signs or artefacts are borrowed from different styles or genres to create something new.

Another useful term associated with postmodernism is 'bricolage' (see section on Intertextuality, p. 72). The term was used to describe the punk movement and the way in which punks took a variety of different objects (e.g. dustbin liners, safety-pins, Mohican haircuts and bondage trousers) and by combining them made a new style or fashion. Bricolage is quite a useful way of looking at certain media forms such as music videos and advertising that increasingly seem to mix together a wide range of different images that do not appear to have any connection, except that they are somehow 'modern'.

Another film that is often called postmodern is Quentin Tarantino's *Pulp Fiction* (1994), which also mixes pieces from various different types of genre: gangster films, sporting films, comedy, etc. Part of the 'pleasure' in watching this film is its 'intertextuality' (see p. 72), identifying the references to other types of film. An example of bricolage might be the scene at a restaurant, 'Jack Rabbit Slim's'. In this scene John Travolta is dressed like a cowboy and 'copies' his *Saturday Night Fever* dance routine surrounded by images of dead film stars from the 1950s and 1960s. Later he does 'the twist', a dance from the 1960s. The people working in the restaurant are dressed like Disney cartoon characters.

Postmodernism is quite a difficult term to understand as it is still quite vague and can seem to include everything that is happening in early-twenty-first-century life. However, it can be a useful tool for analysing some aspects of the media and highlighting their importance in our life today.

HOW TO STUDY THE MEDIA

One of the key aspects of studying the media is that there are no 'simple answers'; often there is no obvious 'correct' answer at all. The skills that you are developing are the skills of analysis, interpretation and being able to argue a particular position regarding some aspects of the media. If, for example, we take the censorship debate (see p. 141), it becomes clear very quickly that there is no one answer but that it is a matter of looking at various points of view, various pieces of evidence and opinion, and perhaps coming to your own conclusion which you can then justify. Quite often it is case of raising more questions than you started out with, but often a sign of success is knowing what questions to ask. This means that studying the media can be both quite exciting and empowering for you as a student but that at times it can be quite frustrating and difficult to grasp.

NOTEBOX

One of the keys to success for a Media Studies student is to develop a wide knowledge of the media 'out there'. Most of us have a few favourite radio stations, television channels, newspapers or magazines that we consume regularly. Most of us are reluctant to change or to try something different, rather we develop a routine or habit in our media consumption. However, as a media student you should take risks, try different types of newspapers, magazines, radio stations or television programmes. You might be pleasantly surprised and discover something new that you like and it will help you understand the range and variety of media products that are available to us all. Having a wide knowledge of media products will also help you to use your own examples instead of relying on those given to you in this book or by teachers. Independent thinking and the ability to transfer concepts and apply them to different examples is a characteristic of the successful Media Studies student.

Media Study skills

Let us now look at the skills you will need to make you an effective and successful student of the media. In addition to skills such as note-taking, we will consider:

- How to look at media texts
- How to plan and get the best from your own media consumption
- Using textbooks
- Using the Internet
- Getting information first hand.

The world is full of media texts waiting to be studied. For the student of media this provides easy access to a wide range of texts for consideration. For most people media texts exist simply as a source of information and entertainment. For the media student, however, they are also a source on which to base serious academic study. It is important, therefore, that you bear this in mind whenever you are considering a media text.

By the end of your course, it is very likely you will say: 'I can never look at a media product in quite the same way again.' So what is the fundamental shift that you need to undergo to change from being a media consumer to a media student? Well, the first step you have to take is to start thinking more deeply about the media you consume. When you go to a restaurant and eat a meal, you will likely think that it was good or it was bad: 'I enjoyed eating that' or 'That tasted awful'. A chef having an evening out eating the same meal may well have a similar response. However, because the chef understands the process of cooking and serving food, s/he will probably be thinking about the raw ingredients that were used, the cooking process, the way the food is presented and even how much profit the restaurant is making on the dish.

Similarly a media student should look beyond a superficial response to a media text in terms of pleasure and enjoyment, and be prepared to consider a broad range of issues and concepts relating not only to the text itself, but also to its production and consumption. Media consumption becomes a much broader consideration of how different people consume a media product, how it is constructed, and the conditions under which it was produced.

The hard bit is to identify the difference between enjoying a media text and applying the skills you have learned to look at the text in a more considered or academic way. In this chapter we hope to consider ways in which you might think about doing this.

General skills

Studying the media is an important skill that you, the would-be student, need to develop. Some academic disciplines define reasonably clearly how you should study. You may need to refer to books on the subject, or perhaps undertake practical or research work. In some cases it even may involve watching a video or a television programme. For the media student, however, watching television, going to the cinema, reading a magazine, or even looking at the billboard at the side of the road can all claim to be part of any study of the media.

Media Studies is an academic discipline with its own language and terminology and its own conceptual understanding. To be a good media student you need to develop a set of skills that will enable you not only to look at the media and its texts with a critical and discriminating eye, but also to grasp the principles of academic study which consider how media products are produced and consumed.

Many of the important skills you need to develop in order to study media will be very similar to the skills you need for other academic disciplines. A wide variety of self-help guides are available to help you develop these broader study skills. Some suggestions are given at the end of this chapter. Consequently our focus here will be on identifying some of the basic skills you need for media and other subjects.

Note-taking

The ability to make notes from a range of sources, such as lectures, class discussion and reference books, is a key skill for every student. Similarly, your ability to make sense of your notes from these sources over a period of time can mean the difference between success and failure.

The key to effective note-taking is to be conscientious and to stick to an organisational method that works. For many students, this means not only taking an initial set of notes, but also revisiting these notes while they are fresh and expanding or developing them in such a way that they will make sense later. Many students find the most efficient method of doing this is to transfer hand-written notes on to a computer at the earliest opportunity. If no computer is available, then writing them up in long hand into a logical and clear format is the next best thing.

ACTIVITY...

Choose a topic you have covered recently, either in Media Studies or another subject. Now look through your notes and see how easy it is to retrieve information on the topic. What has the result told you about your level of organisation?

Organisation

Organisation is a skill closely linked to note-taking. The most accurate and detailed set of notes imaginable will be quite worthless if you cannot retrieve them for use when you want them.

Whatever system of storage you have, be it a computer or simple A4 binder, you need to develop a method of filing and organising your notes in such a way that you can confidently gain access to them whenever you need to refer to them. If you are able to store information on a computer hard disk, don't forget to make a back-up copy on a floppy disk, especially if you are not the only person to use the computer.

The need for organisation, however, goes far beyond simply filing your notes for easy retrieval. Probably the single most effective way to improve your ability to study lies in organising your time, or time management as it is often called. The simple act of drawing up a timetable or a daily action plan can help you optimise the use of your time. This can be especially important to a media student; time spent on recreational activities and time spent on study can sometimes become blurred. A visit to the cinema, for example, might well be considered a pleasurable social activity as well as a feature of your study of the media. It is up to you to try to make sure you get the best of both worlds.

Information retrieval

We live in an information-rich society. Indeed, many people see a new division within society between those who have access to information and those who don't. In general, students belong to the former category, especially where they have access to the Internet and the skills and knowledge necessary to retrieve information from it. However, the privilege of such access has its downside. So much information is now available through the average student's PC that it is very easy to suffer from an overload of information and data. It is important to learn how to be selective in gaining access to and retrieving information. Equally important is how to make the most effective use of the information you have obtained.

Later in the chapter we consider some of the more useful and reliable sources of information available to the media student, as well as offering some words of caution about the uses to which this information is put.

Despite some potential drawbacks, the Internet has become a real boon to students, allowing instant access to information 24 hours a day. For the student who has taken the trouble to learn how to use it effectively, it is a valuable shortcut to rich sources of information. Compare this to the situation just a few years ago, when a student often had to wait several weeks for a library to transport a book across the country or even across the world.

Learning to discriminate

Now let us get back to some of those specific study skills that are so useful to the media student. There are a number of good habits you can develop that will help your study of the media. As you gain an understanding of some of the underlying principles of Media Studies, through using this book for example, you will begin to realise that there are a number of key concepts that can be applied to media. For example, look at the three main areas that this book is divided into:

> Reading the Media (or textual analysis)
> Media Audiences
> Media Institutions

These three headings can be used to provide you with a framework for looking at any media text you encounter. For example, when you are considering a media text, you may want to ask yourself:

- How is it constructed?
- Where was it created?
- How is it consumed?

If you can get into the habit of applying these questions to media texts you encounter, you will be making an important step towards looking at them in a Media Studies context.

Second, it is important to ensure that you have some method of making a note of your responses to and thoughts about media texts that you find particularly interesting. Many media students find a diary or log in which they keep a note of these on a daily or weekly basis is a useful method of keeping track of important aspects of their media consumption. Such information can be very useful later in your course when, for example, you may be looking for ideas for coursework or production, or perhaps some texts that may illustrate an essay you are writing.

Third, it is a good idea to be thinking of ways you can preserve some of the key texts that you come across. You will probably want to keep copies of important texts that you can use as examples in essays, such as copies of TV programmes, newspaper or magazine articles and radio programmes. You are also likely to come across quite a lot of material in the media about the media itself, such as a documentary about the launch of a new magazine, a newspaper article about a new television programme, or a radio programme discussing the ethics of the press. All of these are potentially valuable sources of information and ideas that can be used in your media work. It is important, therefore, to keep a look-out for them and ensure that you either record them or save particular articles in a scrapbook.

One important way in which you can make yourself a better media student is to select your own texts for use when you are illustrating a particular point in an essay or piece of coursework. Far too many students limit their examples to those discussed in class. Inevitably that leads to a whole class of students writing essays that are very similar to one another. If you can show you have understood a concept or principle by providing an example from a text that you have chosen, this is likely to be rewarded much more than the student who has relied on the teacher's example. Indeed, if the example you choose is an appropriate contemporary text, you will have demonstrated clearly your own up-to-date engagement with a study of the media.

Planning ahead

It should now be clear just how important it is to plan your media consumption. Of course, there will be recurring texts you need to look at, for example the *Media Guardian* every Monday or a monthly film magazine such as *Empire*. Remember that these should be available in libraries, so you don't have the expense of buying them regularly and you can also look at back copies.

Keeping up to date with key issues and debates in the media is an important aspect of your study and looking in such places as the media sections in the broadsheet newspapers is a particularly good way of doing this. A list of other recommended information sources is given at the end of this book.

Getting hold of a good listings magazine that has details of the week's television and radio programmes is an effective way of identifying useful programmes that are likely to help you with your study. Don't forget to look in some of the places you might not normally consider. Radio 3, Radio 4 and some of the local radio stations have quite a lot of speech-based output, some of which you may well find interesting, stimulating and probably quite accessible, once you have given it a try.

Some sources of information

Even though we live in an age of electronic information, books are still an important source for the media student. Indeed, many publishers believe that books are set to grow in importance and popularity as society is keen to have access to more and more information, encouraged by such innovations as the Internet.

For the media student, using a textbook is an important skill that needs to be developed. The first challenge is to find the right book. You will need to consider both the content of the book and the level at which it is pitched.

A lot of Media Studies books are aimed at students who are well ahead of A Level and are used to a much more sophisticated level of language and concepts than people at your stage of study. Unless you are prepared to spend hours wrestling with the ideas and looking up unfamiliar words, these books will not be very helpful. Equally there is a wide range of media books across a variety of different media topics. Finding the best one for your needs is bound to be tricky. Here are some tips to help you select the right book at the right level.

- **Check jacket or cover copy.** If you are browsing in a library or bookshop, read it to see if the book covers the topics you are looking for.

- **Check the contents page** to assess if it covers the right ground. You may also find information about the level the book is aimed at. Ideally you want a book that is geared to the needs of a reader looking for an introduction to the topic. You can check this further by reading half a page of the text inside the book to see how easy or difficult you find it.

- **Check name of the writer(s).** This may also be a hint about the usefulness of the book. Is this a writer whose name you have heard mentioned in other books or in class, perhaps? You will find in the Resources section at the end of this book some suggestions for further reading. Most of the authors mentioned in it have produced books that are accessible to students at your stage of study.

Once you have found the right book, the next step is to learn how to get the best from it. It is always a good idea to read the introduction to any textbook. This should tell you about the approach the writer is going to take and what s/he intends to cover.

It is unlikely that you will have the time to read a whole book, so you need to learn how to select the sections that are especially relevant for what you are doing. One device that may help here is the index. This will outline for you all the references to a particular topic. Where these are fairly detailed you will find they span several pages (e.g. 68–73), so that is always a good place to start looking. Note also that most textbooks give a chapter summary at the beginning of every chapter, outlining what is covered. It is a good idea, therefore, to check each chapter in turn to see if it is likely to contain any relevant material. To help you with this, look at the section headings within each chapter as a way of navigating your way to the information you are looking for.

The next stage is to make some notes. Some students like to photocopy useful sections of books. If you do this, you need to check with your school or college that you are not infringing copyright laws. Whilst photocopying can be a useful tool, it is often much better to make some notes from the book you are using. The reason is that the process of transferring information in this way helps to reinforce your learning. Not least because you need to read and understand the original before you can write down your own version. Second, it is important to learn the skill of summarising other people's ideas in your own words. Taking notes will help you to perfect this skill. On a very few occasions you will want to lift direct quotations from a book. When you do so, don't forget to remind yourself they are direct quotes, by putting them in inverted commas. In this way you will not forget to attribute the ideas to their original source.

NOTEBOX

Don't forget to write down all the publication details of a book you use. In the section on coursework we look at the important art of reference and writing a bibliography. Every time you use a book, make a note of:

- author
- title
- publisher
- date of publication
- ISBN.

It is also a good idea to make a note of the page numbers from which your notes have been taken. Don't forget, if you are using a reader or collection of essays by different people, you also need to note down the name of the individual contributor whose work you are using.

An important reason why you need to make a note of the source of your information is that when you come to use it in an essay or a piece of coursework you have to attribute it. That means that you should not try to claim that it is an original idea of your own but that you should acknowledge the source from which it comes. Otherwise you can be accused of plagiarism, which means taking and using other people's ideas without properly acknowledging them.

The Internet

The Internet is a great boon to all students, but for the media student it also offers some unique advantages as well as disadvantages. The chief advantage is the way it provides swift access to contemporary information. A problem with much of the information in a textbook is that it may become out of date. In a subject like Media Studies, important issues like patterns of consumption or audience figures can change rapidly as new media products are launched and gain popularity. The Internet is an especially useful way of keeping up to date with important data. For example, a site such as www.abc.org.uk offers details of up-to-date circulation figures for a wide range of magazines.

Similarly, most of the bodies who are responsible for the regulation of the media industries (the Press Complaints Commission, or the Radio Authority for example) all have useful websites. Not only do these offer background information about codes of practice and complaints procedures, but they also provide details of recent cases on which they have adjudicated. Certainly it is worth while book-marking these sites, the addresses of which are given in the Resources section (p. 309).

NOTEBOX

If you are using a computer that doesn't belong to you, make sure you have a plentiful supply of disks to store information. It is a good idea to reserve one disk for keeping a list of book-marked sites that you have found especially useful. If you download information to a disk for future reference, keep a detailed note of the contents of that disk on the label so you can find it again without having to search through each of your disks in turn.

Just as you will find that the many textbooks available to you are pitched at a range of different levels, so it is with Internet sites. Many sites that deal with media-related issues are aimed at a general audience. This is especially true of many of the cinema-related sites, such as the Internet Movies database (www.imdb.com). Other sites are directed towards students with quite a sophisticated level of understanding. Just as you will have found it necessary to dip into a textbook to find if it is useful or not, so it is with a website.

Before you do this, however, it is a good idea to learn how to use a search engine to the best effect. Search engines, for example Yahoo or Lycos, are the means by which you can enter keywords to identify what you are looking for and they will list all of the sites on the Internet that seem relevant to your search. Often this can number several thousand, so it will pay you to do some initial research into how to get the best from the search engine you have chosen to use. Click on the help icon on the home page of the search engine and it will tell you how you can use such devices as inverted commas and plus and minus signs to limit your search. It is really worthwhile getting familiar with these devices if you are going to make searches that produce a manageable amount of information for you to follow up.

Google℠

Advanced Search   Preferences   Search Tips

media studies   Google Search

I'm Feeling Lucky

Tip: Use Google to find street maps! Just enter a street address with city/state or zip (e.g. 165 University Ave Palo Alto CA) into the search box.

Searched the web for **media studies**.   Results **1 - 10** of about **814,000**. Search took **0.09** seconds.

Categories: Science > Social Sciences > Communication   News > Current Events > Media and Free Speech

Who we are: **Media Studies** Center
...special events World center **Media Studies** Center First Amendment...
...PRESS/FAIR PRESS DIVERSITY **MEDIA STUDIES** JOURNAL PUBLICATIONS...
www.freedomforum.org/whoweare/media.asp - 24k - Cached - Similar pages

University of Wales, Aberystwyth
...ar <http://users.aber.ac.uk/dgc/**media**.html> Cewch eich cyrchu i'r...
...at <http://users.aber.ac.uk/dgc/**media**.html> You will be forwarded...
Description: This is a comprehensive hypertext introduction to semiotics.
Category: Science > Social Sciences > Language and Linguistics > Semiotics
www.aber.ac.uk/~dgc/media.html - 2k - Cached - Similar pages

CCMS - Communication **studies**, cultural **studies**, **media**
...**studies**, cultural **studies** and **media studies** includes...
... **studies** includes communication theory, semiotics, mass **media**...
Description: Extensive list of interlinked definitions of concepts related to cultural **studies** and **media** ecology.
Category: Science > Social Sciences > Communication
www.cultsock.ndirect.co.uk/MUHome/cshtml/ - 7k - Cached - Similar pages

Voice of the Shuttle: **Media Studies** Page
...THE SHUTTLE: **MEDIA STUDIES** PAGE The "Voice of the Shuttle:...
...Film **Studies** Depts. & Programs Johns Hopkins U. Film and **Media**...
vos.ucsb.edu/shuttle/media.html - 92k - Cached - Similar pages

New **Media Studies**, for web info, reviews, design, and culture
www.newmediastudies.com is the site for the study of new **media**, containing book
reviews, website reviews, web design guides, internet information, and more. -- www...
Description: A site for the study of new **media**, containing book reviews, website reviews, web design guides, internet...
Category: Arts > Design > New Media > Resources
www.newmediastudies.com/ - 5k - Cached - Similar pages

Faculty of Information and **Media Studies**
...Doctoral Program UNDERGRADUATE **STUDIES Media**, Information &...
...Faculty of Information and **Media Studies** Middlesex, College...
www.fims.uwo.ca/ - 10k - Cached - Similar pages

Welcome to the **Media Studies** Program!
... **Media Studies** @ University of Southern Maine Welcome to the...
...This new interdisciplinary **Media Studies** program, at the...
Description: University of Southern Maine's Visual and **Media studies** program. Portland area, Maine.
Category: Regional > North America > ... > Maine > Business and Economy > Visual and Media
www.usm.maine.edu/~ms/home.html - 7k - Cached - Similar pages

Welcome to Poynter.org
About This Site Bookstore Poynter Information 2001 Course Schedule 2000 Course Schedule
Apply Online Seminars About Us Who's Who How to Apply Contact Us Areas of Study...
Description: News, analysis, advice and other resources regarding journalism and **media** from the Poynter

http://www.google.com/search?q=media+studies&hl=en&lr=&safe=off   02/11/00

Figure 4

Warning: As well as information that you are likely to find useful, there is also an awful lot of irrelevant material on the Internet. One thing you must learn quickly is how to discriminate. In many cases it is only experience that can teach you this, so you must learn to be cautious in the early stages and keep an open mind about the value of the information a site is offering. One useful test is to ask yourself if you have come across this information source elsewhere. Another is to consider how long the site has been in existence. A site such as the BBC or *The Times* would clearly have credibility on both counts and could be considered a source of reliable information. If you are not sure, it is probably a good place to start looking at some of the sites indicated in the Resources section (p. 309).

One difficulty that the Internet is likely to present to you is probably also its chief attraction. Using hypertext links allows you to move quickly from one site to another in search of related information. Simply clicking on the link will transfer you immediately to a related site. The danger is that, unless you adopt a very disciplined approach to your use of the Net, you can end up skipping from site to site until you lose all sense of what it was you were originally seeking. Fortunately the back button on your browser will allow you to retrace your steps, or alternatively you can pull down the history menu and find your way back to a relevant site that way. You will get the best from your session exploring the Internet if you can avoid getting sidetracked and keep to a focused exploration of the topic you are concerned with. One way to do this is to set yourself a time limit; staring at a computer screen in a tired frame of mind is not conducive to getting the best from the Internet.

Finally, remember that, although the Internet is about freedom of speech and ideas, it is still necessary to acknowledge any information you intend to use in your own work. So remember to make a note of all the details, including the URL or address, just as you would when using a textbook.

A contact from overseas is doing some research into British media and the bodies that regulate them. Find three website addresses for regulatory bodies that might be useful.

Other sources of information

There are a number of other ways in which information can be obtained by the Media Studies student. These tend to involve primary sources of information, which means getting information firsthand, direct from someone who knows. In the section on research skills you will see how important information obtained from interviewing people can be, for example to find out about audience consumption.

Another important source of information is when you go on a visit, say, to a media organisation such as a local newspaper, or a museum that exhibits media issues, or you have the opportunity to go and hear someone speak at a conference or workshop. Similarly your teacher may arrange for someone with a media interest to visit your class. Make sure that you prepare for such an event by making a list of some pertinent questions that you would like to ask. Make sure also that you get down some detailed notes, including, for example, any useful information on follow-up opportunities.

Another source of primary information is to approach an organisation or individual directly for help. This is especially relevant when you are undertaking coursework and need some special information about an organisation or its products. Before you get in touch, think carefully about what you are doing:

1   Make sure that the information you want is not readily available elsewhere, in a magazine or on the Web for example.
2   Be very specific about what you want to know. Letters that begin 'I am doing a Media Studies project on advertising' rarely produce anything more than a very general response, if any response at all. Remember that some information is likely to be commercially sensitive, so a firm may not want it to fall into the hands of a competitor.
3   Address your request to the right department or individual; the Press or Public Relations Office is always a good place to start.
4   Don't waste people's time. Media organisations are nearly always busy, so only ask for information if it is essential and there is no other way to find it. Be specific about what you want and why you want it.
5   Consider enclosing a stamped addressed envelope so that it is easy to reply.

CONCLUSION

Studying the media is a popular and enjoyable pastime. Like any other course of advanced study, it is also hard work for the student who wants to do a good job. The important issue is make sure that you get the balance right between your own enjoyment of media texts and the task of serious study you need to undertake to ensure you succeed in the course you are taking. If you can manage to do this, then you will find Media Studies an enriching experience which will not only make your own media consumption more informed and enjoyable, but will also provide a useful skill that you can share with your family and friends.

FURTHER READING

Barrass, R. (1984) *Study!*, E & F.N. Spon.

Chambers, E. and Northedge, A. (1997) *The Arts Good Study Guide*, Open University Press.

Drew, S. and Bingham, R. (1997) *The Student Skills Guide*, Gower.

Fry, R. (1999) *The Great Big Book of How to Study*, Career Press.

▼ IMAGE ANALYSIS (CODES ETC.)

In this section we will:

- explore the use of semiotics in analysing media texts

- consider the history of semiotics and its significance as a critical tool in the understanding of how texts create 'meaning'

- look at different kinds of sign, the way we read codes and the concepts of connotation, denotation and anchorage

- identify some of the limitations of semiotics as a critical tool for textual analysis.

WHAT IS A MEDIA 'TEXT'?

As mentioned on p. 3, we usually associate the word 'text' with something that is printed or written. In Media Studies, however, the word 'text' is used to describe any media product such as television programmes, photographs, films either on video or in the cinema, newspaper articles, radio programmes, advertisements, video games or web pages.

'Texts' are, therefore, the main point of our study in understanding how media languages create meaning. One of the keys to understanding the meanings in texts is the use of codes.

KEY TERM

CODES Rules or conventions by which signs are put together to create meaning.

The English language itself is a set of codes: letters made up into words, words made up into sentences and sentences made up into paragraphs. Just as we learn to read the letters, words and sentences, so, too, we learn to 'read' media codes and languages. We learn that sounds or images can be put together in particular sequences, working as codes to give particular meanings.

Just as there is a great variety in the forms and style of media texts, so the codes used to construct meanings are varied and frequently depend upon the form of the media text. In most cases the text will use a variety of codes – visual, audio and written – that 'fit' together in a certain way to create a particular meaning.

Look at the Tribe advertisement (Figure 5). We see that this is a text that is print-based but contains visual and written codes. Its exact meaning may be quite difficult to 'fix' except to say that it is an advertisement and is trying to 'sell' a product, a particular brand of Cologne. In this advertisement additional meaning is given through the use of colour codes and the written text at the bottom of the advert.

Some adverts do not even seem to be trying to sell a specific product but are, presumably, just trying to make us aware of a particular company or name, for example the United Colors of Benetton campaign (see below).

Most of us living in western society at the beginning of the twenty-first century are sophisticated media consumers and will be able to 'read' the Tribe advertisement fairly quickly. We would probably normally only glance at it as we skim through a magazine. However, as media students, we now have to distance ourselves from our daily and often unreflective consumption of media texts like the Tribe illustration. Our task is to break down or 'deconstruct' the illustration into its component parts and fully to 'reveal' and understand how the advertisers have used the various signs and codes in their attempt to create a particular meaning or set of meanings.

One of the key theoretical tools to assist us in this process of deconstruction is semiology, or, as it is often called, semiotics.

SEMIOTICS

The word 'semiology' is derived from the Greek word *semeion*, which means sign. Semiology is an attempt to create a science of the study of sign systems and their role in the construction and reconstruction of meaning in media texts. Semiology concentrates primarily on the text itself and the signs and codes that are contained within it.

NOTEBOX

One of the most influential theorists of the way visual images transmit meanings was Roland Barthes (1913–1980). Barthes was influenced by the structuralist work of the Swiss linguist Ferdinand de Saussure (1857–1913), who first promoted the idea of semiology in the book *Course in General Linguistics* (1954).

Saussure saw language as a cultural creation rather than something innate and as a social system that was ordered, coherent and governed by sets of rules. The

Figure 5

American Charles Peirce (1839–1914) took Saussure's ideas and expanded them to include not just language but other 'social constructs' in society such as the way society itself is ordered, labelled and governed by sets of rules. Peirce introduced the term 'semiotics'.

Roland Barthes took these ideas still further and in *Mythologies* (1972) applied them to areas of daily life and popular culture such as the face of the actress Greta Garbo and soap detergents advertising.

KEY TERM

STRUCTURALISM This approach argues that identifying underlying structures is all-important in undertaking analysis. In linguistics, for example, it can be argued that all languages have a similar underlying grammatical structure that we are born with the capacity to learn. Similarly, certain social structures, such as the family unit, may be common to many cultures.

For students of the media, semiotic analysis is a useful tool in the deconstruction of texts as it helps to reveal the underlying meanings that are 'suspended' within a text. You can then take this analysis further and consider the ideologies that underpin texts and their construction.

It is important to be aware that most sign systems, like the Tribe advertisement, do not necessarily have one particular 'fixed' meaning. Part of the meaning of the sign is dependent upon the social and cultural background of the 'reader' of the particular sign system.

As part of the process of semiotic analysis we, the audience, are called 'readers' because this helps to suggest a greater degree of creativity and involvement in the construction of the text's meaning. 'Reading' is something we learn to do and is influenced to a large extent by our social and cultural background. As the reader of a text, we are likely to bring something of our own cultural and personal experiences to a text.

ACTIVITY . . .

Choose an advertisement from a magazine and show it to a range of different people. These should include people of different gender, age, ethnic and social background. Ask them what they think the text 'means'. How might you account for the different readings that you are offered by each reader?

SIGNS

The Tribe advertisement is a sign. It consists of a signifier, the printed magazine advert itself, and something that is signified, the 'idea' or 'meaning' behind the set of images used in the advertisement.

Fiske and Hartley in *Reading Television* (1978) describe the sign as being made up of two components: the signifier and the signified

signifier + signified = sign

The signifier is a physical object, e.g. a sound, printed word, advertisement. The signified is a mental concept or meaning conveyed by the signifier.

Peirce differentiated between three different types of signs: symbolic (or arbitrary); iconic; indexical. Symbolic signs have no obvious connection between the sign and the object. For example, the word CAT has no obvious link with a small furry animal usually domesticated as a pet. It only works because we understand the rules that say the letters C-A-T, when put into a certain order, mean or 'signify' that small furry animal. If it was a different 'we', for example a group of French speakers, then the 'rules' would be different and we would use the letters C-H-A-T to signify that small furry animal.

SYMBOL A sign that represents an object or concept solely by the agreement of the people who use it.

KEY TERM

These types of signs Peirce also called 'arbitrary' as their 'meaning' is the result of agreement amongst their users. These types of signs do not have any direct or intrinsic connection with what is being 'signified'. This means that some arbitrary signs can have several meanings that are 'contested', or about which people might not agree. The Union Jack has a variety of meanings depending upon who is using it – the British monarchy at a national ceremony, the Unionists in Ulster, the mods in films like *Quadrophenia* (1979), or a group of football supporters.

The symbol A referring to anarchy will have different meanings for different groups of people. Think of other signs that may be arbitrary and then list all the different groups of people and the different readings that they may apply to these signs.

Iconic signs are like the religious paintings, statues, and stained-glass windows found in churches that display pictures of the holy family. Photographs are a good example of an iconic sign. They have a physical similarity to the objects that they 'signify'. We are familiar with iconic signs in our everyday lives, for example the use of a wheelchair to signify facilities for disabled people. Wherever we are in the world, we can usually find the men's and women's toilets by looking for the iconic signs on the doors.

Indexical signs are the signs that have some kind of direct connection with what is being 'signified'. Smoke is often used as an indexical sign for fire, and a tear running down someone's cheek can be an indexical sign for sorrow.

So why is it useful to know about these signs in order to study media texts? Let us look at some of the reasons here. Media texts are usually complex messages. Most texts are composed using all of the types of sign that we have indicated. Printed words or a spoken commentary both employ arbitrary signs to communicate with an audience. Photographs in magazines or moving images on film or television are iconic signs, which work because of their similarity with the thing they represent. We may also see or hear indexical signs; someone sweating profusely may be an index of either extreme temperature or high levels of stress. Similarly, tears or the sounds of sobbing provide an index of grief.

An audience consuming the media by watching television, for example, is creating meaning from a complex system of signs that they have become use to 'reading'. By understanding the nature of signs and how they work, we can gain some insight into the process by which media messages are interpreted.

As you may have realised, iconic signs are especially significant in our study of the visual image, in photography, film and television. It is because iconic signs so closely relate to the object that they represent, that they seem so natural. In the process it is easy to forget that we are looking at a sign and confuse the sign with reality itself. As we will see in later sections, this has important implication for the way in which we read the representation of reality in the media.

John Fiske in *Introduction to Communication Studies* (1990) uses the example of a road-sign (Figure 6) to illustrate how a seemingly simple familiar sign is in fact composed of all three of these different types of sign.

Fiske suggests that this road sign is symbolic because it is in the shape of a triangle which, according to the *Highway Code*, indicates a 'warning'. The cross in the middle is iconic in that its shape is determined by the shape of the object that it signifies, a crossroads, and the road sign is also indexical because it is related to the physical presence of the actual crossroads further along the road.

Media texts can have several possible meanings depending upon the way in which the signs are read and the background of the individual 'reader'. This means that signs are polysemic, or are open to many interpretations. Sometimes, however, a particular or preferred meaning is indicated by the way in which the text has been produced and presented to the reader.

Figure 6

Crossroads

The photograph used in the Dolce & Gabbana advertisement (Figure 7) could have many different readings and can be considered, therefore, to be polysemic. We are directed, however, towards a particular or preferred reading by the inclusion of the name of a well-known fashion company and the fact that this text would have probably appeared in lifestyle magazines such as *Company, FHM* or *Elle*.

It is the name Dolce & Gabbana that provides the anchorage for this text in the same way that the wording at the bottom of the Tribe advertisement, along with the picture of the product itself, directs us towards its preferred reading.

KEY TERM

ANCHORAGE is the fixing or limiting of a particular set of meanings to an image. One of the most common forms of anchorage is the caption underneath a photograph.

ACTIVITY . . .

Without the wording the Dolce & Gabbana photograph could be very ambiguous and difficult to put into context. Try putting different captions to the photograph to illustrate some of its possible meanings and suggest where else the photograph might appear.

CODES

Signs often work through a series of codes that are, like signs, usually socially constructed and, therefore, agreed upon by society as a whole. There are many different types of code at work in media texts; some of the most common are: dress codes, colour codes, non-verbal codes, technical codes.

Figure 7

Dress codes relate to what people wear in particular situations. If we see people in evening dress we usually make the association of glamour, wealth or sophistication. Sometimes these dress codes are deliberately flouted, for example the title sequence to *Blind Date* where a couple are seen in swimming costumes in the middle of a busy city street.

Colour codes in particular vary within different cultures. Black, for instance, is usually the colour of mourning in most western countries, but in some Asian countries mourners will often dress in white. Red is a particularly strong colour in terms of what it signifies: depending upon the context it can mean danger, stop (as in traffic lights) or socialism. It can also mean excitement and glamour if it is included in a fashion picture of a woman perhaps with red glossy lipstick, painted fingernails or a red dress. Part of the way in which the Tribe advertisement works is through its use of bright colours like red, pink and blue.

Non-verbal codes are to do with gesture and body language, and again these vary from culture to culture. In some countries it is normal to shake hands every time you meet someone whereas in other societies you may kiss on the cheeks each time you meet. In some Muslim countries on the other hand such open gestures of intimacy between couples would be frowned upon.

In a media text such as the Tribe advertisement, non-verbal codes would include facial expressions, different postures or gestures, and proxemics (the way in which the people appear close together or keep their distance).

Technical codes relate to the way in which particular texts are reproduced and the media used. This may be a photograph or a film (such as *Schindler's List*) that is shot almost entirely in black and white to convey an idea of documentary 'realism'. It may be the use of a close-up in a film or television programme to convey a character's strong emotions. (See Production Skills for further discussion.)

NOTEBOX

Andrew Crisell in *Understanding Radio* (1994) identifies silence as an important code used in radio texts alongside more obvious codes such as words, sounds and music.

ACTIVITY

Look at the Tribe advertisement again (Figure 5).

- How important are the dress codes in this advertisement?
- Why does the advertisement use bright colours like red, pink and blue?
- In what ways do you think the body language and facial expressions (i.e. non-verbal codes) are important here?

As particular media have their own sets of codes and sign systems, we can see that the Tribe illustration 'works' in the context of a fashion magazine. It is read by (predominantly) women readers who are familiar with the signs and conventions of this type of illustration. The advertisement would work less well in a newspaper like the *Big Issue* because its 'glossy' image would not work on the recycled newsprint the *Big Issue* uses and readers would possibly not respond to the advert in the way that the advertisers planned.

Part of the 'meaning' generated by the Tribe advertisement is dependent upon (a) where it is placed and (b) who 'reads' it.

DENOTATION AND CONNOTATION

According to Roland Barthes we, the 'reader', go through various stages when we deconstruct the meaning of a sign.

The first stage he called denotation, which refers to what is actually reproduced in the text. In the case of the Tribe illustration, the denotation consists of three young women in a car, brightly dressed, smiling and laughing, surrounded by shopping bags and with one of the women holding up a bubble blower. We may be tempted to say that the car is on a road but we cannot confirm this as, in denotational terms, we cannot see the road, we only *assume* that it is there.

KEY TERM

DENOTATION   What an image actually shows and is immediately apparent, rather than the assumptions an individual reader may make about it.

We may say that the women are fashionably dressed and are wearing jewellery and make-up. We should also notice that at the bottom of the page is the slogan 'a fragrance uprising' written in a wavy line and a picture of the product and its packaging.

The next stage that Barthes identified, connotation, is where we, the 'reader', add our own pieces of information. We fill in what is missing from the denotation stage and attempt to identify what the sign is signifying. In the case of the Tribe advert this will probably mean that we 'add' the information that this is an illustration of three fashionable, attractive, happy-go-lucky young women, who are having fun, have been shopping and who presumably use Tribe Cologne.

KEY TERM

CONNOTATION The meaning of a sign which is arrived at through the cultural experiences a reader brings to it.

We should be able to identify the various codes that are at work in this sign, particularly those to do with the clothes that the three young women are wearing, the use of primary colours in the advert and the body language of the three women.

Look at the woman using a bubble-blower in the Tribe advertisement. Carry out a small-scale piece of research by asking various people what connotations they associate with this image.

- Do their responses vary? If so, why?
- Why do you think the advertisers have included this image?
- Can you think of other ways in which the same meaning could have been created?

We may wish to add other connotations that say that the three young women seem to be reasonably affluent, they are not working but appear to have the time to enjoy themselves. They have the money required to go shopping and drive the type of car illustrated in the advertisement. The car itself looks like an American-style convertible.

The idea of alternative ways of presenting an image is also important in the analysis of moving images. For example, a director may choose to shoot someone's face in close-up. All the other possible sizes of shot, mid-shot, long shot, etc., have all been rejected in favour of the close-up. It can be argued that at some level we are aware of all the shots that have been rejected in order to include the one that has been selected.

There may be different connotations that other 'readers' add. It is sometimes helpful to ask what has been excluded from the image or how it might have been presented differently.

For instance why is the car set in a kind of limbo that seems very unrealistic? Would the advertisement work better if the car were situated in a local high street? Would other models of cars work as well? A four-wheel 'off-roader'? A 'people-carrier'? Or a small hatchback like the Renault Clio or Ford Fiesta?

We also need to consider the connotations associated with the written slogan. We need to look at the words 'a fragrance uprising' and the typeface that is used. We may identify connotations that suggest carefree, happy-go-lucky, revolutionary, stylish, sophisticated, expensive, fashionable and possibly desirable.

We have, through our reading of the connotation of the Tribe advertisement, added 'extra' layers of meaning beyond that denoted by the images themselves.

Collect a selection of adverts from various magazines and then, using the worksheet on p. 41, describe what you can see in terms of the denotative content of the adverts. Remember that denotation only means what is there and you must be very disciplined in not adding information or assuming more than is shown. This can be quite a difficult exercise as most of us have learnt to become very sophisticated in reading in the additional information that advertisers intend us to supply ourselves.

One way of noting everything that is contained in the illustrations is to cover each advert and slowly reveal it bit by bit. This will help you to identify some of the smaller details that are often overlooked when we glance or skim through printed material.

Using the same set of adverts, now describe what the connotations of the adverts are. Again try to look at all the aspects of the illustrations and try to say why the advertisers put them in.

Compare your interpretation of the same advertisement with a colleague's. This can be a useful means of illustrating how meaning is not 'fixed' but partly dependent upon the individual reading.

THE PROCESS MODEL OF COMMUNICATION

Semiotics with its emphasis on the text and its codes and signs can be seen as a move away from earlier analyses that saw the media as a 'process' model of communication. The model suggested that the medium used was perhaps more important than the message itself (see Part 2: Media Audiences).

KEY TERM

PROCESS MODEL This model considered the audience's interaction with the media as part of a linear process SENDER–CHANNEL–MESSAGE–RECEIVER where the meaning of a text was thought to be 'fixed' by the producer.

In the Tribe example, the sender is the producer of the advertisement, i.e. the agency that created it on behalf of the perfume manufacturer. The channel is that of magazine advertising. Other channels such as television and billboard advertising are also likely to have been used. The message is basically 'buy this perfume and you will be like these people'. The receiver is the reader of the magazine. The process model assumes that the message created by the sender and the message received are likely to be the same. The meaning of the message is thought to be set by the producer.

You may like to compare this idea with some of the theories about media effects (p. 141) in Part 2, on Media Audiences.

You can see that semiotics offers a much more sophisticated view of how media texts communicate meaning and are interpreted by audiences, However, just as the process model has been criticised for being too simplistic, so the semiotic approach has itself been criticised.

CRITICISMS OF SEMIOTICS

Critics have suggested that it is not really a 'science' in the way that Barthes claimed, and because all signs can have different meanings depending upon the individual reader's interpretation there is some difficulty in judging which interpretations are the most 'valid'.

Another weakness of semiotics is that it can sometimes be difficult to measure the effect or influence of the audience or reader in creating signs. For instance, the flowers left outside the various royal palaces after the death of Diana, Princess of Wales, could be seen as 'signifying' national mourning but only after the event had started and became widely publicised in the media. This seemed to create a snowball effect, where many people decided to join in. In this case it is difficult to say whether this 'signification' originated with people expressing their sorrow or through media manipulation of that sorrow.

Critics have also suggested that the denotation stage is not very useful because it is so artificial and all readers automatically 'add' connotations.

ACTIVITY...

Consider some of these criticisms and suggest ways in which they may be answered. Suggest reasons why you think semiotics may be a useful tool for analysing media texts.

WORKSHEET...

WORKSHEET FOR ANALYSING ADVERTISEMENTS

Use the worksheet below to help you with the analysis of an advertisement of your own choice. Consider each of the following aspects:

Portrayal of people in the advertisement:

- How old are they?
- What gender are they?
- What racial group do they come from?
- Which social classes are represented? How do you know?

- What do the clothing codes tell you?
- What are their facial expressions? Why?
- What is their posture? Why?
- What roles and stereotypes are being represented?
- How would you describe the relationship between the people?
- What other people could have been included? Why have they been excluded?

Technical codes:

- Is the illustration in colour or black and white? Why?
- How have the images been framed and cropped?
- Are all the elements in the image in focus? If not, why?
- Has anything been left out of the illustration? Why?
- How has it been lit and what is the camera angle? Are these important?

Text included in the advertisement:

- How does the slogan relate to the images?
- What other information are we given to help explain the images?
- Who is being addressed?
- What typeface has been used? Why?

Objects that are included:

- Where is the advert set? How do we know?
- What objects are included in the advert? Why?
- Does the product appear in the advert? If not, why not?
- What else could have been included but has not? Why?
- What do the background colours and textures signify?
- What colour codes are at work?

The function of the advertisement as a whole:

- What kind of advert is this? Does it refer to any other adverts or media texts?
- What is the narrative and how do we make sense of it?
- Who are we supposed to identify with?
- What is being promised by this advertisement?
- What are the values that underpin it?
- Who is in control in this image and where does the power come from?

The audience for the advertisement:

- Who is the advert aimed at? How do we know?
- Is any prior knowledge required to understand the advert? If yes, what?

- In what publications might the advert appear? Why?
- Whereabouts in the publication might the advert appear?
- Is the advert part of a larger campaign? If so, what are the other components of the campaign?

▼ NARRATIVE

In this section we:

■ consider the significance of narrative in both fiction and non-fiction texts
■ look at narrative construction and mode of address
■ examine the relationship between narrative and genre.

NARRATIVE CONSTRUCTION

From our earliest days narrative is an important part of our lives. For many people, their earliest recollections relate to bedtime stories or stories told by their teacher in primary school. Another reason why narrative is so important to us is that it acts as an organising principle that helps us make sense of the world. To a child the world is a mass of unconnected and incomprehensible events, some pleasurable, some frightening, none of which makes a great deal of sense. Narrative, or storytelling, performs the important function of interpreting the world and shaping it into a comprehensible and comfortable form that allows us to see the forces of light and dark, and good and evil, battle against each other. Usually we are rewarded with the comforting outcome of the triumph of good and the reassurance of an equilibrium in which all will live 'happily ever after'.

KEY TERM

NARRATIVE The way in which a story is told in both fictional and non-fictional media texts.

As we grow up, narrative remains an important source of reassurance in a hostile universe, in much the same way as it did when we were children. Indeed, satisfying our need for narrative can in itself become associated with reward or punishment. Bad behaviour at school or at home may be punished with the denial of an end-of-day or bedtime story. Good behaviour on the other hand is rewarded with a narrative. Narrative, therefore, plays an important role in our growing up and consequently in forming our social values.

Indeed so commonplace and natural does story-telling appear that it may seem invisible to study. Yet story-telling is a complex process with important implications.

(Tilley 1991)

ACTIVITY

Watch on television a children's programme that involves some element of storytelling. Paying particular attention to the narrative, consider how conflict within the narrative is developed. What devices are used to indicate to the audience where their sympathies are expected to lie between the characters?

Clearly narrative is a powerful force not only to help us make sense of our world, but also with the potential to influence our behaviour. Similarly, for the media producers, narrative is an important tool for organising seemingly random and incoherent events into a coherent and logical form that an audience can assimilate. Consider, for example, a news story which has occurred in some remote part of the world. It may be a disaster, such as an earthquake or a famine that has damaged the lives of many thousands of people in a terrifying way. A journalist writing a newspaper story has to explain what has happened in a few hundred words and, perhaps, a couple of photographs. Often the journalist will do this by focusing on specific detail about the impact of the disaster on the lives of individual people or families. In this way the audience has a clear point of reference by making a comparison with themselves or their own families. The scale of the disaster, too vast to comprehend, is understood in terms of the individual human being with whom we, the audience, can empathise.

NOTEBOX

Narrative can be used as a potent means of influencing the responses of an audience to a particular event. This is often determined by the way in which the information is presented. Certainly when we are being told about a conflict, in a western or gangster movie for example, the narrative often unfolds in such a way as to make us 'take sides' in support of one party or the other. The narrative can thus be used to position an audience in such a way as to limit the range of readings available to them from the text.

It is important to note that, although the term 'narrative' is associated, through its literary origins, with fictional texts such as films and novels, it also plays an important part in non-fiction texts such as newspaper stories. Consider how the news photograph

Figure 8

(Figure 8) exploits the moment of conflict between the police and the protesters to achieve its effect.

So we have seen that narrative is a means by which media producers shape and control the flow of information to an audience. At a basic level, narrative can be seen as the sequencing of information about events into a logical and cohesive structure in time and space. Indeed, it has been argued that the underlying structure of all narratives is basically the same, with variation only taking place in terms of character and setting. The Bulgarian theorist Tzvetan Todorov reduced the concept of narrative to a simple recurring formula:

Equilibrium → Disequilibrium → New Equilibrium

A narrative starts with a state of equilibrium or harmony, for example a peaceful community getting on with and enjoying life. A firm sense of social order is established. Into this world of stability comes a force of disequilibrium or disruption, an evil outsider, intent on destroying the sense of well-being. By some mechanism such as the intervention of another outside agency, such as a lone gunfighter, the force of evil is overcome and order and harmony, in the form of a new equilibrium, are restored.

Clearly you will see the plot of many Hollywood movie genres, for example Western, sci-fi or even musical, fitting into this structure. Less obviously, the plot of the television news follows a similar pattern. The opening shot (see Figure 10) introduces us to the harmony of the studio as the news programme opens. The tragic events of the world news,

MEDIA STUDIES: THE ESSENTIAL INTRODUCTION

Figure 9 *Still from* **The Evil Dead II (1987)**

reports of wars, famines, social unrest and political intrigue, invade our living space and disrupt the harmony. Finally we are offered a light and comic story to provide relief from this narrative of world disorder and disaster before we are returned to the newsreader shuffling papers and calmly saying good night. The equilibrium of the familiar world – our living room – is re-established, disrupted only briefly by the tragic events of world at large. Similarly, in a programme such as *Crimewatch*, despite depicting the nightmare deeds of the criminal community, the narrative closes in the security of the studio with a familiar and friendly presenter reassuring us that we are unlikely to become victims ourselves. We may have experienced the dangers of the world, but are told that we can still sleep soundly in our beds.

In their book *Film Art: An Introduction* (1979), Bordwell and Thompson offer a technique for looking at film narrative in segments or sequences. These are called scenes, or distinct phases of the action occurring within relatively unified space and time. The segmentation allows us to see major divisions within the plot and how scenes are organised within them. This is a useful device that can be applied to a number of different narratives in order to reveal the way in which they are constructed. Few films or broadcast texts are likely to break down into the complex narrative structure of *Citizen Kane*, however (see Figure 11).

As you can see, this film relies heavily on flashback as an organising principle for the narrative. Instead of presenting a chronological life of Kane, common in biopics, the structure employs elements of the detective story as each flashback signals a different phase in the investigation of Kane's life and the meaning of his dying word, 'Rosebud'.

Figure 10 *Trevor McDonald on ITV, opening shot*

ACTIVITY

Using Figure 11 as a guide, produce your own narrative segmentation of a film or fictional television programme you have watched recently. A comedy film or situation comedy might make an interesting example. What have you learned about the structure of the text from breaking it down into segments?

This activity should help you to understand that even seemingly simple and straightforward programmes often reveal quite complex narrative structures. It also serves to suggest how narrative works across a range of texts, some of which are non-fictional. Consider for example how in a programme like *Jerry Springer* a narrative unfolds in each part as each of the characters adds to the conflict that is the mainspring of the show. This provides a good example of narrative flow whereby the unfolding of the narrative is carefully controlled by the production team. Real-life characters designed to provide further opportunities for conflict are unleashed and duly move the narrative forward to its climax. The show, of course, ends with Jerry Springer's homily which serves to restore the equilibrium.

Character is an important aspect of narrative, particularly in fictional texts such as films, TV and radio drama. In soap operas, for example, certain character types consistently recur to the point where they almost become stereotypes. For example, grumpy old people and angst-ridden teenagers are to be found as stock characters across the range of television soap operas. Grouping people into different categories like this is called

CITIZEN KANE: PLOT SEGMENTATION

C. Credit title
1. **Xanadu: Kane dies**
2. **Projection room:**
   - a. "News on the March"
   - b. Reporters discuss "Rosebud"
3. **El Rancho nightclub: Thompson tries to interview Susan**
4. **Thatcher library:**

First flashback
   - a. Thompson enters and reads Thatcher's manuscript
   - b. Kane's mother sends the boy off with Thatcher
   - c. Kane grows up and buys the *Inquirer*
   - d. Kane launches the *Inquirer*'s attack on big business
   - e. The Depression: Kane sells Thatcher his newspaper chain
   - f. Thompson leaves library

5. **Bernstein's office:**

Second flashback
   - a. Thompson visits Bernstein
   - b. Kane takes over the *Inquirer*
   - c. Montage: the *Inquirer*'s growth
   - d. Party: the *Inquirer* celebrates getting the *Chronicle* staff
   - e. Leland and Bernstein discuss Kane's trip abroad
   - f. Kane returns with his fiancée Emily
   - g. Bernstein concludes his reminiscence

6. **Nursing home:**

Third flashback
   - a. Thompson talks with Leland
   - b. Breakfast table montage: Kane's marriage deteriorates
   - c. Leland continues his recollections

Third flashback (cont.)
   - d. Kane meets Susan and goes to her room
   - e. Kane's political campaign culminates in his speech
   - f. Kane confronts Gettys, Emily, and Susan
   - g. Kane loses election and Leland asks to be transferred
   - h. Kane marries Susan
   - i. Susan's opera premiere
   - j. Because Leland is drunk, Kane finishes Leland's review
   - k. Leland concludes his reminiscence

7. **El Rancho nightclub:**

Fourth flashback
   - a. Thompson talks with Susan
   - b. Susan rehearses her singing
   - c. Susan's opera premiere
   - d. Kane insists that Susan go on singing
   - e. Montage: Susan's opera career
   - f. Susan attempts suicide and Kane promises she can quit singing
   - g. Xanadu: Susan bored
   - h. Montage: Susan plays with jigsaw puzzles
   - i. Xanadu: Kane proposes a picnic
   - j. Picnic: Kane slaps Susan
   - k. Xanadu: Susan leaves Kane
   - l. Susan concludes her reminiscence

8. **Xanadu:**

Fifth flashback
   - a. Thompson talks with Raymond
   - b. Kane destroys Susan's room and picks up paperweight, murmuring "Rosebud"
   - c. Raymond concludes his reminiscence; Thompson talks with the other reporters; all leave
   - d. Survey of Kane's possessions leads to a revelation of Rosebud; exterior of gate and of castle; the end

E. **End credits**

(Source: Bordwell and Thompson 1979:87)

Figure 11

character typology, and it should be clear that this principle can be extended across a range of genres, such as the police series or the gangster movie.

Vladimir Propp, the Russian structuralist, studied fairy stories and established a number of character types and events associated with them. He called these events 'functions' and suggested their number was limited to 31. His work has been related to film and media studies, and it is possible for example to use Propp's theory to fit the character types in a range of texts, especially feature films.

Typical Proppian characters and their functions would include:

- the hero
- the villain
- the donor (offers gift with magical properties)
- the dispatcher (sends hero on mission)
- the helper (aids hero)
- the princess (hero's reward)

Using the above list, identify these characters in any Bond or similar action/ adventure film. How well can these characters be related to any other film or TV programme that you have seen?

An important influence that character has on narrative is that of causality, which is concerned with the idea of cause and effect. Characters usually act out of motives. When different characters are introduced to us, we usually get to know what their motives are, for example what goals they have. These motives are likely to be the cause of events that unfold around this particular character. At the beginning of a film or drama we will find out about a character's goal; it may be to get a partner, rob a bank, control the world, murder a spouse, or perhaps all of these. These motives will drive the character and become the cause of action within the text. Clearly this is likely to bring the characters into conflict with other characters who may be acting out of different motives and are intent on achieving different goals. Conflict is central to the functioning of narrative not least because it is conflict that invites us, the audience, to take sides.

As we have indicated, narrative is an important concept in non-fiction as well as in fictional texts. Consider how conflict is used as a basis for telling stories in any of the following non-fiction texts:

- newspaper articles
- TV documentaries
- radio current affairs programmes.

MODE OF ADDRESS

This is an important concept in narrative study. It refers to the way in which a media text can be said to 'talk to' its audience. As such, it also has important implications for the way in which the audience responds to the text. For example, the use of a voice-over, an off-screen narrator who talks directly to the audience, is often seen as an authoritative mode of address, providing the audience with information that is incontrovertible. The authority of this voice is often further reinforced by the use of a well-known actor with a particularly distinctive voice (see p. 137).

MODE OF ADDRESS   The way in which a particular text will address or speak to its audience.

KEY TERM

The use of voice-over is a feature of news, current affairs programmes and some documentaries where this commentary holds the narrative together and develops it. Similarly, voice-over is used as a narrative device in cinema. It is a distinctive feature of the genre *film noir*, for example in Fred MacMurray's commentary on the action in Billy Wilder's *Double Indemnity* (1944). Such a voice-over is an off-screen (asynchronous) voice that directly addresses and confides in the audience. One effect of using this device is to make the audience a party to information that may not be shared by the rest of the characters on screen. It therefore offers us, the audience, privileged information about what is going on. We are positioned to accept, often without question, the information being communicated by this off-screen voice. On occasions the off-screen voice may also make us wary of trusting the character, especially in the opening scenes of a film like *Taxi Driver* (1976), where Travis Bickle reveals his conflicted personality in a tirade against humanity (see Figure 24, p. 106).

ACTIVITY

Make a recording of a documentary that deals with complex medical or scientific issues about which you are likely to know very little.

■   What methods does the commentary use to help the audience understand the complex information being conveyed?

Similarly, consider the use of voice-over in a feature film.

■   How far do we trust what the voice is telling us?
■   How is the off-screen narrator used to make us view the on-screen action from a particular perspective?

The issue of audience positioning is a complex one and is dealt with more fully in Part 2 on Media Audiences. An important effect of narrative, however, is the way in which it can be used to place or position an audience in relation to the text. In the example of *Taxi Driver*, the device is used to provide the audience with the opportunity to be party to information not shared by other characters in the film. This was an important device used in *film noir*. Not only does it provide the audience with information which assists the development of the narrative, it also gives it access to the innermost thoughts of the main character, thus providing the audience with an insight into motivation and psychological make-up.

Roland Barthes explored the concept of narrative as part of his work on structuralism. He argued that narrative works through a series of codes that are used to control the way in which information is given to the audience. Two of these codes are particularly important for our understanding of how narrative functions in media texts. The first is called the enigma code. An enigma is a riddle or puzzle, and some types of narrative make extensive use of this code. An obvious example is a detective story, where we the audience are invited to solve the puzzle of 'whodunnit' by interpreting the clues and pitting our wits against those of the fictional detective whose job it is to find the perpetrator of the crime.

KEY TERM

ENIGMA A narrative device that teases the audience by presenting a puzzle or riddle to be solved.

This is an obvious use of enigma as a narrative device. However, there are many other, less obvious ways in which these enigmas are used. One example is the use of trails for programmes to be broadcast later on television or radio. These often rely on teasing the audience with information that can only be fully understood by tuning in to the programme itself. Similarly a non-fiction text such as the news begins with headlines, which provide cryptic details of the stories that are to follow, ensuring that the audience stays with the programme to find out the full story behind the headlines. Print media use similar devices with newspaper headlines or magazine front covers offering brief information to invite the reader to purchase the product and consume the larger narrative within (e.g. POP STAR IN DRUGS TRAGEDY). Similarly, advertisers often use billboards to tease us with little clues about a product, such as a feature film, to be launched on to the market.

One of the pleasures that an audience receives from consuming a media text is that of predicting the outcome to a particular narrative. Clearly this is much of the appeal of crime-based texts, where the audience is positioned alongside the detective in trying to solve the crime or mystery.

Another code that Barthes writes about is the action code. This code suggests how narratives can be resolved through action, often on the part of the protagonist or hero. Typically a resolution is achieved through an act of violence, such as a gun battle. The action code is, therefore, often considered to be a male genre where problems are resolved through action, such as physical violence or a car chase.

MEDIA STUDIES: THE ESSENTIAL INTRODUCTION

ACTION CODE A narrative device by which a resolution is produced through action, e.g. a shoot-out.

Figure 12 Still from Police Story (1985)

RELATIONSHIP BETWEEN NARRATIVE AND GENRE

A study of different genres in film and television will suggest that the formula requires the narrative to be closed in a different way for each different genre. For example, a soap opera will always end with a cliff-hanger, a narrative device designed to create suspense for the audience and ensure that they tune in to the next episode.

Narrative is also often recognised for the different devices it employs to engage the audience with the text. Alfred Hitchcock spoke of a device which he called 'the bomb under the table'. Here suspense is built for the audience by making them party to information not shared by the characters on screen. In this case, a bomb under the table ready to explode but about which the on-screen characters are wholly unaware.

Most narratives will move in a straight line, following the basic chronology of a story unfolding. This is often called a linear narrative because it moves in a straight line.

However, in controlling the flow of information, a number of devices can be employed to realign the narrative. An obvious example is flashback, where the narrative allows a character to remember events that have happened in the past, usually to shed light on events 'currently' taking place within the narrative. Similarly, a complex narrative may allow events taking place in two different locations at the same time to be shown alongside each other. This is called parallel action and provides the audience with a privileged view. An extreme form of this is the use of split-screen techniques where two narratives can literally be shown simultaneously on screen.

LINEAR NARRATIVE A plot that moves forward in a straight line without flashbacks or digressions.

KEY TERM

PARALLEL ACTION A narrative device in which two scenes are observed as happening at the same time by cutting between them.

KEY TERM

Some media texts play on the need of the audience to find logical sequencing in narratives by denying this. For example, if we are watching a film, and a character we know to have been killed suddenly and inexplicably reappears, we find it hard to make sense. Indeed the contract that we, the audience, agreed to whereby we suspend our disbelief is clearly threatened by this.

ANTI-NARRATIVE describes a text which seeks deliberately to disrupt narrative flow in order to achieve a particular effect, such as the repetition of images or the disruption of a chronological sequence of events.

KEY TERM

Pulp Fiction is an example of a film which uses this device, confounding the audience by the reappearance of a character whose death we had witnessed earlier.

▼ GENRE

In this section we:

- consider and explain the concept of genre
- look at the function of genre in relation to audiences and the producers of media products
- consider the role of genre as a critical tool in the analysis of media texts.

Figure 13 *Robert De Niro and Ray Liotta in* Goodfellas *(1990)*

Look at the image in Figure 13. Try to identify the type of film this image is taken from.

- Can you work out what sort of storyline the film is likely to have?
- Can you determine who the villains may be?
- Can you make any suggestions as to the actors or directors that might appear in this type of film?
- What else can you deduce about the film?

THE FUNCTION OF GENRE

In working out the answers to the questions above, you will have used your knowledge of genre. The concept of genre is useful in looking at the ways in which media texts are organised, categorised and consumed. It is applied to television, print and radio texts as well as to film. The concept of Genre suggests that there are certain types of media material, often story-types, which are recognised through common elements, such as style, narrative and structure, that are used again and again to make up that particular type of media genre.

KEY TERM

GENRE The term used for the classification of media texts into groups with similar characteristics.

An important element in identifying a genre is the look or iconography of the text. Iconography constitutes a pattern of visual imagery which remains common to a genre over a period of time.

KEY TERM

ICONOGRAPHY Those particular signs that we associate with particular genres, such as physical attributes and dress of the actors, the settings and the 'tools of the trade' (cars, guns, etc.).

Look at a selection of films that are currently being shown in your area and try to categorise them into different genres.

- What types of stories do the films tell?
- Where are the films set?
- What type of characters appear in the films?
- What particular actors and/or directors are associated with the films? Have they been involved with similar types of films before?
- What is the 'look' or iconography of the film?
- What music is used?

Genre is a formula which, if successful, is often repeated again and again and can be used over a long period of time. For instance in a gangster film, like the one in Figure 13, (*Goodfellas*, 1990), we expect to see some, or all, of the following elements that will also probably have been in a gangster film from the 1930s:

Car chases	Urban settings
Guns	Mafia
Heroes	Corrupt police/politicians
Villains	Beautiful women
Violence	Italians

There are also certain actors that we may associate with this genre of films (James Cagney in the 1930s, Robert de Niro in the 1980s or currently Vinnie Jones) as well as certain directors (Martin Scorsese and Guy Ritchie).

ACTIVITY . . .

Take two examples of films of the same genre from different eras that interest you, for instance *War of the Worlds* (1953) and *Independence Day* (1996), and identify their similarities and differences. Suggest reasons for these similarities and differences.

GENRE AND AUDIENCES

Audiences are said to like the concept of genre (although we may not identify it by that name) because of its reassuring and familiar promise of patterns of repetition and variation.

The concept of genre is important in arousing the expectations of an audience and how they judge and select texts. Placing a text within a specific genre plays an important role in signalling to an audience the type of text that they are being invited to consume. Audiences become familiar with the codes and conventions of specific genres. Familiarity through repetition is therefore one of the key elements in the way audiences understand and relate to media texts.

Audiences not only come to expect certain common codes and conventions but these can also provide a short cut which saves the audience (and the producers) time in developing a new set of conventions each time they consume a new text in that particular genre. This can be seen where two existing genres have been brought together to create a new one. For example, TV docu-soaps, which combine elements of documentary and soap opera. These rely on an audience's understanding and ability to read each specific genre – they understand how documentaries work and they understand how soap operas work. Therefore docu-soaps are able to satisfy their expectations of both.

Look at the promotional material that is used to market either a new radio, TV or cinema product.

■ Identify those elements that are recognisable as belonging to a particular genre by the audience.
■ Are there any elements that distinguish it from other established products of the same genre?

Often the promotion and marketing for new texts invite the audience to identify similarities between a text and predecessors in the same genre. The audience can then take comfort in the fact that what they are being offered is something that they have previously enjoyed and the producers hope that they will enjoy it again.

It has been suggested that proficiency in reading texts within a genre can also lead to the audience's pleasure being heightened as they recognise particular character types or storylines.

Select a magazine or newspaper that you read regularly and consider how you consume it:

■ Make a list of the features that you most look forward to reading. In which order do you read them? Why?
■ Do you read a range of magazines or newspapers from the same genre? If so, what are the similarities/differences between them?
■ Do similar stories/features appear in similar places in different publications? If so, why?
■ Are similar products advertised in these magazines or newspapers? If so, why?

MEDIA STUDIES: THE ESSENTIAL INTRODUCTION

Genre and producers

Producers are said to like the concept of genre because they can exploit a winning and minimise taking risks. The concept of genre also helps institutions budget their finances more accurately and helps them to promote new products.

One of the main functions of most of the mainstream media is to make a profit. Just as a high-street retailer has to sell goods that the customers will want to buy, so a media producer has to create texts that audiences will want to consume.

One way to do this is to find what audiences already enjoy and offer something similar. Genre is an easy way of doing this. Where a formula has been proved popular with audiences it makes sense for the producer to use that formula again and to create a new product that contains similar recognisable features which it is hoped will have an immediate appeal to an established audience.

ACTIVITY

How might the use of a proven formula apply to the popular music industry? Is this also the case when listening to radio music stations? Give examples.

It is for this reason that certain genres seem to be continually popular, such as hospital dramas on television. Some genres, like wildlife programmes, although popular for many years, have changed over time as technology has changed, although the codes and conventions or the presenter may have stayed the same. Indeed, genre is such a useful tool that it is now the case that small niche audiences are targeted by themed cable and satellite channels carrying programmes of just one genre. These niche audiences are groups of people with specific media interests, such as holiday, history or 'adult' programmes. This has the very real advantage of delivering a ready-made audience to advertisers marketing specific products. For example, a channel dedicated to travel programmes will clearly attract an audience in the market to buy holidays.

Other changes in genres over a period of time may be due to the changes in society itself. Consider, for example, the police series on television. The representation of police officers in programmes like *Dixon of Dock Green* (Figure 14a), broadcast in the early 1950s, is quite a long way removed from the way they are represented in some more contemporary programmes like *Cops*, although some might argue that there are still many similarities between *Dixon of Dock Green* and *The Bill* (Figure 14b and 14c).

The dominance of genre, coupled with the caution of many media producers, can mean that some new texts are marginalised because they do not fit into the generic conventions that audiences recognise and accept. However, there are always new combinations of programmes being produced that can be difficult to fit into a particular genre but yet are successful. For instance, where do *The Young Ones* or *Third Rock from the Sun* fit?

a

b

Figure 14

c

Some texts such as the television series *Police Story* or the films *Airplane* and *Scary Movie* deliberately adapt or parody genre conventions and characteristics. It could be argued that texts that fail to fit into a particular genre are often the most successful. For instance, the popularity of Ridley Scott's film *Blade Runner* or the television series *Absolutely Fabulous* might be due to the fact that they failed to fit neatly into audience expectations.

GENRE AS A CRITICAL TOOL

The idea of genre has been used for a long time. For example Literary Studies categorises texts into such genres as sonnets, tragedies, picaresque novels. It was the film theorists of the 1960s and 1970s who recognised the importance of genre to Film and Media Studies. They saw genre as important because media texts are the product of an industrial process, rather than the creation of an individual, as typified by the Hollywood studio system or indeed Bollywood today!

Grouping texts according to type makes studying them more convenient, recognises the industrial constraints upon producers of media texts and also allows these texts to be looked at in terms of trends within popular culture (e.g. the Western). Genre theory acknowledges that, while an individual text may not be worthy of detailed study, yet a group of texts of the same genre can reveal a good deal, especially in terms of audience appeal (e.g. Hammer films).

For example, recent studies suggest that categories of programmes can be gender-specific in that they appeal particularly to either male or female audiences. Males, it is suggested, prefer factual television programmes, sport or action-based narratives, and fictions where there is a clear resolution at the end, i.e. all the villains are killed and the boy gets the girl.

NOTEBOX

David Morley in *Family Television* (1986) found that men often disapproved of watching fiction on the grounds that it was not 'real life' or sufficiently serious. He also found that men tended to defined their own preferences (sport, current affairs) as more important and more 'serious'. Morley suggests that men do in fact enjoy more 'feminine' genres but are perhaps not prepared to admit it.

ACTIVITY

Select a group of males and females from a range of age groups. Using a questionnaire that you have designed, conduct some research into the popularity of a particular genre across any medium. You should be trying to establish whether consumption of genre in the media is gender-specific.

LIMITATIONS OF GENRE

1   The concept of genre can have limitations when applied to a range of media texts because of the variety and the need for constant updating of texts that are being produced. Many texts may look similar but are too different to be put together.

2   Sometimes the category becomes too generalised to be helpful. For instance, soap opera could be described as a genre because there are many common characteristics (domestic settings, continuing storylines, cliff-hanger endings, familiar characters, etc.) but how helpful is it to say that *Sunset Beach* and *EastEnders* belong to the same genre? We need to be able to distinguish between subgenres within a genre, e.g. American 'fantasy' soap operas and British 'realism' soap operas. How would you describe Australian soap operas, such as *Neighbours* or *Home and Away*?

3   Although we have used the concept of genre for all types of media text, it has been argued that genre is most useful for film and television and is of limited use when applied to newspapers, magazines or radio.

ACTIVITY . . .

If you are interested to know more about this, research the early days of newspapers like *The Times* or the *Observer*. Look up references to 'The Radical Press', which was a series of illegal, untaxed or unstamped newspapers like *The Poor Man's Guardian* or *The Working Man's Friend*, aimed at the working classes.

OR

Carry out a survey of the television schedules and try to categorise the main genres that appear. Also look at satellite, cable and digital channels.

■   What are the most common genres?
■   Why is this the case?
■   How can these genres be linked to particular audiences?
■   What effect does this have on shaping the schedules?

▼ REPRESENTATION

In this section we consider the important concept of representation in examining media texts. We look at

- how the media represent to us the world at large
- the significance and accuracy of such representations
- the use of stereotyping
- how minority groups may be affected by media representation.

REPRESENTATION The process by which the media present to us the 'real world'.

KEY TERM

MEDIA REPRESENTATION OF THE WORLD AT LARGE

For many of us, the media are an important source of information about the world in which we live. Indeed, it has been argued that the media are one of the chief means by which we reach an understanding of this world. In consequence, many people believe the media are a powerful means of shaping our attitudes and beliefs.

This process by which the media can be said to interpret the world, or external reality, for us is called representation. There is a wide philosophical debate about what constitutes 'reality' and whether, in fact, reality ultimately exists. If, however, we assume, for the convenience of looking at representation, that there is an external reality, then one key function of the media is to represent that reality to us, the audience. The means by which it does this are discussed in the earlier section on Image Analysis, where we identified a series of sign systems that are used by the media to represent the world.

As we have seen, each medium, such as television or print, is composed of an elaborate system or code, by which it represents the world outside. These codes are often a complex combination of symbolic, iconic and indexical signs (see p. 33). Television, for example,

THE RANK ORGANISATION Presents
A PETER ROGERS PRODUCTION
SIDNEY JAMES · KENNETH WILLIAMS · CHARLES HAWTREY
JOAN SIMS · HATTIE JACQUES · TERRY SCOTT
RICHARD O'CALLAGHAN · BERNARD BRESSLAW · JACKI PIPER
IMOGEN HASSALL
in "CARRY ON LOVING" A
Screenplay by Talbot Rothwell
Produced by Peter Rogers
Directed by Gerald Thomas

Figure 15 *Still from* Carry on Loving (1970)

uses iconic images of a world we can recognise, often anchored by spoken language to shape and limit the meanings it is communicating to the audience. The use of iconic images is an important element of the televisual message because it has the impact of making the images seem very like the world it represents. The television screen gives the audience a two-dimensional representation of the three-dimensional outside. The image can, therefore, be said to be very 'naturalised' as we have grown up to 'read' two-dimensionality as a realistic representation of what we know to exist in the outside world. A similar argument can be made about still photography. 'The camera never lies', we are told, although we all know that it can and does. Indeed the French film director Jean-Luc Godard described film as truth 24 times a second, alluding to the number of individual frames used to create a second of screen time.

In his book *How to Read Film* (1977), James Monaco points out that anyone, even a cat, can watch a film. If we are to make sense of the film, however, we must learn to comprehend the visual images with which we are presented.

Consider a situation in which you have been involved in an argument or fight with a classmate. Imagine you are asked to describe the altercation to:

■ your parents
■ a close friend
■ your teacher.

What factors might influence your representation of the events that took place in each of these contexts? Consider carefully how you are likely to select, edit and prioritise the information that you choose to provide.

HOW ACCURATE?

Clearly an important debate in any study of the media is about the accuracy of the representation it offers us. (The issue of realism is dealt with more fully in the section on p. 87.) What must be borne in mind is that the media offer us a representation of reality rather than reality itself. The information communicated by a media text is a constructed reshaping of the world; in the same way as in the above activity, where you will have reshaped your own experience to communicate it. There are a number of questions that we can usefully ask ourselves when we look at examples of media representation:

■ Can we trust the representation that is being made to be an accurate portrayal?
■ How far have the institutional context and audience expectations determined the nature of the representation?
■ In whose interests is it that the representation is made in this way?

MEDIATION The process by which a media text represents an idea, issue or event to us. This is a useful word as it suggests the way in which things undergo a change in the process of being acted upon by the media.

Consider an event that takes place and is shown on television, for example a sporting fixture, protest/demonstration or concert.

■ In what ways is there a difference between being at the 'live' event and watching it on television?
■ Are there qualities that are present in the live event that cannot be experienced through watching television?
■ Are there some things in the televisual representation that may not be experienced by 'being there'?

ENCODING The process by which the media construct messages.

Encoding involves re-presenting ideas and events from the world outside into a form that can be decoded by an audience. As we have seen in the section on Image Analysis, the audience has to learn the code in order to take meaning from a media text. Once this has been learned, however, the process of decoding media texts can make them appear extremely natural, as though the process of encoding had not in fact taken place and that the audience were experiencing directly reality itself.

Take, for example, a location interview on the television news. Often this will have been filmed using just a single camera. The process of this filming is usually to conduct the interview with the camera framing the interviewee.

What you have is a highly constructed presentation of an event that most people watching television would identify as quite 'natural', simply because the audience have become so familiar with this method of presenting an interview. Note, too, that in terms of fictional dialogue in the cinema and on television the concept of shot/reverse shot is the standard or even 'natural' way of presenting two people in conversation.

ACTIVITY . . .

It is interesting to contrast the technique of shot/reverse shot with the intrusive and self-conscious production techniques employed on programmes such as *The Big Breakfast*. This programme actually highlights the presence of the technology and production personnel in the studio by involving them in the programme. How do you think this affects the way in which the programme represents the world to us?

Not only are most media texts highly constructed representations of the world, they are also quite carefully selected. In the example above, we have considered how a constructed representation can be made to appear natural through the simple convention that we are used to seeing it that way and its iconic form convinces us of its naturalness. Prior to the image ever reaching our screens, however, a process of selection has taken place that determines which aspects of the world are chosen to be represented.

As we will see in the case study on news in Part 4, a careful selection process takes place which will determine which events on any one day will be reported on television, in the newspapers and on the radio. In putting together a news report, a television news crew will then make a series of decisions about what images and information are going to be gathered by a reporter and film crew to represent a particular news item. Back in the television studio images and information will be selected (and others rejected) and then combined on an edit suite to produce a representation of the event. These processes of selection may heavily mediate the original event that took place. What we see on our evening news bulletin is a highly refined representation of an event that has taken place, selected and shaped to be represented in a particular way to the audience.

This process of selection and refinement inevitably involves a large element of simplification in order to produce a text that is clear and manageable enough for the audience to consume. A good example is television highlights of a sporting event, or a report of such an event in a newspaper. Here the process of representation will involve the selecting and highlighting of important details. Inevitably, therefore, those elements that in some way are controversial or dramatic will be included at the expense of more mundane and run-of-the-mill events. As we have noted in the section on Narrative (p. 44), dramatic and controversial events usually involve conflict between people. In consequence, it is often this conflict that becomes the main focus of the media's attention in representing the world at large. In this way a violent tackle, a controversial decision or a brawl on the pitch will almost certainly be highlighted rather than an example of skilful play or sportsmanship.

NOTEBOX

When we consider tabloid newspapers, this highlighting of conflict is often called sensationalism. The tabloid press is accused of seeking to sensationalise events that they represent.

STEREOTYPING

An important result of the media needing to simplify in order to make a representation is in the production of stereotypes. The process of simplification in order to make events and issues more digestible for the audience in this case is extended to the representation of groups of people. Rather than representing them as individuals, sections of the media use a kind of shorthand in the way in which they represent some groups of people. These groups of people come from all walks of life, but significantly they are often minority groups (for example, gay men or ethnic groups). What stereotyping does is to characterise whole groups of people by attributing to them qualities which may be found in one or two individuals. These characteristics are often exaggerated, and entire racial groups or nationalities become reduced to single characteristics. For example, the Jewish race and people from Scotland are both characterised as being tight-fisted.

In their book *Media Studies* (1999), Taylor and Willis consider images of youth as examples of stereotyping. They base their analysis on the work of two Cultural Studies writers, Angela McRobbie, who produced an influential study of the influence of the magazine *Jackie* on teenage girls, and Dick Hebdige, who wrote extensively about media representations of youth (see Hebdige 1988).

Figure 16 Wakefield Express, *21 April 2000*

ARMED COMBAT. Huddersfield-Sheffield Giants' Karl Lovell gets to grips with Wildcats centre Tony Tatupu during the side's high-scoring encounter at McAlpine Stadium last Sunday. The Giants clawed their way back into the game and pinched it at the death with a decisive drop-goal.

Countries and even whole continents are often represented in the media in a stereotypical way. Consider, for example, the most common media representations of Africa, which is often presented through images of starvation and war.

Youth has tended over the latter half of the twentieth century to suffer from a rather negative representation in the media. From the Teddy Boy images and panics surrounding Elvis Presley movies in the 1950s, through mods and rockers, punk and the representation of 'E' and related drug culture today, youth in revolt has always provided the media with ample opportunities for negative representation of young people. Typically, much of this stereotyping has been based on the activities of one or two individuals whose activities have provided a source of newspaper headlines.

- Is it possible to find media representations of youth that are positive?
- If so, where are these mostly to be found?
- Do you feel these are accurate representations?

Stereotyping is obviously a useful short-cut for media producers to reproduce and represent groups of people in the media. What a stereotype allows them to do is to condense a lot of complex information into a character who not only is easily recognised but also is simple to deal with. Minor characters in films are often presented as stereo-types. The unfortunate side-effect of this is to dehumanise people by denying them the complex psychological make-up that an individual possesses by reducing them to a few generalised personality traits. As Tessa Perkins has pointed out, some stereotypes are based on truth that can be observed. For example, France has produced many talented chefs and most French people enjoy gourmet food and wine. However, like the rest of us, French people are complex individuals with more to their lives than indulgence in food and drink.

An even more worrying aspect of stereotyping is the way in which it can be used to marginalise and devalue the worth of whole groups of people in society. In addition, it tends to disregard the causes of stereotypical behaviour, making the group a potential scapegoat for broader ills within a society. For example, the stereotyping of some members of ethnic minorities as living all together in crowded and substandard accommodation can suggest that, where this is the case, it is a matter of choice rather than a result of economic and social deprivation.

This use of stereotypical representation can be seen to reflect the power relations within our society; it tends to subordinate certain groups. Often this will involve some element of ridicule by suggesting that certain groups of people are intellectually challenged or more prone to criminal activity than the rest of the population.

In the 1970s in America, George Gerbner produced a quantitative survey, using content analysis techniques, to investigate the representation of violence in the American media. One of his findings was that the victims of violence were often minority groups that society considered most expendable.

Make a list of groups that you feel are most often stereotyped or represented negatively. In what ways can these groups be said to be subordinate within our society, e.g. economically or socially?

You may like to link this activity to the content analysis activity on p. 279.

CONTENT ANALYSIS A method of collecting, collating and analysing large amounts of information about the content of media products, such as television advertisements, in order to draw conclusions about such issues as the representation of gender roles.

ACTIVITY . . .

The end of the twentieth century was dominated by the emergence of so-called 'Girl Power'. Discuss the extent to which this phenomenon represents the emancipation of women and to what extent it can be seen as another form of exploitative representation in the interests of patriarchy (i.e. male domination in society).

Another important issue has been the under-representation of people from minority groups in the media. Certainly television representation of ethnic-minority groups and the gay community has increased in recent years. However, some would argue that this is in fact mere tokenism. This implies that the increased presence of such groups is simply to give the illusion of fairer representation, rather than being a genuine attempt to produce a more even balance. Many, for instance, would point to the relative absence of people with disabilities in the media other than in texts aimed at audiences with a disability. People with a disability have traditionally been represented in a particularly negative way by the media. Commonly they are depicted in films as evil and dangerous people intent on causing harm to able-bodied people.

The representation of groups, however, is not fixed for ever, and it is possible to observe changes over periods of time. The emergence of specific groups and subcultures is often accompanied by a challenge to existing stereotypes and a challenge to the media to produce more positive representations. It can be argued that this may be linked ideologically to such things as legislation promoting equal opportunities. Some people would argue that these groups remain marginalised; it is simply that the negative representation of them becomes less overt.

ACTIVITY . . .

Consider the media representation of minority groups:

■ Do you think the high-profile media representation of outwardly gay figures such as Graham Norton and Julian Clary is a positive development for gay people?

■ In the programme *Goodness Gracious Me* the Asian actors direct much of the humour at their own culture and stereotypes. Do you think such a programme might have been called racist (and been censored) if the programme had featured white actors?

■ What is your reaction to the *Ali G Show*?

To some extent the work of many activist groups fighting on behalf of minorities has at least drawn attention to the extent of negative stereotyping. For example, the feminist movement on both sides of the Atlantic has served to highlight the exploitation of women through the media in such forms as page 3 girls in the tabloid press, and more recently the emergence of 'lad culture' with magazines such as *Loaded* using images of women in an exploitative way.

Certainly it is an interesting exercise to compare some of the stereotypical representation from the recent past with today. For example, *Carry On* films or 1970s television sit-coms such as *Mind Your Language,* frequently rerun on cable and satellite networks, were much more overtly sexist and homophobic than today. However, many people would argue that the difference lies in the extent to which such negative attitudes are made manifest.

ACTIVITY . . .

Choose a group of people that you consider to have been negatively represented in the media. Can you identify any members of the group who feature in the media and can be said to present a positive representation? For example, you might like to consider Victor Meldrew or Miss Marple as representatives of elderly people.

▼   MEDIA INTERTEXTUALITY

In this section we look at the concept of intertextuality and explore its role in media studies through:

- mimicry
- parody, pastiche and homage
- marketing of media texts
- the treatment of fictional soap opera stories in the tabloid press
- reviews of media texts in other media forms
- media performers working in more than one media form.

One of the pleasures that audiences experience in the consumption of media texts is the joy of recognition. One form of this pleasure comes in recognising the reference in one media text to other media texts. This process of referencing is called intertextuality.

KEY TERM

INTERTEXTUALITY The way in which texts refer to other media texts that producers assume audiences will recognise.

MIMICRY

This interdependent relationship between texts can take a number of different forms. It often transcends both genres and media forms so that a text created in one particular medium will be used in some way in another medium. Advertising and music videos are two genres that rely heavily on the use of intertextuality to achieve a particular effect. Often this borrowing of a text to link it to a second one is stylistic. This means that a text will mimic or otherwise copy certain stylistic features of another text. Usually this is done in order to create a particular impact, although there may be instances where this borrowing may seem simply a matter of convenience to give a music video, for example, a particular look. For the reader of the image, however, the connotative power of the original text is likely to be carried through into the new text.

a

b

c

Figure 17

An example of this might be the deliberate playing on the style and content of the film *Thelma and Louise* in advertising a Peugeot 106 car (Figure 17). The original film portrays two women travelling across America seeking to escape from the dominant influence of life in a patriarchal society. The women are seen as emancipated travellers seeking their own destiny in a world free from the oppression of men. The film is often regarded as an example of post-feminist cinema. By deliberately making references to the film in the advertisements, the car comes to symbolise the concept of emancipation, suggesting that any woman who buys it will be able to liberate herself in just the same way as the women in the film.

Clearly we, the audience, experience the joy of recognising the 'cleverness' of the way in which advertisers play with both the style and themes of *Thelma and Louise* in order to link their product to the film. At a deeper level, however, the connotative power and mythological status of a female road movie provides a selling point to a hatchback car. Owning the car will be a statement about lifestyle aspirations to be an independent self-assertive woman just like Thelma and Louise. Advertisers are always keen to sell the consumer a lifestyle to go with the product.

Of course the impact of the car advertisement relies on our familiarity with the film. There may be audiences watching the advertisements who have never seen the film, as well as some who only hear about the link second-hand from those who have. Much of the impact of intertextual reference is determined by our own cultural knowledge or awareness of the texts with which the link is being made.

In the *Thelma and Louise*/Peugeot 106 example above, it can be seen that there is a deliberate attempt on the part of the advertiser to use the meaning of the film to add to the effectiveness of the advertisement. Can you find examples of similar uses of intertextuality?

The Peugeot example is a source of pleasure because it can be said to contain elements of parody. There is a certain tongue-in-cheek comedy about the way in which the characters in the advertisement mimic their cinematic counterparts, perhaps in a subtle way to poke fun at the original. There is perhaps also some element of self-parody in the vaguely absurd notion that owning a car can effect a new emancipated lifestyle. Intertextuality can confront us with some complex readings of media texts.

PARODY, PASTICHE AND HOMAGE

The postmodern critic Fredric Jameson has suggested a differentiation between *parody*, which aims to mock an original in a critical way, and *pastiche*, which he suggests is merely a stylistic mask. Pastiche simply uses images in an empty surface way in order to sell products. Parody for Jameson has substance; pastiche is merely a matter of imitating.

In the introduction to this book we discussed the significance of postmodernism in any study of the media. You may find it useful to look back at that section in light of some of the ideas about intertextuality. Specifically, one of the concepts mentioned is bricolage, the French word for 'do-it-yourself'. The word also carries a more negative connotation of 'patching up'. As you will see, there is an obvious relevance to the idea of recycling earlier texts to produce 'new' ones. For example, the idea of sampling existing pieces of music and mixing them to create new ones is typical of this notion of bricolage. Some people would argue that this recycling represents an act of great creativity, while others would suggest that it is a symptom of the fact that people have run out of ideas, what Jameson calls 'the failure of the new'.

Perhaps what is most significant is the idea that the insatiable demand for media texts in the postmodern media-saturated world requires a large degree of recycling simply to meet this demand.

ACTIVITY . . .

Watch a segment of output from MTV.

- How many of the videos that you encounter make some reference to other media texts you have come across?
- How many of these can be said to be parody?
- How many are pastiche?
- What criteria have you used to distinguish this?

Obviously, parody can only be effective through our knowledge of the text or genre of text being parodied. We take a delight in the recognition of the elements being parodied in what is called the 'shared cultural knowledge' which enables us to enjoy through recognition the relationship between the texts.

Similarly, some texts work through the idea of homage. Homage suggests respect for a particular text, acknowledging the power and importance of the original text by imitating it. Homage is commonly experienced in the cinema, where a director may deliberately create a scene, or even a whole film, in which the intertextual elements combine to pay respect to an earlier creation. The work of Alfred Hitchcock is frequently referred to in this way, through, for example, the work of a director such as Brian De Palma. Similarly more recent examples of *film noir*, sometimes referred to as neo-noir, have paid homage to the Hollywood genre that dominated the cinema in the 1940s and 1950s.

How can we distinguish homage from plagiarism? Consider the many films that have simply copied the successful style of others. What films have you seen that you think develop the style and themes of the original to which they relate?

MARKETING

One area of the media in which intertextuality is important is in the marketing of media texts. In order for a media product to be promoted successfully, it is often advertised extensively. Some of this advertising will obviously be placed alongside existing products of a similar nature and form. Trailers on television and radio for programmes to be shown later in the schedules are a typical example of this. However, it also common to find examples of new media products being promoted through other media forms. For example, trailers for new cinema releases are often shown as advertisements on television or on the radio. More subtle forms of promotion are also brought into play. Celebrity news stories in the press are often linked to the promotion of a new film or album release. Similarly, appearances by stars on chat shows, breakfast television and radio programmes are used to promote newly released texts. Increasingly, new films and television programmes are the focus of billboard campaigns. Such methods of promotion have also been used to make the public aware of new presenters on national radio stations. In all of these instances there is an intertextual relationship between one or more texts.

An interesting example of intertextuality is the way in which stories from soap operas find their way into the tabloid press. Sometimes these stories feature the actors who play the roles of soap characters. At times, however, the fictional characters themselves are featured in the print media. For example, a storyline from *Coronation Street* featured the wrongful imprisonment of the fictional character, Deirdre Rashid. This story was taken up by the tabloid press and the *Sun* newspaper's front page story demanded her release.

REVIEWS

Reviews of media texts appear regularly across different media forms. Cinema releases are reviewed on television, in programmes dedicated specifically to the week's cinema releases. Films and television programmes are similarly reviewed in the press and on radio. Radio output itself is also reviewed in the broadsheet newspapers. In many ways, the media, it has been argued, spend a good deal of time looking at themselves, rather than at the world outside, positioning themselves at the centre of their own universe.

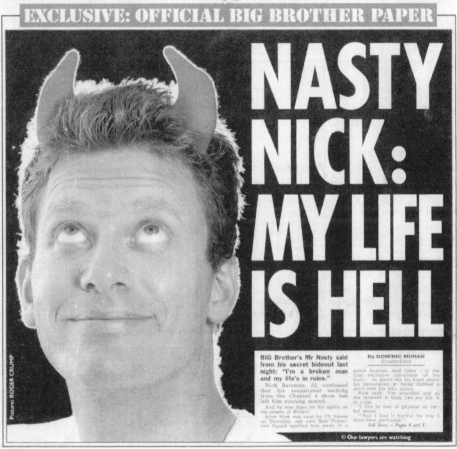

Figure 18

An increasingly common television genre involves programmes about the making of a particular film. These programmes are usually linked to an expensive new blockbuster film and take audiences behind the scenes of the shooting of the film. Often they include interviews with the stars and the director as another method of promoting the film.

Some genres and media forms are so popular that they have whole magazines dedicated to them. Consider, for example, the number of film magazines currently available that not only reflect but also promote interest in the cinema. There is also a range of magazines given over to television soaps. It would seem that the audience for these products has almost an insatiable desire to consume them both in televisual and print formats.

The Internet is another media form that constantly makes reference to other media. Most major newspaper and magazine publishers have a website that complements their existing publications. Film companies are able to show clips of new releases via the Internet, and in a similar way the music industry uses it to promote new music. Many individual fans also have their own websites promoting a whole range of media-related issues. Indeed the Internet has rapidly become a forum for a dynamic exchange of views, some more informed than others, across media forms on a worldwide scale. Some sites of particular interest to media students are given in the Resources section at the end of this book.

Allied to this type of promotion is that of the 'spin-off'. One particularly successful spin-off is the magazine or book that emerges from the television programme. The newsagent's shelves are packed with examples, ranging from *X Files* magazines to cookery books. The former are particularly popular with viewers of cult television series. Similarly, videos of successful television series are often made available for sale or rental, once they have been transmitted.

The BBC publishes a number of magazines linked to television programmes that it broadcasts. What do you think are the advantages to the BBC of doing this?

MEDIA PERFORMERS IN DIFFERENT MEDIA FORMS

It is worth noting the increasing number of performers in the media who appear in different media forms. Commonly journalists are likely to write for newspapers and magazines as well as appearing in, or presenting, television and radio programmes. Working across the media provides opportunities for these performers to promote both themselves as well as the publications and programmes for which they are working. An example is Anne

Robinson, who currently writes a column in the Saturday edition of *The Times* newspaper and is also presenter of the television quiz show *The Weakest Link*. In a similar vein, it is also possible to find examples of media texts that exist in, or have developed through, a number of different media forms. A comic-strip character, such as Batman, has been transformed into feature films and television programmes.

▼ MEDIA IDEOLOGY

In this section we:

- consider the concept of ideology
- explain the nature and function of ideology, and
- assess its significance in studying the media.

BELIEF SYSTEMS

As suggested in previous sections, we as humans experience a need to make sense of the world and the events that take place in it. One important way of doing this is through our consumption of media texts. However, it is often argued that all media texts are in some way ideological. On one level, ideology is the system of beliefs that organises the way in which we view the world and the events that take place in it. It follows, therefore, that in our consumption of media texts we will be subjected to the ideological views of the producer of the text.

Ideologies come in a variety of different forms. Perhaps the most prevalent and obvious examples are the political and economic systems that govern the way in which people live their lives. Capitalism is an ideology that emphasises the importance of people in a society to be free to create wealth by setting up and running their own businesses. Marxism, on the other hand, is a belief system that considers that capitalism exploits the labour of the workers and argues that the state should own and control wealth creation and distribute it fairly among the population as a whole. Clearly these two ideologies are in conflict.

Religion, it can be argued, is an ideology where an organised system of beliefs and values defines to people how they should live their lives and what constitutes appropriate behaviour. The stained-glass windows in a church, for example, portrayed a worldview and a set of values (symbolised by parables, etc.) designed to instruct the local people in how to live their lives in a righteous and morally responsible way.

Today the media have to a large degree replaced stained-glass windows as sources of ideology. Media messages, as we have seen, are constructed. In this process of construction, inevitably selection and shaping take place in order to represent the world outside. This selection and shaping reflect the value system of the originator of the message. An important question we need to ask when considering the ideology that lies behind a media message is 'In whose interest is it that we perceive the world this way?'

Consider a number of texts in which family life is depicted. These might include magazines articles and pictures, radio, television and print advertisements, and feature films.

- Are there consistent elements in the way families are represented?
- Do any of these elements dominate the representation?
- Are members of the family assigned similar roles across media texts?
- Why are families important to our social order?
- In whose interest is it that families are depicted in this way?

You may like to take the illustration of the family on the *Radio Times* cover (Figure 26, p. 113) as your starting point.

Researchers such as the Glasgow Media Group have undertaken investigations that reveal that television news reporting on industrial disputes tends to depict strikers as a disruptive force in society which needs to be resisted. Clearly such a representation is doing a good deal of ideological work to reinforce the belief that it is wrong to take industrial action. Ideologically we are being encouraged to see capitalism as a system that is basically fair and just. Workers who exercise their democratic right to withdraw their labour to achieve social justice through better pay and conditions are seen as disruptive and anti-social. Ideologically they are seen to represent subversive forces that threaten the very fabric of society.

As the vast majority of people in this country are workers, many of whom are likely to be dissatisfied with their pay and conditions, it can be argued that such a view is in the interests of those people who hold power within our society and who benefit from keeping workers on low pay. In a democracy the people who hold power and rule over us have to do so to some extent with our consent. Forces do exist that are capable of coercing people into behaving in certain ways, the police for example, or in extreme cases the armed forces. Generally, people have to be persuaded to allow other people to exercise power over them. Some see the media as a powerful tool to ensure the co-operation of the population in accepting the norms imposed by the ruling elite.

HEGEMONY is the concept used by the Marxist critic Antonio Gramsci to describe how people are influenced into accepting the dominance of a power elite who impose their will and worldview on the rest of the population. He argues that this elite is able to rule because we allow it to do so. It can be argued that the ideological role of the media is to persuade us that it is in our best interests to accept the dominance of this elite.

The American commentator, Noam Chomsky, argues that popular culture can be used to divert people's attention from real issues such as their conditions of employment. It is only the intellectual and educated classes in society, largely the professional classes, who must be persuaded to agree with the ideological values of the ruling elite.

Make a list of some of the mass media texts that could be viewed as a diversion from real issues and social conditions. Which texts do you think are aimed at Chomsky's educated classes?

WATCHING *BIG BROTHER*

Let us look at a particular example of the way in which the media can be seen to shape our attitudes in order to accept what is best for the elite in power.

The idea of 'Big Brother' has always had strong negative connotations in our society. The freedom to go about daily business without being spied on has been considered a fundamental human right. In his novel (and the subsequent film) *1984*, George Orwell offered a nightmare vision of a society in which a citizen's every move was watched, leaving little opportunity to oppose the oppressive power of the state.

Today, however, nearly every public building and every town centre has surveillance cameras that watch every move of the people who occupy these spaces. The majority of people accept the presence of the cameras, and many would argue that they serve the public good, as they are an effective deterrent against crime. Clearly there has been a shift in consciousness on the part of the population from the paranoia of Big Brother to acceptance of the concept of surveillance. An important mechanism by which this change has been brought about is through the media. Programmes such as *Police, Camera, Action* make extensive use of footage from these cameras. These clips are often accompanied by a commentary from a reputable media personality such as a newsreader extolling the advantages of the cameras in detecting crime. Commonly we are presented with a chase in which cameras, for example in a police helicopter, offer the audience a privileged vantage point from which to observe the chase which leads to the arrest of the criminals. As the narrative unfolds we are positioned to identify with the forces of law and order as they use this sophisticated equipment to keep crime off our streets.

The ideology behind surveillance cameras is an example of how the media can be used to shape social attitudes and gain the acceptance of a population for something that may seem to be against their interests. It also demonstrates how ideologies do not remain fixed or static. In many respects, the media are part of a battleground in which different power elites fight for supremacy in terms of the acceptance of their ideas.

The concept of ideology is closely allied to that of representation. One way in which ideology works through media texts is by the simple process of repetition. This is particularly true of repeated representations across media forms which can have the effect of naturalising a way of seeing an issue so that it seems that no other interpretation is possible.

So changed is the ideological meaning of Big Brother that it has been used as the title of one of the most talked-about television programmes at the beginning of the twenty-first century. A group of people locked in a house, trying to win a prize by staying the longest, became the focus of the nation's attention. The filming of their every action provided voyeuristic entertainment for the nation and the media in the summer of 2000. Instead of Big Brother watching us, we took our pleasure from watching *Big Brother*.

IDEOLOGY AND GENDER

Our perceptions of female beauty, for example, are dominated by young, white, flawless size 10 women staring out from the covers and advertisements in magazines, and in newspapers, films and television. Similarly, as we have seen, family life is nearly always depicted as being a happy and desirable state with married couples bringing up children. On the other hand, consider the negative representation of people who do not go out to work and earn a living. They are called scroungers and depicted as people who live off the backs of other people who work hard for a living. Single mothers, for example, have been demonised in this way.

It can be argued that the effect of these representations is cumulative and, as we saw with stereotypes, they deny the complexity of human existence and reduce it to a basic issue of right or wrong. Going to work and using your earnings to support your family is right. Being unemployed and not being able to support your family is wrong.

What do you think is the ideological work of game shows and quiz programmes?

An interesting and useful way of looking at ideology is through its impact on minority groups within society. Despite the ground won by the feminist movement in the emancipation of women, it is generally accepted that we still live in a patriarchal society, that is one dominated by men, who retain most of the power. Clearly it is not in the interest of most women to occupy a position of inferiority to men. However, the ideological work of the media is such that women are represented so as to accept this subordinate position as being both natural and inevitable and in some way 'right'. If we were to make a list of typical depictions of women in the media, we would find a preponderance of images in which women are seen in a domestic situation; as objects for the pleasure of men; and as partners to men.

An interesting comparison can be made with the way in which ageing Hollywood stars are depicted. Generally when a female star ceases to be 'young and attractive' she is seen in fewer and fewer screen roles. She is then replaced with the latest and most attractive young starlet. Male stars, however, go on well past their youth and prime, many working into their old age.

One inference we can make from this is that women in Hollywood movies are seen to be of interest only when they are young, attractive and sexually desirable. In an important essay on the image of women in the cinema, 'Visual pleasure and narrative cinema' (1975), Laura Mulvey uses ideas based on psychoanalysis to argue that the main source of visual pleasure in the cinema is the voyeuristic male viewer enjoying the image of the female body. In order for a woman to experience pleasure from the film she has to position herself in a similar role to that of a male viewer enjoying the spectacle. Ideologically it can be argued that this positioning functions in order to persuade women that by occupying a role similar to that of the women on screen they will become desirable and attractive to men, thus reinforcing a woman's subordinate position within a patriarchy.

In this way, the ideological function of many media texts is to identify for women how they should perform within a patriarchy. Magazines aimed at young girls contain articles and features on how to look attractive and suggest ways in which to develop relationships with boys. Ideologically it is clear that happiness for a young girl is to be found in the arms of a male partner. Similarly the output of both television and magazines aimed at women suggests the importance of their domestic and child-bearing roles. Women who are able to juggle the demands of a career as well as these other duties are celebrated. Men on the other hand are only expected to be successful in their jobs.

Angela McRobbie in 1983 made a study of a magazine called *Jackie*, which was popular with teenage girls. She wrote how girls were being introduced into the sphere of feminine consumption. It can be argued that magazines of this type work ideologically to define for their audience those domestic roles of wife and mother which they should accept and embrace.

Figure 19 Michael Douglas and Catherine Zeta-Jones

Another ideological impact of the media is through what is known as 'moral panic'. This is basically a scare story often with little basis in truth, which serves to persuade people of the need for drastic action to cure a social ill. Horror videos, dangerous breeds of dog, asylum seekers and the drug Ecstasy have all been at the centre of moral panic. This panic is often orchestrated by the tabloid press and has the ideological impact of people demanding immediate action, usually to ban the availability of such things, without any rational consideration of whether this is an appropriate reaction or not.

MORAL PANIC A mass response to a group, a person or an attitude that becomes defined as a threat to society.

▼ REALISM

In this section we look at the concept of realism and consider its particular significance to the genre of documentary. We consider:

■ the accuracy of the representation
■ different types of realism
■ continuity editing
■ documentary film-making and the docu-soap
■ reality television.

In previous sections we looked at the way in which the media use sign systems to provide us with a representation of the outside world. We also noted that, because of a prevalence of iconic signs in visual media such as film, television and photography, these representations of the world can appear so natural that we easily see them as real. In this way, audiences can easily overlook the process of mediation that has occurred in presenting these images to us.

In considering the issue of realism, one of our concerns is to determine just how accurately a media form such as film or television can be said to represent 'reality'. As we have noted in the section on Representation (p. 63), what the media present to us is always a constructed and edited version of the real world. Any enquiry into realism must always take on board this issue. Similarly, when we look at a landscape painting we always bear in mind the fact that it is a painting or representation rather than the landscape itself. In both the painting and a media representation we should always remember that what we are presented with is an illusion of the real world and the events that take place in it.

Figure 20 *Still from an early episode of* **Coronation Street**

We can identify just how constructed and encoded the concept of realism is by considering the significance of monochrome, for example, in press photographs or film and television text. Many people find they associate black and white images with realism. For example some types of documentary photography or 1960s British cinema, in films such as *This Sporting Life* or *A Kind of Loving*, use black and white photography to depict a gritty realism of working-class life or poverty. As most of us see the world in its full spectrum of colour, there is a fundamental contradiction in the perception of black and white being in some way more real than a Technicolor image. Obviously there is something in our reading of monochrome images that serves to make us perceive its starkness as depicting the world in a more realistic way.

To confuse matters further, it has been argued that there is not one single realism, but that realism in media texts exists in a number of different ways.

DIFFERENT TYPES OF REALISM

Some media texts may be considered realistic because they contain 'truth' from the outside world. In this way we would identify a news bulletin as realistic in so far as the information it communicates to us is based on a verifiable external reality. In consequence we could argue that the content of such a text makes it realistic. A similar argument may be made for the realism of documentary films, which like news are concerned with offering factual information about external reality. This realism is sometimes referred to as *realism of content.*

Some media texts may contain material that has little credibility in terms of what we may know of any external reality. Science fiction programmes or action movies are likely to contain material that we perceive as far-fetched or unrealistic. However, the construction of these texts may still be seen as realistic in so far as they are produced in such a way as to remain plausible and to contain detail that we accept as being realistic. For example, the characters, although unreal in appearance, may act out of plausible motives and hence appear realistic. We might ask ourselves the relatively simple question of whether or not we are convinced by the text.

One of the ways in which we judge a text is by its ability to represent reality to us in a convincing way. We expect some degree of verisimilitude or resemblance to things that we know from real life. For example, an anachronism such as motor vehicles appearing inadvertently in a historical drama will create implausibility and can interfere with our ability to believe what we see in the text.

An important aspect of realism in film and television is rooted in the way a text is edited. The use of *continuity editing* is one method of shaping a text in such a way that it appears natural or realistic. Continuity editing requires that the action on screen should appear 'continuous'. In order to achieve this, the editor has to take care to ensure that what we see appears logical, for example by matching the eye levels when using shot/reverse shot for dialogue. The editor must also observe the 180-degree rule, whereby the camera keeps to one side of an imaginary line dividing a scene. This means that the audience has a constant reference point in viewing the action. If the 180-degree rule is broken, the audience will lose this frame of reference and the sense of continuity may be destroyed.

For some critics, discussion of the issue of realism has no relevance in a world where for many people the media themselves have come to represent the real world. The media no longer simply try to represent the real world; they have in fact replaced it. The French writer Jean Baudrillard coined the term 'hyperreal' to describe the way in which the media now dominate our perception of the outside world. For Baudrillard the world of the television represents a reality that is 'more real' than that which we can directly experience in the outside world. In this way a media representation becomes a hyper-reality with the reality encountered in the world itself a pale shadow of this.

DOCUMENTARY FILM-MAKING

Documentary film-making is one area in which the issue of realism is important. As its name suggests, a documentary seeks to document real life. It attempts to replicate experiences in the world in a realistic fashion. So, to some extent, we assess the effectiveness of a documentary film by its ability to convince us that what we are seeing is 'real'.

As a genre, documentary has developed over a period of years, but still functions by seemingly holding up a mirror to the world to show the audience what is 'out there'. Clearly this is an oversimplification, not least because there is a whole range of different types of documentary. However, one feature common to all documentaries is the fact that, like all media products, they have to be constructed. Although this construction may be undertaken in such a way as to make the text seem natural and realistic, the same process of selection and shaping has taken place as in a fictional text.

Indeed, there are important areas in which there is a clear parallel between fictional film-making and documentary. Film-makers like Mike Leigh, for example in *Meantime* (1981), or Ken Loach, in *Raining Stones* (1993), create films that have a strong realistic or naturalistic quality. This is in part due to their subject matter. Many of their films are a celebration of the lives of ordinary people. The filmic style contrives to be naturalistic in that there is little evidence of intrusive camera work or editing. The artifice of film-making is rendered subsidiary to the truth being told on the screen. Similarly some documentaries will use the reconstruction of events where the original footage is either non-existent or needs to be supplemented by more dramatic sequences (e.g. the series *999*). There are also examples of drama documentaries where real-life events are dramatised to enable audiences to relive the experience. Such programmes may draw on court transcripts or eyewitness testaments. *Hillsborough* (1996), written by Jimmy McGovern, is an example.

ACTIVITY

View extracts from a docu-soap and a drama documentary such as the one mentioned above.

■   Which do you consider to be the more accurate representation of reality?
■   What criteria have you used in arriving at your decision?
■   Do you think other readers of these texts would agree with you?

There are a number of issues that need to be explored in relation to the nature of documentary and of realism. There are also ethical and ideological issues to be considered. If documentary seeks to show us some kind of truth, the process of construction is obviously going to represent that truth from a specific viewpoint. As we have seen, the use of a voice-over narrator is a powerful device not only in determining the response of the audience to a documentary, but also in positioning them in such a way as to limit the readings that are available.

Part of the popularity of documentary as a genre is the way in which it allows the audience to get inside other people's lives. We often associate it with the idea of fly-on-the-wall filming techniques, where the participants are seemingly unaware of their being characters in the unfolding drama. Reality unfolds before our eyes, and the function of the camera is simply to capture it. This is not true for a number of reasons. First there is generally a process that takes place before filming, which is about selecting precisely what is to be filmed. The characters who feature in a documentary will be vetted for their charisma and screen presence long before a camera is ever pointed at them. What seems on screen a spontaneous process in which a film crew simply turns up at someone's house and starts filming is in most cases a carefully planned and constructed piece of film-making. A good deal of planning and preparation is likely to have taken place before the expense of committing a film crew is incurred.

It is very likely that the character featured will have been interviewed by a researcher to determine what he or she will say and do on camera. As most people, when confronted by a camera, will either freeze or ramble on for hours, some prompting as to the most appropriate responses may well be necessary. Similarly, as talking heads (i.e. mid-shots of people just talking) tend to be boring in televisual terms, it is often necessary to set up some activity in order to add visual interest. Note how often people in documentary are filmed undertaking some domestic chore while their voice is played over the action.

A second key issue with shooting documentary is the extent to which the camera itself necessarily intrudes and determines how people will respond and react. Your own experience of using video equipment will probably tell you that people 'play to the camera'. There is evidence to suggest that, as they become more accustomed to the presence of the camera, the more likely they are to forget that it is there and to act naturally. Despite this, there will always be a tendency to act differently when a person is being filmed.

A third issue is that at the post-production stage editing will probably be used to cut any of the material that does not fit readily into the narrative or is felt to get in the way of the flow of the programme.

ACTIVITY . . .

In the section on Narrative (p. 44), we emphasised the importance of conflict. Consider the narrative construction of a documentary. How has conflict been presented here? Do you think the conflict has emerged naturally or do you think it may have been contrived for dramatic effect?

NOTEBOX . . .

Most successful media texts are about people. Even when it is ideas and issues that are important, the story is usually told in terms of people. In many ways the docu-soap has become such a successful genre because it engages with the lives of people. The people featured are also ordinary enough for us to be able to relate readily to their lives. Interestingly, for some of them it is their ordinariness that enables them subsequently to become minor celebrities, as happened to Maureen in *Driving School* (Figure 21).

Figure 21 *Maureen in the BBC docu-soap* Driving School

Another issue to take on board in terms of documentary realism is that commonly documentaries are made from a specific standpoint adopted by the film-maker. For example, a documentary may have been made to expose some social injustice. A documentary film-maker such as John Pilger or Nick Broomfield may well be intent on offering a particular viewpoint in order to convince the audience of an argument. Clearly the editorial process is going to impact on what is represented in the film as well as the way in which that representation is made.

An extreme is the actual faking of scenes in documentary films. This may be a deliberate cutting of corners by a film crew in order to make filming easier, less time-consuming and less costly. For example, reconstructing an event that has taken place but filming it as though the action had been caught on camera. Equally, film-makers are occasionally conned by the subjects of their documentaries who manage to persuade them that they are something that they are not.

THE DOCU-SOAP

An interesting recent development in documentary film-making is the advent of a genre called docu-soap, which comprises elements of both the documentary and the soap opera. The common factor here is a strand that is concerned with the lives of ordinary people and the engagement of the audience with their lives. The docu-soap is an example of what is called a hybrid genre, where elements of two or more genres are fused to create a new category of media text.

MEDIA STUDIES: THE ESSENTIAL INTRODUCTION

DOCU-SOAP A hybrid genre in which elements of documentary and soap opera are combined to create a series about the lives of real people.

As Sonia Livingstone has pointed out, one quality of the soap opera is that the perceived realism generates for us a greater sense of involvement. This is a source of pleasure for the audience in that they can readily suspend their disbelief and involve themselves in the characters and the action. Similarly, in a study of *Dallas*, Ien Ang suggests that audiences enjoy pretending that soaps are real in order to heighten the pleasure they get from watching them.

The docu-soap usually focuses on a group of people who have a common interest, for example working for the same organisation. So, like a soap opera, it is concerned with the interaction of a group of people living or working in a community. Just as in a fictional soap, the audience is invited to engage with the lives of these characters, empathising and forming allegiances with these real-life characters. Docu-soaps produce their own 'stars' who can then go on to make appearances in other programmes and in the print media.

ACTIVITY

- Would you be prepared to be featured in a docu-soap about your family or school or college? What reasons do you have for your answer?
- When you watch a docu-soap are you conscious of people deliberately acting for the benefit of the camera?
- What do you think is the appeal of docu-soaps to media producers?

REALITY TELEVISION

A natural extension of the docu-soap is the use of real-life characters in 'reality television'. This genre seeks to replicate or reconstruct real events. Footage shot by the emergency services, such as the police or the fire brigade, is partly used, but this is often enhanced by real people playing their own roles in the event. *Crimewatch* is a good example where people are asked to reconstruct their own roles as victims of or witnesses to crimes. Similarly a programme such as *999* uses real people to re-enact life-threatening disasters and misfortunes that have befallen them. Such programmes clearly have a distinct audience appeal in terms of ordinary people being recognisably similar to us. The audience, therefore, is able to empathise with an ordinary member of the public in a way that they may not be able to do with an action hero or heroine. This may account for the popularity of a series like *Big Brother*, which attracted both large audiences and considerable media attention in the summer of 2000. The opportunity it presented for the audience to observe other people's daily lives in minute detail seemed irresistible to a large proportion of the population.

In making reality television programmes, the television producer is rewarded with a relatively cheap programme, with the public acting out the roles usually played by expensive stars.

FURTHER WORK

1 Choose six different genres of film or television programme. For each identify the most likely generic convention for bringing the narrative to a close. Can you think of any texts that deliberately break the genre conventions in terms of narrative closure?

2 Choose two examples of fictional television series, such as soaps, and outline the main narrative characteristics of the genre.

3 Consider how the representation of a particular group has changed over a period of time. Do you think the change is positive or negative?

4 In what ways can the media be influenced to make more positive representations of minority groups?

5 How far can it be said that professional working practices in the media lead to negative representations?

6 It is argued that genre is a more useful concept to media producers than to media audiences. Do you agree?

7 Genre analysis is of little use when considering contemporary media texts. Discuss this statement by drawing on contemporary media texts to support your arguments.

8 Consider how one particular media genre has changed over a period of time. How do you account for these changes?

9 Create a publicity package for a new film or television programme which fits into an existing genre. Your package should contain a range of work including an advertisement and a press release. Identify where these will appear in order to reach the existing audience for this type of genre.

10 In what ways can narrative be said to be an important element of non-fiction texts? Support your answer with examples from at least two media forms.

11 Choose a minority group that is said to be inadequately or negatively represented in the media. Using examples, outline how the group is represented.

12 Find examples of texts that exist in different media forms. For example, think of some that started life as computer games. Why do you think these texts lend themselves so well to such intertextuality?

13 Consider how your reading of a text is affected by your knowledge from other texts from which borrowing may have occurred.

14 Assess the way in which real-life events and news stories are used as the basis for fictional texts.

15 Are there any texts created in order to oppose dominant ideological beliefs? If so, in what context are these texts likely to be found? At what type of audience are they aimed?

16 Consider some of the ways in which the media have been be used to change ideological beliefs and social attitudes.

17 All media texts are ideological. What do you understand by this statement? Illustrate your answer with examples.

18 In a media-saturated society in which media technology is playing an increasingly important role in our lives, how far do you agree with Baudrillard's notion of the hyper-real?

19 Documentaries have to be constructed in just the same way as fictional programmes. How far do you agree with this statement?

20 Imagine you are creating a marketing campaign for a film, a television series, a radio station or a magazine shortly to be launched. Decide on what you think would be appropriate promotional material. Which media would you use for advertising and promotion?

21 What do you understand by the term 'intertextuality'? Illustrate your answer with examples.

FURTHER READING

Bell, A., Joyce, M. and Rivers, D. (1999) *Advanced Level Media*, Hodder & Stoughton.

Bordwell, D. and Thompson, K. (1979) *Film Art: An Introduction*, McGraw-Hill.

Branston, G. and Stafford, R. (1999) *The Media Student's Book*, 2nd edition, Routledge.

Cohen, S. and Young, J. (1973) *The Manufacture of News: Deviance, Social Problems and the Mass Media*, Constable Sage.

Corner, J. (1996) *The Art of Record: A Critical Introduction to Documentary*, Manchester University Press.

Fiske, J. (1987) *Television Culture*, Methuen.

—— (1990) *Introduction to Communication Studies*, 2nd edition, Routledge.

Herman, E. S. and Chomsky, N. (1994) *Manufacturing Consent*, Vintage.

McRobbie, A. (1991) *Feminism and Youth Culture: From Jackie to Just Seventeen*, Macmillan.

Nelmes, J. (ed.) (1999) *An Introduction to Film Studies*, 2nd edition, Routledge.

O'Sullivan, T. *et al.* (1998) *Studying the Media*, Arnold.

Paget, D. (1998) *No Other Way to Tell It: Dramadoc/Docudrama on Television*, Manchester University Press.

Storey, J. (1993) *An Introductory Guide to Cultural Theory and Popular Culture*, Harvester Wheatsheaf.

Strinati, D. (1995) *An Introduction to Theories of Popular Culture*, Routledge.

Taylor, L. and Willis, A. (1999) *Media Studies: Texts, Institutions and Audiences*, Blackwell.

Tilley, A. (1991) 'Narrative', in D. Lusted (ed.), *The Media Studies Book*, Routledge.

Wilcock, J. (2000) *Documentaries*, Auteur.

Winston, B. (1995) *Claiming the Real: The Documentary Film Revisited*, BFI Publishing.

▼   EXAMPLE: TITLE SEQUENCES

In this section we present a case study of title sequences in film and television programmes. We draw on the concepts we have explored in the preceding chapters on media language. You may find this chapter valuable in considering how you might approach work on the close textual analysis of moving images.

Title sequences offer an interesting and rewarding area of study in our reading of media texts for a number of different reasons. Perhaps most importantly, it is their role in establishing initial contact with the audience and signalling to them what is to follow that makes them worthy of consideration. An audience receives from a title sequence an indication of the content of the text they are about to consume. As we have seen in the section on Genre (p. 55), audiences usually approach a text with certain expectations.

Title sequences play a significant role in both raising the expectations of the audience and indicating how likely it is that these expectations will be fulfilled. Title sequences also signal to the audience an indication of the tone of the text that is to follow. They may suggest that it is light-hearted or serious. In doing so they have a clear function in both preparing and positioning the audience by putting them in an appropriate frame of mind to consume the subsequent text. News programmes have music that is serious and important-sounding. Comedy programmes, on the other hand, employ a lighter, more flippant style of music.

ACTIVITY

Consider how music is used to indicate to an audience the nature of a text and its role in establishing the tone. Think of a situation where you have been in another room and heard the title music for a television programme. How does this impact on you?

NOTEBOX

In communist states in the Eastern bloc, solemn music was broadcast several days before the announcement of the death of an important political figure. Part of the function of this music was to prepare or position the audience in readiness for the national mourning that was expected to follow this news.

Title sequences can also be compared to magazine covers or the front pages of newspapers. All of these have the function of attracting an audience to come and consume the product that is on offer. An effective title sequence on television will call out to or hail an audience, through such devices as music, and invite them to consume the text. This invitation usually indicates the pleasures that lie in store for the audience if they choose to partake.

INTERPELLATION The process by which a media text summons an audience in much the same way as a town crier would ring a bell and shout in order to summon an audience for an important announcement.

Louis Althusser argued that this process of interpellation is important in preparing an audience for the text they are about to consume. Part of its function, he argued, was to position the reader in order to be receptive to the ideological function the text was about to perform.

The idea of repetition also needs to be taken into account when we consider the functioning of title sequences. On television, many texts form part of a series that recurs over a period of time. News bulletins, for example, have individual time slots each weekday. Typically, a programme such as *Newsnight* has its own title sequence signalling to the viewer the programme that is to follow.

ACTIVITY . . .

Look at the title sequences for typical news bulletins broadcast by each of the terrestrial channels.

■ What similarities do they have?
■ In what ways are they different?
■ What does this tell you about the style of news presentation that each adopts?

Similarly, serial programmes such as soaps, sitcoms and quiz shows all have title sequences that are immediately recognised by an audience. It is important to producers that these title sequences remain recognisable to the audience. Even programmes such as soaps, which have run over long periods of time, have maintained very similar title sequences in order to provide their audiences with the reassurance of instant recognition.

When a new series of programmes is launched, it is interesting to consider how the title sequence, although clearly individual to that programme, is likely to rely on links to other title sequences to programmes of a similar genre.

The idea of recognition is obviously not an issue with TV programmes that do not form part of a series or with feature films shown both at the cinema and for consumption at home. In this case the title sequence has other functions to perform. Besides summoning the audience and setting the tone of what is to come, these title sequences often function as the opening of the narrative that is to unfold. In this way they are likely to present a series of enigmas that work to engage us with the narrative in a similar way to a headline on the front of a newspaper. We are teased with information that invites us to involve ourselves in the narrative and to consume the rest of the text. At the same time we are promised that, through consuming the text, the enigmas that are teasing us in the title sequence will be resolved as the narrative is unravelled.

As the name suggests, a title sequence provides the audience with details of the title of the film or programme that they are about to watch. In addition, according to the particular genre of the text, it sometimes provides other information, such as details of the actors or stars, the production company and director/producer. A more detailed list of people who have contributed to the production process is usually given at the end. These are known as the end credits.

■ Why do you think some people remain in the cinema to watch all the end credits?

When we undertake the analysis of a media text, it is always useful to have a checklist of the things we need to look for, similar to the worksheet given on p. 41. When we consider the title sequence of a TV programme or film, it is important to keep in mind the function that the sequence has been designed to perform. For example, it may be a title sequence from a long-running series designed to remind the audience of a familiar programme. Alternatively you may be looking at a sequence for a film or one-off television programme, which, as we have indicated, will work rather differently.

WORKSHEET FOR ANALYSING TITLE SEQUENCES

It is always useful to have any moving image text that you want to analyse available on video. This will enable you to watch it as many times as you wish. In addition you will be able to use the pause and slow-motion facilities on your video recorder to consider the framing of individual shots.

The following ideas may help you when you get started in your analysis of a title sequence:

■ What sort of text is the sequence introducing? For example, a fictional/factual text?
■ What tone is being set? Serious, light-hearted, flippant, or comic?
■ What is the function of the text? Information; entertainment?
■ What type of audience is being addressed? You might like to think in terms of age, gender, background, cultural experience.

Some further points to consider:

1   Is the sequence live action or an animation? If the latter, why do you think this medium has been chosen?
2   How has the sequence been edited? Short fast-moving edits or long sequences? What is the effect of this?
3   What does the soundtrack contribute to the sequence? You should consider use of music, voice-over and sound effects for example.
4   How long is the sequence? Is there a clear division between the end of the title sequence and the beginning of the text?
5   What links does the sequence have to the text itself? How does it work as an introduction to the text? Is it, for example, an opening scene from the film or TV programme?
6   Is any iconography used that will be significant in the text to follow?
7   How does the sequence link to other sequences introducing texts of the same genre?

CORONATION STREET

Coronation Street is the longest running serial drama currently shown on television. It attracts an audience in the region of 15 million viewers for each of its four weekly scheduled slots on ITV. Despite many technical innovations in television production, the title sequence has remained fundamentally the same since the first broadcast, except that the sequence presently used is in colour.

Clearly the main function of this title sequence is to announce to viewers that a familiar programme is about to be broadcast, rather than to entice them to watch a new one. In fact, the sequence introducing *Coronation Street* (Figure 22) will be familiar to the majority of the population, even those who are not regularly part of the vast audience.

The sequence itself runs for approximately 20 seconds. It is preceded by an animation that uses familiar chocolate-coloured images of the street to advertise the sponsor of the programme, Cadbury. The opening shot is a high-angle long shot of the familiar brick-built terraced houses in the foreground. In the background are the high-rise housing blocks that form another type of accommodation for people in an inner city. The two types of housing are set in contrast. The brick-built terraces suggest an old-fashioned, close-knit, working-class community, while the two blocks carry with them the connotations of the alienation of impersonal life in the inner city with all its incumbent social problems. This long shot from a high angle is important in establishing for us the inner-city context of the drama with both its old and new architecture, as well as providing us with the name of the programme which is overlaid on the image. On a connotational level there is a contrast between the lasting values and sense of community represented by the brick-built terraces and the decline of community values in the concrete and impersonal tower blocks.

This establishing shot then dissolves to a similar high-level crane shot, but this time at roof-top height, looking between the rows of chimney pots to an industrial landscape on the far horizon. This time we have camera movement as the image slowly pans left and downwards towards the street. At the same time the title fades as we dissolve into a second shot close to the top of a telegraph pole that looks down into the back alleys of the rows of terraces. At this time a caption appears with the name of the writer. The next shot cranes slowly down to street level where the backs of the houses are framed by a leafy tree on the left of the screen. The shot then dissolves to the final image in which the camera looks into the backyards of the houses, with the homely touches of the occupants' washing on the lines and a cat exploring a pigeon loft in the foreground. A caption giving the name of the director appears over this shot. Immediately after the last shot, the sequence ends by cutting to the opening action of the drama.

The music that acts as a soundtrack to these titles is an instantly recognisable tune associated with *Coronation Street* over its 40-year history. The brass instrument playing in a minor key provides a plaintive accompaniment to the images on screen. The association of brass instruments with northern industrial life is clearly an element contributing to the effectiveness of the title sequence. Allied to the images, it presents us with a sense of timeless northern working-class life with its connotations of a down-to-earth community in which the lives of people are played out against a backdrop of industrial grime and squalor. The sequence of shots moves from out of the sky with the wide-ranging image of the northern landscape through to the individual street, and then down at street level into the very backyards of the inhabitants. Clearly the audience are being invited into an intimate engagement with the lives of the people who inhabit this community.

ACTIVITY . . .

Look carefully at a video of the title sequence for *Coronation Street*.

■ Why do you think there are no people featured in any of the shots?
■ Why do you think dissolves have been used as transitions between each shot?

a

b

Figure 22 Coronation Street *opening shots*

MEDIA STUDIES: THE ESSENTIAL INTRODUCTION

NEIGHBOURS

The title sequence to *Neighbours* (Figure 23) makes an interesting contrast to *Coronation Street*. *Neighbours* is an Australian-produced soap, broadcast on BBC1 at lunch-time each weekday and repeated early-evening. The early-evening time slot and the preponderance of characters in their teens and early twenties have made it popular with a young audience. In fact the slot it occupies in the early evening follows immediately the end of children's television.

The programme is based on a community who live in a suburban street of an Australian city. Unlike *Coronation Street* in which no one appears in the title sequence, *Neighbours* uses its opening credits to introduce all the major characters currently featuring in the serial.

The title sequence opens with three 'dramatic' sequences from recent episodes of the soap. Each presents the audience with an unresolved narrative conflict involving characters who appear in the episode that follows. Each is a narrative enigma designed both to tease and remind the audience, and to ensure their interest in the current episode which promises some development or even resolution of the conflicts.

Accompanying this opening is the instantly recognisable *Neighbours* theme tune. The melody is much more upbeat and jolly than the plaintive tones of *Coronation Street*. It also contains lyrics that celebrate and idealise the virtues of neighbourliness, suggesting that *Neighbours* 'can become good friends'. Frequently, however, the subsequent narratives suggest that this is not always the case, despite the insistence that everybody needs good *neighbours*, a sentiment that clearly seeks to universalise the theme.

The reprise sequence runs for around 45 seconds before giving way to a montage of approximately 20 seconds which introduces us to the characters at play. A typical title sequence has ten or so scenes in which central characters currently in the series are seen, usually in family or domestic groupings. These short scenes are set outdoors, in contrast to the grim urban landscape of *Coronation Street*; the bright sunshine of Australia beats down on the *dramatis personae* as they gather round the pool or the barbecue. Each of these scenes is linked by means of a dissolve which is so fast that, to all intents, it acts as a cut.

The title sequence is brought to an end by another fast dissolve – this time into a still of Ramsey Street, a cul-de-sac which is the setting of the drama. It is interesting to note that both soaps, *Neighbours* and *Coronation Street*, end by emphasising the setting of the drama and with it the connotations of communities and the people who live in them.

a

b

c

Figure 23 Neighbours *title sequence*

ACTIVITY

Now watch the title sequences of the two soaps yourself, checking for any changes in style or content that may have been made.

- How do you account for the different approaches of the two programmes?
- What do you think this tells the audience about the themes and content of the two programmes?
- What do the title sequences tell us about the way in which each programme addresses its audience?
- Do you think the audience for the two programmes is likely to be similar?

Now consider two more soaps, such as *EastEnders*, *Brookside*, or *Home and Away*.

- What similarities and differences does each have with *Neighbours* and *Coronation Street*?
- What does this tell you about the nature of the programme?

As we have noted previously, title sequences for films and one-off television programmes function differently from those for a television series. The latter work through a form of interpellation which relies on audience familiarity and recognition. The title sequence of a feature film will almost certainly be new to the audience when they encounter it. It therefore needs to perform several important functions, not the least of which is to gain and hold the attention of the audience. This is especially true where a film is being shown domestically rather than at the cinema. When we watch a film at home, even by means of a rented video, it has to compete not only with other choices of media consumption (other TV programmes, radio, computer games), but also with a multitude of distractions, such as the telephone or unexpected visitors.

The title sequence of a film, however, does much more than grab the attention of the audience. It is an important signalling device to show us what we can expect from the text we are about to consume.

TAXI DRIVER

Taxi Driver is arguably one of the most important films of the last century. Released in 1976 it is director Martin Scorsese's study of an obsessive loner, alienated from society by his experiences in the Vietnam War. He finds work as the eponymous taxi driver, and the opening to the movie provides the audience with an insight into the man who is to be the focus of attention in the action that follows (see Figure 24).

The opening shot is a cloud of steam emerging from a New York street which fills the screen. From the steam emerges a yellow cab which drives in slow motion towards us and across our field of vision, in close-up, leaving us with the screen again filled with the steam. Both the steam from the street and the yellow cab are powerful, almost indexical images of New York. The image is accompanied by a discordant soundtrack of percussion instruments which adds to the eerie nature of what we see on the screen. The title credits in the same yellow as the taxi appear on screen against the backdrop of the white steam and accompanied initially by the discordant music, which itself gradually develops a clearer melody until the screen dissolves into an extreme close-up image of Travis Bickle's

Figure 24 Taxi Driver (1976)

(Robert De Niro's) face bathed in a red light, as his eyes scan across the screen. The music has now become a mellow-sounding and harmonious saxophone solo. The scene then dissolves into a point-of-view shot through the windscreen of the cab.

The image through the screen is blurred by rain on the windscreen itself. Even when the wipers clear the screen, the image remains distorted and unworldly as we try to pick out the New York night-time street scene with its garish lighting and ghostly figures. As the scene dissolves into a clearer and closer shot of people crossing the road in front of the cab, the music again shifts from melodious sax to discordant percussion. The figures crossing the road are shrouded in the steam and bathed in the same red light, giving them the appearance of creatures of another world, perhaps even some kind of hell. The image again dissolves to an extreme close-up of Bickle's face as his eyes pan across the screen. Again his face is coloured by the same red light that pervades the night-time street. Finally the image dissolves into the dense white steam that again fills the screen, as the music hovers between the melody of the sax and the discordant sound of the percussion.

This opening sequence runs for a little over a minute and a half before dissolving into a shot following Travis Bickle into an interview for a taxi-driving job. On a denotational level we can read the sequence as a man driving a taxi at night through the streets of New York. On a connotational level, however, this title sequence is rich in themes and ideas that prepare the audience for much of what is to follow in the film. There are a number of images in which what we see on screen is blurred or distorted, for example, the clouds of steam and the rain on the windscreen. Psychologically, Travis Bickle is a man who finds it hard to see the world clearly, at least from a moral perspective. His experiences in Vietnam have clouded his judgement. The blurred images on the screen can be read as a metaphor for the confusion that exists inside his head. Similarly the recurrence of the colour red, on two occasions on Bickle's face, suggests the anger which is pent up inside him – an anger that ultimately finds its release in a bloodbath, when Bickle decides to play the avenging angel. The music's movement between harmony and discord again suggests the volatile state of Bickle's mind, moving between controlled calmness and sudden bursts of anger.

The sequence creates a sense of weirdness: familiar images are filmed in such a way as to seem dislocated or out of context. The effect is achieved in several ways, such as the use of slow motion and the garish colours. The sequence seems to have been constructed specifically to suggest the hero's emotional and psychological state as well as to introduce us to the nature of his job and the environment in which he works.

NOTEBOX

The reason that Robert De Niro's eyes move so slowly and deliberately across the screen is that the camera was over-cranked in order to shoot the scene in slow motion to create this particular effect that the director wanted.

FURTHER WORK . . .

Taxi Driver is a rich and complex film that rewards detailed study and analysis. This is not the case with many films. It is, however, still a useful and worthwhile process to look closely at the opening of a film or TV programme to identify:

■ how it has been constructed
■ why it was done in the way
■ how this affects the audience's reading of the film.

In Part 2 we look at:

- how audiences are made up

- the ways in which audiences have changed over time and how our engagement with media forms is patterned and determined

- 'passive' and 'active' views of the audience

- some of the issues around the 'effects' debate

- some of the research that has been carried out on audience behaviour

- terms like the 'hypodermic needle theory', 'uses and gratifications', 'mode of address' and 'situated culture'.

DIFFERENT TYPES OF AUDIENCE

In one sense everyone is part of the audience in that we are all, to some degree or another, exposed to media texts. However, it can sometimes be difficult to stand back and think about the different ways in which our daily lives interact with the media. It is well worth considering the extent to which, in an average day, we will be part of many different audiences for a wide range of media. This may include being part of a radio audience in the morning as we get ready for college or work, watching breakfast television or reading the newspaper, listening to music on the radio in a car, or glimpsing advertising hoardings as we travel to school or work.

Throughout the day we will be, either consciously or unconsciously, exposed to different media products – becoming part of many different types of audience. As we mentioned in the Introduction, it may be as part of an audience of over 18 million people all watching the same episode of *EastEnders* at the same time. It may be as part of an audience sitting alone in their cars listening to the same radio show or as one of 200 people watching a film in a cinema. It can also be through the more personal and private consumption of

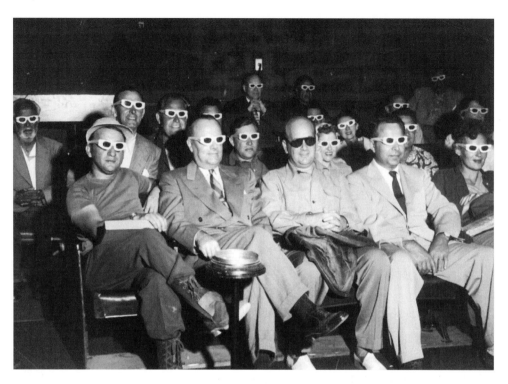

Figure 25 *Cinema audience wearing 3D glasses*

newspapers, either local or national, or magazines, or through the one-to-one communication of the Internet. We may work in an environment where a radio is on in the background or somewhere – for example, a hospital or a shop – which has its own radio station.

WHY ARE AUDIENCES IMPORTANT?

There are several reasons why audiences are important. The first is perhaps the most obvious.

- Without an audience why would anyone create a media text? What is the point of a film that no one sees?
- Audience size and reaction are often seen as a way of measuring the 'success' (or otherwise) of a media product. One of the reasons why we say that the *Sun* newspaper is successful is because it sells over 3 million copies a day and is read by nearly 12 million people.
- Audiences who buy media texts are providing income for the media companies who produce them.
- Much of the media available to us, however, is free or subsidised; it is financed by advertising, and the advertisers want to know that they are getting value for money.

In other words they want to know which, and how many, people are seeing their adverts.

■ As the media become more central to our lives, so many people want to know how we use the media, what we understand of what we consume, and the effects that the media have on our lives.

HOW HAVE AUDIENCES CHANGED?

Concerns about the size and impact of the media on audiences, the 'effectiveness' of advertising, and how audiences interrelate with the media have been with us since the development of a 'mass' audience at the beginning of the twentieth century.

We know that the media are constantly changing, and this means that audiences, too, must be changing, both as a result of the changes in media technology but also because of the changes in the way we live our lives and because we as individuals change.

ACTIVITY . . .

Consider how your media consumption has changed over the last five years. Can you identify those changes that are the result of your own individual changes in age, circumstances, interests etc. and those changes that are the result of changes in technology affecting what is on offer to you?

The word 'broadcasting' implies a 'mass' audience of perhaps more than 30 million people all watching or listening to the same event, at the same time, participating in the same experience. The 1966 World Cup final attracted a television audience of 32 million viewers, while the wedding of Prince Charles and Lady Diana in 1981 attracted 39 million. The episode of *EastEnders* where Den and Angie split up broadcast in December 1986 attracted over 30 million viewers and was voted 24th in a millennium poll of the top 100 television excerpts. Number 1 was the live broadcast of Neil Armstrong and Buzz Aldrin walking on the moon in July 1969. It is estimated that over 600 million people watched this on television.

Today we have a wide range of broadcasting and press services available to us. Radio and television, in particular, have moved away from the original ideas of addressing a large 'mass' audience. Today the concept is one of narrowcasting, where programmes are aimed at specific, specialist audiences in a way that is similar to the range and variety of magazines available in a newsagent's. There is now a wide range of specialist channels and stations aimed at small and specific markets that might be defined on the grounds of age (Classic FM, Disney or Nickelodeon), gender (the television channel Men & Motors), interests (most obviously sport but also television channels like National Geographic, Travel or Home & Leisure) or ethnicity (radio stations like Sunrise in London and Bradford or television channels like PCNE Chinese, Bangla TV or Channel East aimed at Chinese or other Asian audiences).

NARROWCASTING The opposite of broadcasting, where texts are aimed at very small special-interest groups.

ACTIVITY . . .

Research the way people used to consume the media.

- Perhaps using your parents or grandparents, carry out a small oral history project. Ask them to talk about how they listened to the radio, watched television or went to the cinema when they were young. Is the way they watched television then different from the way we watch it now? How have patterns of consumption changed? If so, how do you account for these changes?
- The Coronation of Queen Elizabeth II in 1953 was one of the most important events in introducing people to television for the first time. Try to find people who remember watching the 'live' broadcast of the Coronation and ask them how they watched it. Think also about your own earliest experiences of seeing television and 'special events'.
- You could also try to find out what the television schedules looked like in the 1950s and/or 1960s. What does a comparison between then and now tell us about the changing television audience?

This change from 'broadcasting' to 'narrowcasting' is partly due to the development of new media technologies that have become, or are increasingly becoming, part of our ordinary domestic lives. These include new hardware products such as DVD and video-recorders, computers and satellite and cable television receivers, but there has also been an increase in ownership of existing hardware. For instance, once upon a time it was the norm for a household to have only one television set, often placed in the living room and usually with the furniture organised around it. Before that it was not unusual for households to have just one radio (or wireless) set that again would have been placed in the living room and the furniture arranged around it. The illustration on the cover of the *Radio Times* (Figure 26) represents a view of how families were thought to consume radio in the 1930s and 1940s. It would be interesting to consider what type of image would be used today (see also section on ideology, p. 80).

Today many households have several radios and televisions spread around the house, perhaps in bedrooms as well as in the living room, maybe in the kitchen and, in the case of radios, in cars and as part of personal stereos. Part of the reason for this growth in hardware is that television sets and radios have become increasingly cheap to buy. When colour television sets first came on the market, they cost the equivalent of several weeks' wages, whereas today they represent less than one week's wages. As more and more of our lives become linked with media consumption and as more and more of our peers have several radio and television sets, so there can be a pressure on us as consumers to buy

Radio Times (Incorporating World-Radio) September 30, 1949
Vol. 104; No. 1355.   Registered at the G.P.O. as a Newspaper

TELEVISION EDITION

RADIO TIMES

JOURNAL OF THE BBC   PRICE TWOPENCE

BBC's Plans for Autumn Listening

DRAMA ★	MUSIC ★	RELIGIOUS BROADCASTING ★	FEATURES ★	VARIETY
Val Gielgud	Sir Steuart Wilson	The Rev. Francis House	Laurence Gilliam	Michael Standing

In This Week's Programmes

WILFRED PICKLES	LIGHT PROGRAMME	NATIONAL RADIO	BENJAMIN BRITTEN'S
returns in	DRAMA WEEK	CELEBRITY GALA	entertainment
'Have a Go!'	Famous plays and players every evening, Monday to Friday	Two-hour all-star concert on Sunday evening	'Let's Make an Opera'

Figure 26

more and more of these products – especially when we are told that each new piece of technology is 'better' than the previous one.

ACTIVITY . . .

Carry out research amongst your peers to see how many television sets and radios they have in their households. Work out the average number of people per radio and television set. In Britain according to BBC figures there are more radio sets than adults. Does your research support this?

OR

Consider how one particular media genre has changed over a period of time. How do you account for these changes?

Some of the changes you may have identified in the ways in which we consume media products will be because of the increase in services available to us. When television first started it was only broadcast for a few hours a day, mostly in the evening, and the BBC had something called 'the toddlers' truce' when television closed down at teatime, after children's television, to allow parents to put their children to bed. On Sundays broadcasting was very limited because it was assumed that most people would be going to church services or wanted religious programming.

Gradually over the years the amount and range of television broadcasting have increased. Breakfast television went on air in 1983, and now we have five domestic terrestrial channels that broadcast 24 hours a day. Part of the reason for this is because television companies now recognise that there are many different groups of audiences who watch television at different times of the day and want different types of programmes (see p. 118).

Today the rate of change is becoming faster and it is difficult to predict what our domestic media will look like in ten years' time. The new ADSL (Asymmetrical Digital Subscriber Line) telephone network turns an ordinary telephone copper wire into a high-speed connection for Internet, broadcasting and video-on-demand services. Already the Internet is available via our television sets through the various digital packages, and soon we will be able to download films and other programmes from the telephone line as well as play 'interactive' film formats like DVD and digital VHS.

Increasingly developments like Internet-based radio services, more digital television channels and MP3 players will mean that audiences for traditionally popular 'mass' programmes will become more fragmented. The 'free' audience for *Match of the Day* is likely to decline as more and more football clubs offer their own subscription channels like Manchester United's MUTV, or because of the growth of 'interactive' digital channels that offer the viewer a choice of camera-angles, instant replays and additional information about players or the teams. It is already possible to select your own 'news story' on some digital news channels.

Title	Day	Time	Viewers (m)	Channel	Last week
1 Friends	Thu	2100	1.85	Sky One	1
2 Super Sunday Live	Sun	1130	1.26	Sky Sports 1	2
2 FA Cup Special Live	Sun	1600	1.26	Sky Sports 2	–
4 Doctor Doolittle	Sat	2000	1.19	Sky Premier	–
5 ER	Thu	2130	0.87	Sky One	5
6 Stargate SG-1	Wed	2000	0.85	Sky One	7
7 The Strangerers	Tue	2100	0.73	Sky One	–
8 The Simpsons	Wed	1900	0.72	Sky One	–
8 The Simpsons	Sun	1800	0.72	Sky One	3
10 The Simpsons	Mon	1900	0.70	Sky One	11
11 Monday Night Football	Mon	2000	0.71	Sky Sports 1	–
12 Buffy the Vampire Slayer	Fri	2000	0.63	Sky One	6
13 Rugby Union: France v England	Sat	1300	0.61	Sky Sports 2	–
14 The Simpsons	Thu	1900	0.60	Sky One	11
15 The Simpsons	Sat	1800	0.57	Sky One	14
16 Super Sunday pre-match	Sun	1100	0.54	Sky Sports 1	18
17 Dream Team	Tue	2000	0.52	Sky One	–
18 FA Cup Special post-match	Sun	1805	0.51	Sky Sports 2	–
18 Prickly Heat	Sun	2100	0.51	Sky One	13
20 Super Sunday post-match	Sun	1330	0.50	Sky Sports 1	–

Figure 27 BARB Top 20 Satellite Programmes

Perhaps eventually we will rely upon the mobile phone instead of *Top of the Pops* to give us the latest record charts and we will be able to download the latest releases and order ticket concerts at the same time.

This increase in choice may suit those who can afford to pay monthly cable or satellite subscription fees of around £35 per month – in addition to pay-per-view fees of perhaps £3.50 per film. However, there are some observers who are concerned that those who are less affluent may end up with an inferior and limited, but 'free', choice. It also raises questions about the role of concepts like Public Service Broadcasting (see p. 190).

Look at BARB's Top 20 satellite programmes (Figure 27).

■ Can we draw any conclusions as to the most popular types of programme for satellite viewers?
■ How do the audience figures compare with terrestrial programmes?
■ What do you think is the attraction of these programmes for satellite viewers?

(You can access more up-to-date viewing figures at the BARB website www.barb.co.uk)

Part of the change that has occurred over the years is also due to the way in which the technology that produces media texts has changed. The introduction of such innovations as the 'Steadicam' or high-definition portable video-camera has made news, documentaries and 'live' programming much more 'action-packed' and attractive to viewers. There was a vogue a few years ago for investigative programmes that used small 'hidden' cameras to expose various malpractices. Consider, for example, the technology required to produce a programme like C4's *Big Brother*.

Another example of how our patterns of consumption have changed is cinema attendance in this country.

Look at the figures for cinema attendances in Britain between 1933 and 1999 in Figure 28.

■ Can you suggest reasons as to why admissions almost halved between 1956 and 1959? Or why they have more than doubled between 1984 and 1999?
■ Consider how the cinema audience has changed. Look at the development of multiplexes and the types of film they show. How might these have helped shape the cinema audience and to what extent is it similar to/different from 10 or 20 years ago?
■ Find out about cinemas other than multiplexes, for example, independent, 'art house' cinemas and/or clubs. What sort of films do they show? What types of audience are attracted to these cinemas?
■ How has the introduction of video recording changed the way in which we consume films?
■ Consider the different formats that one film may appear in: the cinema version, on video, on cable or satellite television, on terrestrial television or shown in an airplane. Are there different audiences for different formats of the same film?

- Increasingly films are being released on DVD. How does this technology alter the way in which audiences watch films?
- What are the differences for audiences between seeing a film in the cinema and on a television set in a domestic setting?
- Is there a difference between the ways in which we consume a film video that is rented and one that is bought?
- Choose a particular film and consider the way in which it is being marketed. This should provide you with clues as to the type of 'imagined' audience the producers are aiming at.

UK cinema admissions 1933–1999

Year	millions	Year	millions
1933	903	1970	193
1934	950	1971	176
1935	912.33	1972	156.6
1936	917	1973	134.2
1937	946	1974	138.5
1938	987	1975	116.3
1939	990	1976	103.9
		1977	103.5
1940	1027	1978	126.1
1941	1309	1979	111.9
1942	1494		
1943	1541	1980	101
1944	1575	1981	86
1945	1585	1982	64
1946	1635	1983	65.7
1947	1462	1984	54
1948	1514	1985	72
1949	1430	1986	75.5
		1987	78.5
1950	1395.8	1988	84
1951	1365	1989	94.5
1952	1312.1		
1953	1284.5	1990	97.37
1954	1275.8	1991	100.29
1955	1181.8	1992	103.64
1956	1100.8	1993	114.36
1957	915.2	1994	123.53
1958	754.7	1995	114.56
1959	581	1996	123.8
		1997	139.3
1960	500.8	1998	135.5
1961	449.1	1999	139.7
1962	395		
1963	357.2		
1964	342.8		
1965	326.6		
1966	288.8		
1967	264.8		
1968	237.3		
1969	214.9		

Source: Screen Digest/Screen Finance/*bfi*

Figure 28

HOW IS AUDIENCE CONSUMPTION 'PATTERNED' AND DETERMINED?

We have already mentioned how we, as audiences, use different media at different times of the day. It is worth spending a little more time exploring the relationship between our patterns of media consumption and the routines of our daily lives. One of the measurements of the extent to which we now live in a 'media-saturated' society is the degree to which our routine daily activities are interlinked with the media.

Many of us wake up in the morning to the sounds of a radio rather than an alarm clock. We may have possibly gone off to sleep with the same radio playing and set to its 'sleep' function. Many televisions also have the same feature, although it may be harder to imagine drifting off to sleep part way through a television programme or a film. We have also already mentioned breakfast television, which many of us now take for granted as a way of getting the latest news over our breakfast or whilst getting ready for college or work.

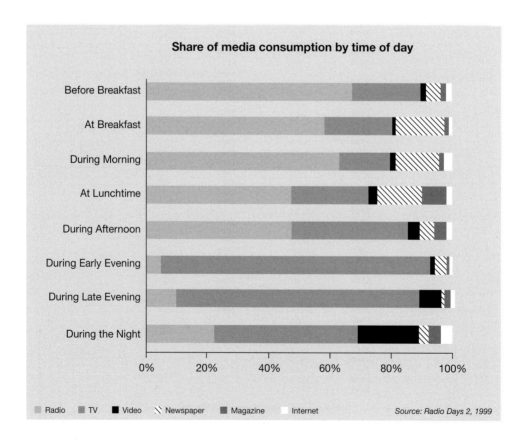

Figure 29

The programmes we watch and/or listen to in the morning often have regular features or segments that are broadcast at the same time each day. In this way we are able to measure our progress each morning by their regular appearance, for example the news headlines, reviews of the day's newspapers or spoof 'wake-up' calls made to unsuspecting members of the public.

It is interesting to reverse the equation and to consider to what extent the media 'organise' our daily routines rather than just fitting in around them. Some people will refuse to go out in the evening or to answer the telephone or speak to visitors until their favourite programme has ended. Mid-morning television shows encourage housewives to sit down with a cup of coffee and relax after getting the family off to work and/or school.

Schedulers for channels like BBC2 and C4 assume that young people will watch their channels between 5 pm and 7 pm in the evenings, presumably as a means of relaxing after a day at school or work or as a break between day and evening activities.

ACTIVITY . . .

Consider your own daily/weekly routine and the manner in which the media interweave with it. Do you sometimes plan your activities around particular media output?

If you look at the radio or television schedules, you will notice that particular categories of audiences are addressed and particular genres of programmes are featured at particular times. We are all familiar with the notion of 'peak viewing time' but it is perhaps more interesting to look at the schedules outside this period to see what types of audience are being addressed, say, between 9 am and lunchtime on a weekday on the different channels or on a Saturday or Sunday morning.

Children's television, for example, is mainly broadcast in the late afternoon and early evening when schoolchildren are expected to have finished school. There are, however, also children's programmes shown on terrestrial television at other times during the week and at weekends.

ACTIVITY . . .

Study the schedules of the terrestrial television channels and identify what groups are being addressed at particular times.

- Is there a difference between the children's programmes transmitted between 4 pm and 6 pm and those transmitted in the middle of the morning or at the weekend? When do the children's satellite channels broadcast?
- Why are programmes like *Frasier* or *So Graham Norton* on C4 on a Friday evening?

Popular media like television and the press try to make the most of special occasions like royal or sporting events or, more recently, the Eclipse and the Millennium. They attempt to turn these occasions into rituals in which the media play a central part. The idea of a typical Christmas Day that centres around the television is one example, where it is assumed that the family cannot fully celebrate Christmas without watching the Queen's Speech, film premieres and special editions of popular programmes.

Sporting events like the World Cup or the Olympics are other occasions where we, the audience, are encouraged to celebrate the success (or otherwise) of our teams through our participation in a 'television event' that often has special theme tunes (*Nessun Dorma* for the 1990 World Cup is perhaps one of the best-known examples) and a special presentation studio for links and interviews (see section on Title Sequences on p. 97). The normal schedules may be changed to highlight the importance and uniqueness of the occasion. There will probably also be special 'souvenir' editions of television listings magazines or newspaper supplements where we can get background information and keep a record of the progress of the events.

One of the reasons that media companies like to turn these occasions into 'rituals' is that by packaging them in this way they hope to attract larger audiences than normal. These can then be sold on to advertisers. Another reason is that, as pay-per-view becomes increasingly available, it is a way of making these broadcasts look 'special' and worth paying extra money for. This is increasingly the case with sporting events like world championships in, for example, cricket, boxing or golf.

ACTIVITY...

■ List all the different media texts that you have consumed in the last week. Divide your list into those texts that you had to pay for individually (cinema, newspapers, magazines, books, etc.) and those that were available to you free of charge (television channels and radio stations). Are the services provided by the BBC 'free'?
■ Compare the prices of the television licence and the various subscription packages for satellite, cable and digital television and radio.

WHO IS THE AUDIENCE?

Many commentators suggest that in any text there is an implied or inferred audience, that the producers of media texts have a 'typical' audience member in mind when they start to create a text. (Look at the section on Production Skills (p. 284) – you are asked to do the same thing in terms of your target audience.)

Figure 30

Ien Ang (1991) in *Desperately Seeking the Audience* discusses the manner in which media producers and institutions view audiences as an 'imaginary entity', as a mass rather than as a set of individuals. They will, however, often have a 'typical' audience member in mind when they produce their texts.

Trainee ILR (Independent Local Radio) presenters were supposed to have an imaginary person, 'Doreen', whom they were told to consider as the 'typical listener'. Presenters were told about her age, her likes and dislikes, her habits, her household and her husband. They were told that 'Doreen' is 'typical'. She is educated and intelligent but may only listen to the radio with half an ear and does not necessarily understand long words or complicated discussions. They were told that this does not mean that 'Doreen' is stupid and should be talked down to, but that they should make sure that she understands and be engaged with what is happening on the radio. They were encouraged to address 'Doreen' and her husband personally as if they knew them.

Academic research, however, has produced another version of this 'imaginary entity'. Hartley (1982) in *Understanding News* identified seven types of what he called 'subjectivities' that are used by media producers to help define the social position of the individual audience member and to engage with them:

■   self-image
■   gender
■   age-group
■   family
■   class
■   nation
■   ethnicity.

Fiske (1989) in *Television Culture* added four more:

■   education
■   religion
■   politics
■   location (geographical and local).

However, Hartley acknowledged that sometimes these categories can get mixed up or can conflict with each other; for instance, some notions of nationhood and some types of ethnicity (Hartley 1982: 69). It is also not clear to what extent these subjectivities are equal or whether in some circumstances some may be more influential than others.

These categories are useful in identifying the way in which individual members of mass audiences are identified both by themselves and by media producers and advertisers. Fiske, talking about television, says that it 'tries to construct an ideal subject position which it invites us to occupy, and, if we do, rewards us with . . . the pleasure of recognition' (Fiske 1987: 51).

ACTIVITY . . .

Using the subjectivities above, try to deduce an 'ideal viewer/reader' for particular programmes. Consider what 'clues' there are in programmes such as *Newsround* or *The Bill*.

- Apart from the categories listed above, consider also the likes and dislikes the 'typical' members of these audiences might have, their interests, their tastes in clothes and music, the types of books and/or magazines that they consume.
- Give your 'typical' viewer a name and a place to live.
- Compare your profile with those produced by others. Discuss and account for similarities and/or differences.

'TELEVISION DOESN'T MAKE PROGRAMMES, IT CREATES AUDIENCES' (JEAN-LUC GODARD)

Advertising is important to a whole range of media products because these products are financed by advertising revenue or are subsidised by the revenue that advertising brings in. The media therefore spend a lot of time and money looking at the circulation and ratings of their products.

Even if you pay for some media products, the advertising can still have subsidised the price and made the product cheaper for you to buy. Take a local weekly newspaper like the *Wiltshire Times* that costs 40p a copy and is probably considered a good buy for that price. It will have lots of local information, stories and photographs. However, if we look through the *Wiltshire Times*, we see that nearly 40 per cent of it is made up of adverts, either for products like cars, computers, or shop goods, or classified ads that include job vacancies, private car sales and other services. One of the reasons why people buy this newspaper is for the information contained in the advertisements. If we want to buy a new car, find somewhere local to live, or see what is on at the local cinema, we can look through the adverts in our local paper and see what is available.

The cover price of the *Wiltshire Times*, 40p, probably represents about 15 or 20 per cent of the true cost of printing an edition of the paper. Without the advertising the reader might have to pay about £3 a copy, and at that price it is unlikely that the *Wiltshire Times* would sell many copies. A few years ago there was an enormous growth of 'free' local newspapers that were financed purely through their advertising revenue. The *Wiltshire Times* has a circulation of about 16,000, but the company that publishes it also publishes several other local 'free' newspapers whose circulation varies between 20,000 and 60,000.

ACTIVITY . . .

Investigate the local newspapers that are available in your area.

- List those that are 'paid for' and those that are 'free'.
- Either contact the companies that publish them or, using reference books like *Benn's Media*, compare circulation figures and advertising rates.
- Can you identify any connections between the advertising rates and the size of circulation?

Similarly, if you buy magazines you are certainly not paying the full cost of producing that magazine. The advertising revenue is probably paying up to three-quarters of the production costs.

The attraction for the advertiser is that these media outlets provide an opportunity to advertise their products to particular social groups of people. In relation to the *Wiltshire Times*, it is a group of people defined by the particular area in which they live. The newspaper will probably have a lot more additional information about its readers in terms of demographics – age, social class, gender, income – similar to the 'subjectivities' that Hartley and Fiske identified. The newspaper will have spent a lot of time and money trying to identify and categorise its readers so that it can then 'sell' these readers to its advertisers.

You may think that this does not apply to the BBC because they do not take advertising. Certainly it is true that at present on its terrestrial services the BBC does not have 'paid for' advertising but it is moving into other types of services and many commentators feel that eventually it will have to take on advertising in some form or another. BBC programmes are already available on cable/satellite via subscription, and many of its magazines like *Top Gear* or *Gardener's World* carry commercial advertising.

The BBC is also in competition with the commercial channels in an attempt to prove its popularity and to justify the licence fee. If the BBC's audience share falls below a certain level, the criticisms of its licence fee increase. (See Public Service Broadcasting, p. 190.) This was a particular problem in 1999 as none of the top ten programmes in terms of audience share was made by the BBC.

Being able to identify both the size and type of their audience is very important for both the BBC and commercial media. There are various organisations who carry out this research and whose findings are sold to the media companies. Some of this information is also available to the public. BARB's tables of weekly top television programmes are published in *Broadcast* magazine (see the section on BARB in Research Skills, pp. 274–6).

Currently BARB measures the audiences for the five terrestrial channels and 45 other channels. The way we consume television is changing with the introduction of many more digital channels, 'narrowcasting' and the 'shuffling' of programmes (where they are repeated several times a day or over several days). Television companies and BARB will therefore have to develop ways of measuring much smaller, but more specialised audiences. It is estimated that of BARB's 4,500 panel homes only 1,500 currently have multi-channel television, and of these only 600 are digital. As there are over 200 television channels now available, most of them digital, this means that a very small section of the BARB panellists represents a large percentage of the digital television audience. Some digital services, such as those available through cable, are not currently included in the BARB figures.

Both NRS (National Readership Survey) and ABC (Audit Bureau of Circulation) carry out a similar function for the newspaper and magazine industry, producing circulation figures, but using different methods. ABC measures the sales of newspapers and magazines whilst NRS interviews a sample of approximately 40,000 people about their reading habits. RAJAR (Radio Joint Audience Research) also uses the sample method and compiles both BBC and commercial radio listening figures.

Figure 31 Top 20 TV programmes of 1999

Title	Audiences (Millions)	Date of transmission
Coronation Street	19.82	Sun Mar 7
Who Wants to be a Millionaire?	19.21	Sun Mar 7
Coronation Street	19.03	Mon Jan 4
Coronation Street	18.22	Wed Jan 13
Heartbeat	17.01	Sun Feb 23
Touch of Frost	16.85	Sun Mar 21
Coronation Street	16.75	Fri Jan 8
Who Wants to be a Millionaire?	16.24	Tues Mar 16
Who Wants to be a Millionaire?	16.05	Thur Mar 11
Who Wants to be a Millionaire?	16.01	Wed Jan 13
EastEnders	15.72	Thur Jan 7
Big Match Live Man U v B Munich	15.62	Wed May 26
Coronation Street	15.60	Sat Dec 25
Who Wants to be a Millionaire?	15.41	Fri Jan 8
EastEnders	15.40	Mon Oct 25
EastEnders	15.38	Tues Jan 26
Walking with Dinosaurs	15.09	Mon Oct 4
Euro 2000 England v Scotland	14.60	Wed Nov 17
EastEnders	14.39	Sun Sep 5
Vicar of Dibley	14.37	Mon Dec 27

According to the Radio Advertising Bureau all commercial radio stations have a clearly defined 'core' target audience – those at the centre of its market and who, it is hoped, will become station 'loyalists'. Around this core are other, secondary listeners.

All of these organisations use the same categories for classifying audiences. These are based on the National Readership Survey's social grades used in advertising and market research. This divides the adult population of Britain into six grades and identifies

National Newspaper Circulation

	October 2000	October 1999	% change	May 00-Oct 00	May 99-Oct 99	% change
Dailies						
The Sun	3,589,204	3,608,880	-0.55	3,628,097	3,666,189	-1.04
The Mirror	2,252,627	2,307,901	-2.39	2,278,542	2,346,970	-2.92
Daily Record	610,950	642,154	-4.86	618,132	637,112	-2.98
Daily Star	648,632	613,562	5.72	635,401	617,009	2.98
The Daily Mail	2,391,229	2,378,428	0.54	2,389,489	2,370,695	0.79
Daily Express	1,039,369	1,069,099	-2.78	1,055,336	1,082,024	-2.47
London Evening Standard	442,467	465,421	-4.93	437,273	439,796	-0.57
The Daily Telegraph	1,014,767	1,034,923	-1.95	1,026,634	1,042,002	-1.47
The Times	718,213	735,162	-2.31	721,505	724,996	-0.48
Financial Times	476,460	426,328	11.76	461,733	400,007	15.43
The Guardian	401,567	403,692	-0.53	395,770	391,908	0.99
The Independent	240,272	230,677	4.16	227,519	224,563	1.32
The Scotsman	103,202	75,387	36.90	101,756	77,712	30.94
Sundays						
News of the World	4,068,042	4,151,230	-2.00	4,027,585	4,106,937	-1.93
Sunday Mirror	1,940,808	2,037,172	-4.73	1,932,761	1,997,098	-3.22
Sunday People	1,492,437	1,578,741	-5.47	1,510,772	1,597,958	-5.46
Sunday Mail	723,553	768,421	-5.84	730,658	761,546	-4.06
The Mail on Sunday	2,292,001	2,332,506	-1.74	2,284,680	2,290,698	-0.26
Sunday Express	967,178	979,143	-1.22	971,183	993,224	-2.22
The Sunday Times	1,411,942	1,374,310	2.74	1,356,010	1,343,119	0.96
The Sunday Telegraph	801,866	824,754	-2.78	804,814	822,021	-2.09
The Observer	460,427	414,537	11.07	435,851	400,296	8.88
Independent on Sunday	270,640	262,762	3.00	247,061	245,543	0.62
Scotland on Sunday	103,751	109,246	-5.03	106,699	113,430	-5.93
Sunday Business	56,807	60,011	-5.34	59,372	56,658	4.79

Source: ABC

Figure 32

(You can access more up-to-date circulation figures from the ABC website at www.abc.org.uk)

MEDIA STUDIES: THE ESSENTIAL INTRODUCTION

Figure 33 Radio listening share

	Oct–Dec 1998 %	Oct–Dec 1999 %
All BBC	48.5	51.3
All BBC Network	39.1	40.5
BBC Radio 1	10.6	10.9
BBC Radio 2	13.1	12.8
BBC Radio 3	1.3	1.3
BBC Radio 4	10.5	11.0
BBC Radio 5 Live	3.6	4.4
BBC Local/Regional	9.3	10.8
All Commerical	49.3	46.7
All National Commercial	9.3	8.3
Atlantic 252	1.4	0.6
Classic FM	3.7	4.3
Talk Radio (now Sport)	1.6	1.5
Virgin Radio (AM only)	2.6	1.8
All Local Commerical	40.0	38.4
Other Listening	2.2	2.0

Source: Rajar/RSI

(You can access more up-to-date listening figures from the RAJAR website at www.rajar.co.uk)

the types of occupation that each grade represents and the percentage of the population that fits that particular grade:

A	Higher managerial, administrative or professional	3%
B	Intermediate managerial, administrative or professional	15%
C1	Supervisory or clerical, junior managerial, administrative or professional	23%
C2	Skilled manual workers	28%
D	Semi-skilled and unskilled manual workers	18%
E	Casual labourers, unemployed, state pensioners	13%

Sex and Age are also important. Age is generally divided into the following categories:

    <15
    15–24
    24–35
    35–55
    55>

Carry out your own research to test the validity of the information contained in Fig. 34. Try to account for any differences you may find.

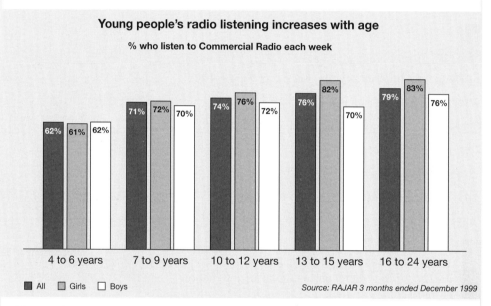

Young people's radio listening increases with age

% who listen to Commercial Radio each week

	4 to 6 years	7 to 9 years	10 to 12 years	13 to 15 years	16 to 24 years
All	62%	71%	74%	76%	79%
Girls	61%	72%	76%	82%	83%
Boys	62%	70%	72%	70%	76%

■ All ▨ Girls ☐ Boys   *Source: RAJAR 3 months ended December 1999*

Figure 34

One of the reasons for the debate over the position of *News at Ten* was not because ITV wanted to give viewers a better news programme or evening's entertainment but to allow ITV to get better ratings for the time-slot so that they could charge advertisers more money. If *News at Ten* remained in its original slot, ITV had to break its 'adult', post-watershed programmes at 10 pm, and often viewers did not return to the film or programme after *News at Ten*. In effect 'peak viewing' ended at 10.30 pm. With the main evening's news programme moved to 6.30 pm, ITV could start its 'adult' programmes at 9.00 or 9.30 pm, and audiences would stay with the film or drama through to its end at 11 pm. This in effect extended peak viewing time by half an hour and allowed

ITV companies to charge higher amounts for advertising space at 10.30, 10.45 and 11.00 pm. Although the audience for *ITV's Nightly News* was one million less than that for *News at Ten*, the audience for ITV between 10.00 and 10.30 pm rose by over 1 million. These new viewers were mainly younger and more downmarket, belonging to the C2DE social grades. Although generally advertisers prefer to reach ABC1 audiences, they are also keen to reach young viewers in their late teens and early twenties as they are considered to have a large amount of 'disposable income'.

The BBC, although not driven by the financial need to attract advertising revenue, had a similar problem in that *The Nine O'Clock News* 'interfered' with its main evening schedules. They were therefore very keen to move into the gap created by the move of *News at Ten*. However, since *News at Ten* is back at its old slot, at least for some evenings, there is now a direct clash between the two channels.

ACTIVITY

Read the section on News (p. 215) and then consider your own consumption of television news.

■ Do you ever watch it?
■ If so, is it a conscious decision to find out what is going on in the world or just because you couldn't be bothered to switch over/off?
■ Which news bulletin(s) do you watch?
■ Are there some news bulletins that you feel are more directly aimed at you?
■ What types of audience do the other bulletins address?
■ Are the news items of interest to you?
■ If you could choose your own news items, what would they be and to what extent would they differ from what is usually presented?

OR

Research the latest viewing figures for both ITV's and BBC's main evening news broadcasts.

■ Which one has the higher audience viewing figures?
■ Why do you think this is?
■ Using old newspapers or listings magazines, identify how the BBC1 schedule has changed since the move of *The Nine O'Clock News*.
■ Explain why you think the new schedule has (or has not) improved the BBC's overall audience figures.

The statistical information provided by organisations like BARB and RAJAR is then supplemented by more detailed and qualitative data about audiences (see Research Skills, p. 274). This is often carried out by advertising or marketing companies for particular broadcasters and media companies, and focuses on the audience's lifestyle, their habits, opinions and sets of values and attitudes. Advertising companies claim that they can segment audiences on the basis of 'socio-economic values' such as:

- **Survivors**   Those that want security and like routine.
- **Social climbers**   Those who have a strong materialistic drive and like status symbols.
- **Care givers**   Those who believe in 'caring and sharing'.
- **Explorers**   For whom personal growth and influencing social change are important.

These socio-economic groups may be given a variety of names (Mainstreamers, Aspirers, Achievers and Reformers is another version) but they are all based on the work of the American psychologist Abraham Maslow and his idea of a 'Hierarchy of Needs' (see Figure 35). Maslow suggested that we all have different 'layers' of needs and that we need to satisfy one before we can move on to the next. In other words, we all start at the bottom of Maslow's hierarchy, having basic *physiological* needs like food and shelter to survive. We can then move up the hierarchy where we have *safety* needs, probably to do with having a regular income, like a job, that guarantees us a regular source of food and shelter – perhaps being able to pay the rent or mortgage. The next level is to do with belonging to a *social* group, whether it is our family, work colleagues or peer group. In fact most of us belong to a variety of different social groups, for example as students, family members, social groups, work groups, etc.

Our *esteem* needs are to do with wanting to gain the respect and admiration of others, perhaps through the display of status symbols like expensive consumer goods. Maslow argues that many people stop at particular levels and only a very few reach 'self-actualisation' at the top of the hierarchy. These are the people who are considered to be in control of their lives and have achieved all their goals.

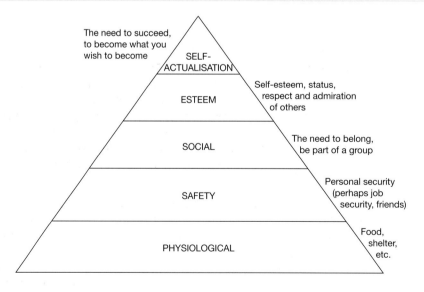

Figure 35 Maslow's 'Hierarchy of Needs'

MEDIA STUDIES: THE ESSENTIAL INTRODUCTION

Advertisers are increasingly using ideas like Maslow's and combining both demographics and lifestyle categories in an attempt to be more effective and efficient in the way in which they target particular groups of people. They are trying to sell their products in a way that meets the target audience's perceived needs. (See Advertising case study, p. 236.)

ACTIVITY

Some commercial media organisations may be willing to let you have media packs or out-of-date rate cards. You could then use these to plan a campaign for a new product. (See Advertising case study, p. 236.)

> 'We must get away from the habit of thinking in terms of what the media do to people and substitute for it the idea of what people do with the media.'
>
> (Halloran 1970)

The history of audience research is a story of the 'shift' from the view of the audience as passive to one that views the audience as 'active' in its relationship with media texts.

THE HYPODERMIC NEEDLE THEORY The theory that suggests that the media 'inject' ideas into a passive audience, like giving a patient a drug.

Some of the earliest academic studies of media audiences appeared in the 1920s and 1930s and looked at what we understand as the 'mass media' – cinema, radio, popular magazines and newspapers – as they became increasingly available to the majority of people in Europe and America. In these early studies the audience itself was seen as a 'mass' audience – a mass of people, all together, consuming the same product and receiving the same 'mass' message. This seemed to be particularly effective when the Nazis in Germany and the Communists in the Soviet Union used the media as a propaganda tool. They appeared to be successful in making their ideas dominant and 'injecting' large numbers of people with their messages.

The Frankfurt School was made up of German Marxists who, in the 1930s, saw the success of Nazi propaganda and later, in 1950s America, of commercial television. They thought that the media were a force for pacifying the population and restricting and controlling public and cultural life by injecting a 'mass culture' that functioned as a distraction from the mundanity of ordinary daily life. Members of the Frankfurt School like Adorno and Horkheimer suggested that the American 'culture industries', in particular commercial television and popular cinema, moulded people into a standardised, passive state of being that allowed them to be easily manipulated. Although in America most of this manipulation was carried out by advertising and the drive for consumerism, they suggested that, as had happened in Germany, mass media could also be used to manipulate people into accepting particular political ideas such as capitalism. They believed that these 'culture industries' worked against democracy and restricted people's choices and actions.

This view of the media seemed to be reinforced by Orson Welles's *The War of the Worlds*, broadcast on American radio in 1938. The programme, based on the book by H.G.Wells, was broadcast as part of a regular weekly drama slot but was produced to sound like a series of news reports and news 'flashes' about the invasion of America by Martians. The programme appeared to include interviews with people in authority such as politicians and police officers and contained instructions for people to evacuate their homes. Many people did in fact believe that the broadcast was a real emergency and did drive out of New York State. The programme caused considerable panic and also attracted considerable criticism and complaints for being 'too realistic'. It is a good example of the power and the 'authority' that the media had at the time in the mind of the radio listeners. Many commentators have suggested that today we are too sophisticated to make the same mistake but a spoof broadcast of the BBC programme *Ghostwatch* on Halloween in 1992 fooled many viewers into believing that they were seeing real paranormal experiences on television.

In Britain there has been a series of exposés about 'fake' documentaries, the re-enacting scenes in docu-soaps and actors pretending to be 'real' people on chat shows such as *Vanessa*. The 'naming and shaming' campaign started by the *News of the World* is also perhaps a reminder that we still give the media too much authority and credence.

With the introduction of commercial television and in particular advertising, the idea of 'injecting' the audience with a message seemed even more relevant. It was thought that advertisers could 'make' people buy particular products or brands of products merely by repeating the message often and loudly – the 'hard sell' approach. Vance Packard in *The Hidden Persuaders* (1957) identified many of the ways in which advertisers attempted to 'manipulate' audiences. C. Wright Mills in *The Power Elite* (1956) suggested four functions that the media perform for audiences:

- to give individuals *identity*
- to give people goals, *aspiration*
- to give *instruction* on how to achieve these goals
- to give people an alternative if they failed, *escapism*.

However, studies of the various political advertising campaigns in America in the 1940s and 1950s suggested that the audience was not so passive and did not just accept what the advertisers or the programme makers said. Rather, in terms of political advertising, audiences focused on those messages that reinforced their existing beliefs and tended to dismiss those that contradicted their established ideas. This suggested that audiences in fact selected the messages that they wanted to hear and ignored others. The media's effect seemed to be one of reinforcement rather than of persuasion.

This research led to a view that audiences, rather than being simply a 'mass', were composed of different social groups, with particular sets of social relations, and a variety of cultural norms and values. Several American researchers, including Paul Lazarsfeld and Elihu Katz, concentrated on providing evidence that audiences were not simply one large, gullible mass but that messages put out by the media were in fact being received by a complex mixture of different groups and that media texts were themselves mediated by these social and cultural networks. The audience was now being seen as playing an active role in the interpretation of the meaning of particular media texts.

KEY TERM

USES AND GRATIFICATIONS THEORY The idea that media audiences make active use of what the media offer. The audience has a set of needs which the media in one form or another meet.

Uses and Gratifications theory was an important shift in the study of how audiences interacted with texts and was developed by Blumler and Katz in 1974. Through a series of interviews with viewers, they identified four broad needs that were fulfilled by the viewers of television:

- **Diversion** — A form of escape or release from everyday pressures.
- **Personal relationships** — Companionship through identification with television characters and sociability through discussion about television with other people.
- **Personal identity** — The ability to compare one's own life with the characters and situations portrayed and explore individual problems and perspectives.
- **Surveillance** — Information about 'what's going on' in the world.

ACTIVITY . . .

Other Uses and Gratifications research developed models about how viewers use quiz shows for four main gratifications:

1 **Self-rating**   See how well I do.
2 **Social interaction**   Watching/sharing/competing with others.
3 **Excitement**   To see who wins and what they win.
4 **Education**   As a source of knowledge.

Uses and Gratifications theory is seen to have some merit as it supposes an 'active' audience that to some extent provides its own interpretation of the text's meaning. However, as a means of understanding the relationship between the audience and the creation of meaning, it can appear to be rather simplistic and limited in relation to the complexity of how we the audience/reader actually work with a text. One of the main problems with Uses and Gratifications theory is that it assumes that the media somehow identify these needs on behalf of the audience and then provide the material to meet or gratify them. An alternative interpretation could be that we the audience 'create' these needs as a response to the material provided by the media, and that in fact we could have many other needs that are not identified, or met, by existing media texts.

ACTIVITY . . .

Look at the BARB figures on p. 125 or access their website (www.barb.co.uk) for the most popular television programmes. Try to identify the main Uses and Gratifications that these programmes may provide for viewers. Design a questionnaire and test your theory.

In fact many of our 'uses' and 'pleasures' can be seen to be 'making the best' of what is available and putting it to our (the audience's) use, which may be different from the one that the producer intended. For example, consider the unexpected popularity and fashionability of many cheap day-time television shows, such as *Supermarket Sweep* or *Ready Steady Cook*.

KEY TERM

SITUATED CULTURE A term used to describe how our 'situation' (i.e. daily routines and patterns, social relationships with family and peer groups) can influence our engagement with and interpretation of media texts.

In Media Studies there is a lot of debate and research about how the reader/audience consumes and makes sense of particular texts. There have been specific studies by researchers such as David Morley (1986), who studied the way families watched television programmes like *Nationwide*, Dorothy Hobson (1982) on viewers of *Crossroads*, David Buckingham (1987) on *EastEnders'* audience, and Christine Geraghty (1991) on the relationship between women and soap operas.

It is worth thinking a little about the difference in the ways we tend to consume different media. Tunstall (1983) in *The Media in Britain* has suggested that the way in which we consume the media can be divided into three levels: primary, secondary and tertiary.

PRIMARY MEDIA Where we pay close attention to the media text, for instance, in the close reading of a magazine or newspaper or in the cinema where we concentrate on the film in front of us.

SECONDARY MEDIA Where the medium or text is there in the background and we are aware that it is there but are not concentrating on it. This happens most often with music-based radio but also when the television is on but we are not really watching it; maybe we are talking with friends, eating or carrying out some other activity. This could also include 'skimming' through a magazine or newspaper waiting for something to catch our eye.

TERTIARY MEDIA Where the medium is present but we are not at all aware of it. The most obvious examples are advertising hoardings or placards that we pass but do not register.

If we compare our consumption of films and television, there is an obvious difference between the two in that television is generally part of what Raymond Williams (1974) described as a 'flow'. By this Williams meant that television was a constant stream available to us in the home that we can turn on or off at will, like a water tap in the bathroom or kitchen. Sometimes we have it on as background or, as it is suggested that many elderly people do, have it on as 'company'. On other occasions we may turn the television on in order to 'share' our watching with others, particularly with sporting events or perhaps soap operas. This may be a way of sharing companionship or, like *The Royle Family*, a way of being a 'family'.

This, Williams suggested, meant that our reception of television programmes, and the media in general, is mediated through our domestic, situated culture. This means that *who* we are, our sense of our own place in the world, our views and beliefs, as well as *where* we are in terms of our social location, all influence our responses to the media.

Watching a film, in contrast to television, is generally a more carefully chosen and focused activity. A visit to the cinema requires a series of conscious decisions such as deciding to 'go out' to the cinema, choosing who to go with, at what time, to which cinema or multiplex and which film to see. Watching a video also involves a set of deliberate choices such as deciding which video to rent, paying money, putting aside the time to watch the film, perhaps choosing particular companions to watch it with. Even a film on television is often chosen in a much more deliberate way than the rest of the television's 'flow', which is often watched 'because it is on' rather than as the result of a series of deliberate choices.

Figure 36 The Royle Family

Think about the last time you went to the cinema. List the series of decisions that you had to make. How did you make your decisions? Refer back to some of the earlier activities in this section that refer to patterns of film consumption. How do you and your friends consume this medium?

DAVID MORLEY'S *NATIONWIDE* STUDY

In 1978 David Morley and Charlotte Brunsdon investigated how different audiences responded to, and made sense of, *Nationwide*, an early-evening BBC programme. Their research suggested that audiences bought a complex set of knowledge and experience to the programmes that they were consuming. This alongside other factors such as gender, ethnicity and class were, Morley suggested, an important part of the way in which audiences 'consume' and 'understand' texts and 'create meaning'.

ANG'S *DALLAS* STUDY

In 1985 Ien Ang looked at the readers' reception of *Dallas*. Ang put an advert in a women's magazine in Holland asking about viewers' reactions to and reasons for watching *Dallas*. Of the 42 replies that Ang received, she identified three different types of response:

- **The ideology of mass culture** suggested viewers liked the programme because it was successful and a high-profile piece of American popular television culture.
- **The ironic or 'detached' position** where viewers would watch it, knowing that it was 'bad' but wanting to see what it was other people were watching.
- **The ideology of popularism** which is based on people's everyday routines and experiences and the 'pleasure' that they get from watching *Dallas* even though they may recognise that it is 'trash'.

(See also the section on Ang on p. 121.)

Researchers have also looked at the way in which the media 'address' or 'position' their audiences in relation to an event, person or idea. (See section on Narrative, p. 44.) Audiences can be positioned by the point of view used both verbally and visually to create a relationship between the text and its audience. Expressed verbally, these can include words like 'I' used by the narrator or broadcaster; 'You' when addressing the viewer or listener; and 'It' or 'They' when referring to an event, third person or idea. Visually this positioning can be maintained by using camera angles, where the camera follows the action in a particular way or follows a particular person. Editing the flow and sequencing of shots can also position the audience to the extent that they become observers who see more than the participants and are spectators placed outside the action. For example, this occurs in a crime drama where the audience is given 'privileged' information about who committed the crime, or in a soap opera where that someone is lying or has a secret.

The modes of address used in broadcasting are often informal, conversational and open-ended because they are consumed in the private domestic world of the home. (See Figure 37, Listening locations.) To create the necessary sense of intimacy, presenters talk to the audience as if they were individual members whom they know personally (see discussion on 'Doreen', p. 122). Although these modes of address are largely motivated by the producers' sense of their audience, sometimes they are determined by the institution's own sense of itself. For example, the BBC might consider itself representing the nation at a time of crisis and therefore may present its material in a particularly solemn and dignified manner (see section on mode of address in Part 1, p. 51).

Figure 37 Radio listening locations

	Ever listen	Listen most often	Favourite
	%	%	%
Listening places			
At home	81	57	56
bedroom	48	17	18
living room	48	18	18
kitchen	47	20	17
bathroom	10	1	1
garden	8	0	0
study	3	1	1
garage/shed	2	0	0
In the car	44	24	24
At work	24	17	16
Listening situations			
Having breakfast	39	10	10
Doing the housework	36	20	19
Driving to work	34	20	19
Getting ready for work/school	27	7	6
Whilst at work	27	19	18
Radio alarm (on waking up)	25	5	4
In bed at night	18	5	7
Having lunch	15	1	2
Doing DIY	12	2	2
Having evening meal	6	1	1

Source: *Radio Days 2*, 1999

MEDIA STUDIES: THE ESSENTIAL INTRODUCTION

AUDIENCE PARTICIPATION

'Real people' are increasingly appearing on television. Once upon a time it was only certain privileged types of people (politicians, experts, presenters) who appeared on our screens. If the public were seen, they were tightly controlled and mediated through the use of presenters (as in documentaries) or a quiz-master. (Even the early quiz and entertainment shows relied upon various types of 'expert' or personality – for instance the BBC's *What's My Line?*, *Juke Box Jury* or *Brains Trust*.) It was largely with the introduction of more American-type quiz-shows on ITV in the 1950s that 'ordinary people' started to appear in front of cameras and then usually only to answer a well-rehearsed and tightly controlled set of questions.

Today, however, the public, ordinary people, are increasingly the stars of the shows. They may appear as the victims in humorous or emotional situations as in *You've Been Framed* or *Surprise Surprise*, or in fly-on-the-wall documentaries like Paul Watson's *A Wedding in the Family* (2000). A recent popular genre has been the 'make-over' show, where ordinary people change their looks (*Looking Good*), their homes or gardens (*Home Front* or *Changing Rooms*) or even find new partners (*Blind Date* or *Street Mate*).

Many shows now encourage their audience to 'come on down' and become involved with the show, as in *TFI Friday* or *The Priory*. *The Big Breakfast* has a 'family of the week' and 'lost in telly' participants as well as competition winners who appear on the show.

Docu-soaps have turned 'ordinary people' into stars and personalities like Maureen from *Driving School* (see Figure 21, p. 92). Ordinary people also appear in the various 'real-life' programmes that may contain actual footage or reconstructions, such as *Jimmy's*, *It Happened to Me*, *Condition Critical* or *Police, Camera, Action*. They may also appear in programmes like *Video Nation* talking directly to the camera, or recounting their experiences in history programmes like *The People's Century* or *Out of the Doll's House*. A recent popular genre has been programmes such as the BBC's *Castaway 2000* or C4's *Big Brother*, which 'isolate' ordinary people and then record their experiences of being together. Forty-five thousand people applied to appear in *Big Brother*, nearly 6 million viewers watched 'Nasty Nick' leaving the show and 7 million watched Craig win (see Figure 18, p. 77).

There are many possible reasons for this increase in 'ordinary people' appearing on television. One explanation is that they are a lot cheaper to use than professional entertainers and presenters. They may also help the audience at home identify with the participants and the programme and they may help to encourage audience loyalty through their familiar situations and characters.

ACTIVITY...

Look through the television schedules and identify those programmes that make a feature of incorporating 'ordinary' people.

■ Can they be divided into different types of programmes?

- Ask members of your family and friends whether they like this emphasis on 'ordinary' people on television.
- Can they identify what the attraction is of these types of programmes?
- Are the schedulers successful in using these types of programmes to attract audiences?

OR

Other people's pain, grief and misfortune make good television. However, as the television seeks to fill more and more broadcasting hours and programme-makers chase audience ratings, are there limits to what 'reality' can be presented on screen?

OR

In what ways are popular genres like docu-soaps and game shows important in determining television schedules in Britain?

OR

Why do you think docu-soaps are so popular? Use examples to illustrate your answer.

GENDERED CONSUMPTION

There has been much research on how gender affects our consumption of the media. Studies such as Hobson (1982) and Gray (1992) suggest that women prefer 'open-ended' narratives like soap operas whereas men prefer 'closed' narratives like police dramas (see Narrative, p. 52). Soap operas are considered popular among women because they conform to what Geraghty (1991) calls 'women's fiction' and have certain common conventions:

- They have strong female lead characters.
- They focus on the private, domestic sphere.
- They deal with personal relationships.
- They contain an element of fantasy and/or escapism.

(See section on Genre, p. 55.)

Other research, such as Radway's (1984) study of a group of readers of romantic novels and Stacey's (1994) work with women cinema-goers from the 1940s and 1950s, also explores this notion of escapism or 'utopian solutions'.

KEY TERM

UTOPIAN SOLUTION A term taken from Dyer (1977), who suggested that entertainment genres are popular because of their fantasy element and the escapism that they provide from daily routines and problems. He suggested that particular genres such as Musicals or Westerns offered particular types of utopian solution.

These studies suggest that women audiences welcome romantic texts as a means of reasserting positive aspects of their lives. Radway suggests that heroines in romantic novels are seen as victorious because they symbolise the value of the female world of love and human relationships as being more important than fame and material success.

Males are considered to prefer factual programmes like news and current affairs, although, as Morley (1986) notes, many men may watch soap operas but are not prepared to admit it. Mulvey (1975) suggests that most Hollywood films are based on the idea of a male viewer and that the camera shots and editing are 'positioned' by a male perspective. This she called the 'male gaze' which automatically positions women as passive and as objects.

All this research suggests the complex nature of the relationships between audience and media text. As you will have read in Part 1, texts are polysemic (see p. 35) in having a variety of meanings, and the audience is an important component in determining that meaning.

THE 'EFFECTS' DEBATE AND MORAL PANICS

There has long been concern about the supposedly bad effects that popular culture may have on 'ordinary' people (see p. 131). This concern has grown with the increase in 'mass media' and the availability of cheap fiction books, popular magazines, the cinema, popular music, television and, more recently, the Internet.

In the 1950s American comics like *Tales from the Crypt* or *Haunt of Fear* with their depiction of violence were seen as dangerous. So a law was introduced called the 1955 Children and Young Persons (Harmful Publications) Act to control which comics were allowed to be on sale in this country.

In fact we can trace panics about the effects of the media back to the introduction of newspapers in the eighteenth century, when a tax or stamp duty was put on newspapers by the government to make newspapers so expensive that only rich people could afford to buy them.

The term 'moral panic' comes from *Folk Devils and Moral Panics* (1972) by Stan Cohen. Cohen looked at the media reaction to the fights between mods and rockers at various seaside resorts in Britain during the mid-1960s. His term 'moral panic' came to mean a mass response to 'a group, a person or an attitude that becomes defined as a threat to society'.

Once a threat has been identified, a panic is then often created through press coverage, particularly the tabloid press, and then taken up by other newspapers and/or television programmes. Newspapers may start campaigns saying 'something must be done' and then politicians may become involved, offering support to the campaigns, and often legislation is introduced as a result.

In recent years we have had panics over refugees 'flooding' into Britain from Eastern Europe seeking asylum, as well as over dangerous dogs, illegal raves and video nasties. As a result of these 'panics', legislation has been introduced to try to control dangerous dogs, make rave parties illegal, control the activities of asylum seekers and the classification and distribution of certain types of video. One recent 'moral panic' was the 'naming and shaming' of paedophiles by the *News of the World* (see pp. 215–16, 'Name and Shame' headline).

The moral panic over video nasties like *Driller Killer*, *Zombie Flesh Eaters* and *Texas Chain Saw Massacre* in the early 1980s led to the Video Recordings Act of 1984 that limited the kinds of videos on sale in this country (see Regulation of the Media, p. 184). Other moral panics can be more subtle, for instance, the campaigns over unmarried mothers who, it is claimed, get pregnant for the welfare benefits or the panics about Supermodels and 'heroin chic' which, it is claimed, encourage young girls to over-diet and can result in anorexia.

Perhaps the most well-known case is the murder of James Bulger in 1993 and its association with the film *Child's Play 3*. In this case neither the prosecution nor the police presented any evidence to support the supposition that the two boys who had killed James Bulger had actually seen (yet alone been influenced by) *Child's Play 3*.

The two boys came from socially and environmentally deprived backgrounds. Jon Venables had been referred by teachers to a psychologist because at school he banged his head against a wall to attract attention, threw objects at other children, and had cut himself with scissors.

Even if it had been proved that the two boys had seen *Child's Play 3*, it is difficult to know how the court could have separated the influence of this video from all the other factors that made the two boys who they were. It was the judge in the case who, in his summing up, made the connection which was then taken up by the tabloid press and MPs. This eventually led to the law being changed so that the British Board of Film Classification now has to take into account 'the influence' of videos as well as their content.

There has been a large amount of research trying to identify the 'effects' of the media on audiences, particularly in relation to violence. However, such research tends to be either inconclusive or contradictory (see for instance Barker and Petley 1997). Part of the problem with any attempt to prove the effects of watching violence or sex on television, video or film is trying to isolate the effect of the media from all the others that are involved in shaping us as individuals – family, home, education, religion, peer groups, etc. In America there were several cases of supposed 'copycat' killings after the release of the film *Natural Born Killers*. In fact many of those convicted of murder already had a history of violence before seeing the film.

Two of Britain's worst murder cases were the shootings of schoolchildren and their teacher in Dunblane by Thomas Hamilton in 1996 and the murders of elderly women carried out by the doctor Harold Shipman over a number of years. In neither case was there any suggestion or evidence at all that either Hamilton or Shipman had ever watched any violent videos.

Much of this 'effects' debate seems to assume that somehow if 'we', the audience, watch a violent film, then we will carry out violent acts. This seems very simplistic in view of the complicated relationship that we, as audiences, have with the media. The most we can possibly say is that people with violent tendencies may watch violent videos, but that does not mean that everyone who watches violent videos is (or becomes) violent.

ACTIVITY . . .

What do you understand by the term 'moral panic'? By referring to one or more specific examples, illustrate how the media can be said to be responsible for creating moral panics.

One of the panics today is focused around access to the Internet. Over 40 per cent of adults in this country now have access to the Internet, and it is available in schools and public libraries. There does perhaps need to be a debate about how media like the Internet are controlled and monitored, but the real difficulty lies perhaps in deciding who should be in charge of regulation. Many people are probably fully in favour of censorship – as long as they are the ones who make the decisions!

AND FINALLY . . .

Let us return to *The Royle Family* as this programme highlights many of the key themes in this section on Media Audiences and how audiences interact with media texts. In one episode of the situation comedy, the family members settle down after Sunday lunch to watch the BBC's *Antiques Roadshow* but instead of admiring the antiques they bet on how much they are valued at, and the family member who is nearest takes the winnings.

This episode is a good example of how the fictional family members are using a programme as a means of both entertainment and diversion from the mundane routines of daily weekday life as well as bringing themselves together as a family and sharing in the experience of betting on the antiques in the *Antiques Roadshow*. Their particular use of the programme, to see who can best guess the value of the antiques, is their own 'negotiated' meaning of the programme but one that is shared by all the members of the family. Their 'situated culture', the family together, affects the meaning of the programme, and their social background affects their interpretation of what the notion of 'antiques' means – not something to own but a way of sharing pleasure and winning money.

We could also say that in fact the members of the Royle family are making quite an astute comment on the *Antiques Roadshow* itself – middle-class people bring out their antiques and pretend surprise when told how much they are worth – but actually the money 'value' of the antiques is the whole point (and attraction?) of the programme. So really we could say that the Royle family is getting to the hub of the programme and exposing its hypocrisy.

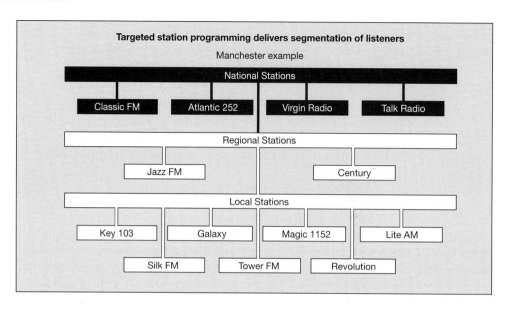

Targeted station programming delivers segmentation of listeners

Manchester example

National Stations

Classic FM · Atlantic 252 · Virgin Radio · Talk Radio

Regional Stations

Jazz FM · Century

Local Stations

Key 103 · Galaxy · Magic 1152 · Lite AM

Silk FM · Tower FM · Revolution

Figure 38

1   Write a detailed clarification of the information contained in Figure 29 (p. 118) 'Share of media consumption by time of day'. Analyse the ways in which the media might be said to organise the everyday lives of its audiences. Your analysis could be based around one specific individual or could be discussed in more general terms.

2   Figure 38 contains a diagram of the commercial radio stations available in the Manchester area. Create a similar diagram for your own area and include the BBC stations.

■ For each station draw up a profile of the 'core' audience. You will be able to make some judgements about the core audience from the types of programmes, the types of advertisements and the shows where listeners are in contact with the station. You can use Hartley's and Fiske's 'subjectivities' (p. 122) but should also try to and research demographic information. (You can also contact the stations themselves to check how accurate your profiles have been.)

■ On what basis are the different listener audiences segmented?

■ Are there any particular groups not catered for? Why do you think this is? If so, draw up a design for a radio station that would meet the needs of this group.

Consider the types of programmes, presenters, advertisers and promotional material that this station would need.

3   Working as a group, imagine that you have been asked by a film company to provide the outline for a new film aimed at audiences between the ages of 18 and 25. Draw up an outline that includes:

■ the main situation or narrative of the story and its dramatic potential

■ descriptions of the main characters, any major supporting roles and the relationships between them

■ ideas of two or three main settings, explaining their visual impact, the reasons for using them and any technical difficulties that they may present

■ the opening sequence of the film (both in terms of sound and images), explaining how it will attract the audience's attention. (You may wish to read the section on Title Sequences, p. 97.)

Then explain the ways in which you think the film will appeal to its target audience and suggest ways in which the film could be marketed. You may wish to present your outline to other students and ask them to choose the one most likely to be commercially successful. You may also consider filming the opening scene on video.

4   Using a selection of examples from a range of different genres in either radio or television, discuss the role that 'ordinary people' have in contemporary media texts.

5   'The media have become a central part of everyday life.' Discuss this proposition using specific examples.

6   Examine the ways in which social and cultural factors influence the ways in which audiences use and interpret media texts.

7   Explain what is meant by the term 'the active audience'. How useful is it as a concept in understanding how audiences interact with the media?

FURTHER READING

Ang, I. (1985) *Watching Dallas: Soap Opera and the Melodramatic Imagination*, Methuen.

Barker, M. and Petley, J. (eds) (1997) *Ill-Effects: The Media/Violence Debate*, Routledge.

Buckingham, D. (1987) *Public Secrets: EastEnders and its Audience*, BFI Publishing.

Fiske, J. (1987) *Television Culture*, Routledge.

Geraghty, C. (1991) *Women and Soap-Opera*, Polity Press.

Halloran, J. (1970) *The Effects of Television*, Panther.

Hartley, J. (1982) *Understanding News*, Methuen.

Hobson, D. (1982) *Crossroads: the Drama of a Soap Opera*, Methuen.

Morley, D. (1980) *The Nationwide Audience*, BFI Publishing.

Radway, J. (1984) *Reading the Romance: Women, Patriarchy and Popular Literature*, Verso.

Williams, R. (1974) *Television, Technology and Cultural Form*, Routledge.

▼ EXAMPLE: MAGAZINES

In this section:

- we apply some of the theories about audiences to magazines
- we concentrate on 'lifestyle' magazines and in particular those aimed at women readers.

Estimates of the number of magazine titles available in Britain vary between 8,000 and 10,000, of which about one-third are consumer and lifestyle magazines, the remainder being professional and business publications or 'giveaways' such as the AA magazine or periodicals for companies like Sainsbury's or Safeways.

ACTIVITY...

Carry out a survey about people's magazine-reading habits. You could look at:

- What magazines people read
- How much they spend on magazines
- How they choose which magazines to buy
- When and where they read them
- Why they read them or, if they don't read magazines, why not
- Which parts of the magazines they read first
- Which parts of the magazines they find least interesting
- How much influence they think the magazines have on their 'lifestyle'; for example, do the features or advertisements influence the products they purchase?
- What is their 'history' in terms of magazine-reading, i.e. what magazines and/or comics have they read in the past?

Do any patterns emerge? Is there any significant difference between the sexes in terms of magazine consumption?

'LIFESTYLE' MAGAZINES

This is one of the most popular and competitive areas of the magazine publishing market. Lifestyle and consumer magazines are second only in terms of consumer sales to the television listings magazines (such as *What's on TV* and *Radio Times*), but the lifestyle market has many more titles competing for its readers. On pp. 111–12 we talked about 'narrowcasting': as new magazines come on to the market they are increasingly trying to narrow down the market and provide advertisers with more and more specific reader 'profiles'. Like most newspapers (see p. 123), the revenue which lifestyle magazines get from advertising is far more important than the income they receive from the cover price and individual sales. It is estimated that women spend £230 million a year on monthly 'glossies' and that the magazines 'earn' another £190 million from advertising.

'Lifestyle' is a very broad category that can include *FHM*, *Gardener's World* or *Woman's Realm*. However, all these magazines are trying to do the same thing, using a consumerism based on particular lifestyles to deliver particular groups of audiences to advertisers.

Consider what the term 'lifestyle' means. What is it that these magazines offer their readers? On the surface they seem to offer information and advice about certain types of 'lifestyle': what products to buy; where to buy them; the types of goods and services that might be available to someone leading that particular 'lifestyle'. However, as Lazarsfeld and Katz suggest (see p. 133), the relationship between audience and text is often much more complex and more intimate, offering a range of 'Uses and Gratifications' for the reader. Lifestyle magazines often offer their readers not only advice but also a sense of identity and possibly companionship and reassurance. They appear to share with their readers the problems and issues of other similar people who also read the magazine. The magazines also appear to offer guidance and instruction on how to live a particular lifestyle as well as entertainment and escapism. The magazines also offer aspiration in a variety of different spheres, such as relationships, careers, material possessions or looks.

One of the attractions of lifestyle magazines is that they are usually a secondary media (see p. 135) and require little effort or concentration to consume. They are designed to be 'browsed' through, with regular features signposted and articles and advertisements designed to attract the reader's attention. These magazines will possibly be kept until the next edition arrives and so may be left lying around a home for some time. The magazines will therefore be looked at several times by the same reader or glanced through by new readers. Readers may have different patterns of reading magazines, perhaps when they do not want to be disturbed and can go somewhere quiet or perhaps in the mornings over a cup of coffee.

The readership of a magazine, therefore, is important as well as its circulation. The readership of magazines aimed particularly at one market may have a significant number of readers from another market, i.e. the men who read women's magazines. Sometimes this is done 'secretly', as some men are reluctant to admit that they enjoy reading some of the features of women's magazines or they may only admit to reading the problem pages. There may be an element of titillation and vicarious pleasure from gaining glimpses of other people's sex lives. Sometimes this reading may be more open, for example, the Letters Page in the July 2000 edition of *Red* included a

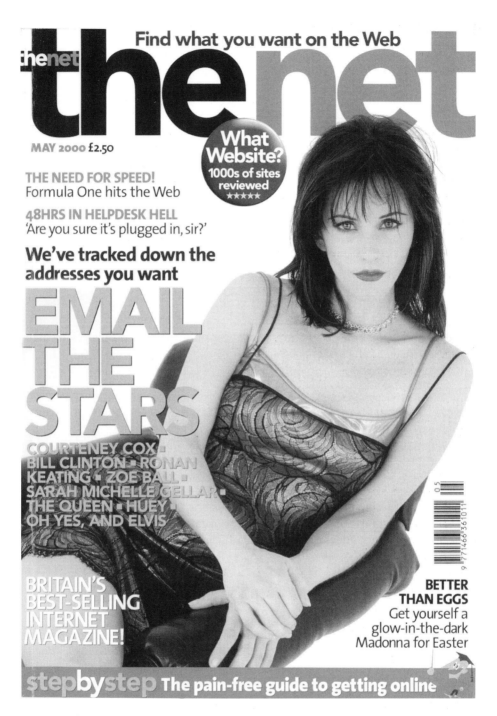

Find what you want on the Web

thenet

MAY 2000 £2.50

What Website?
1000s of sites reviewed
★★★★★

THE NEED FOR SPEED!
Formula One hits the Web

48HRS IN HELPDESK HELL
'Are you sure it's plugged in, sir?'

We've tracked down the addresses you want

EMAIL THE STARS

**COURTENEY COX •
BILL CLINTON • RONAN
KEATING • ZOE BALL •
SARAH MICHELLE GELLAR •
THE QUEEN • HUEY •
OH YES, AND ELVIS**

**BRITAIN'S
BEST-SELLING
INTERNET
MAGAZINE!**

**BETTER
THAN EGGS**
Get yourself a
glow-in-the-dark
Madonna for Easter

stepbystep The pain-free guide to getting online

Figure 39

contribution from a man, and some magazines have included sections aimed specifically at male readers.

Ask a selection of your peers how they 'consume' magazines.

- Do they have a particular pattern to how and when they read?
- Does it vary for different types of magazine?

You may wish to ask them if they read magazines aimed at the opposite sex.

- Do men 'confess' to reading women's magazines? Which ones? What, if any, particular aspects of the women's magazines do they look at?

- Do women read men's magazines? Which ones? Again what particular features interest them?

- Are women influenced by the articles supposedly addressed to the opposite sex?

It might also be interesting to ask men and women if they buy magazines for their partners and, if so, which ones and why.

'Lifestyle' magazines are primarily consumer magazines that aim to make a profit by 'selling' particular types of audience to advertisers. The magazines are offering their readers literally a 'lifestyle': in other words a model on which to base their lives at this particular moment and the goods necessary to accommodate it. To do this successfully, magazines need to be able to make their readers identify with the lifestyle on offer, but at the same time offer them slightly more than they may already have. The magazines offer both guidance and aspiration: 'You, too, can be like this if only you do this/buy that', etc. The way this works for successful magazines is to have a clear sense of the target audience, Ang's 'imaginary entity' (p. 121), and to adopt an appropriate mode of address.

'THE MOST FUN A GIRL CAN HAVE WITH HER CLOTHES ON!' – TEENAGE MAGAZINES

More! and *J-17* are both commercially successful magazines aimed at teenage girls. They are notionally in competition with each other but in fact are both owned and published by EMAP. They are both very carefully aimed at separate, distinctive niche markets defined by age. This market is very competitive; and EMAP's Elan Youth group that is responsible for their teenage magazines has recently closed down two titles, *Big!* and *Minx,* because of falling sales. They still publish *Bliss, Looks* and *Smash Hits* but are planning new Internet titles through EMAP Digital (see p. 11). It is estimated that 72 per cent of girls in the UK read magazines compared to 58 per cent of adult women.

Discuss with others why you think that a magazine publisher may have more than one title aimed at a particular social group. Try to find examples, perhaps using the Internet or your local newsagents.

Although the style of contemporary popular 'teen mags' may have moved away from the photo-stories of *Jackie* and *My Guy*, much of the content deals with similar issues, albeit in a more up-to-date manner. McRobbie (1983), writing about the ideology underpinning *Jackie*, noted that it socialised female adolescents into a 'feminine' culture.

> [*Jackie*] sets up, defines and focuses exclusively on the personal, locating it as the sphere of prime importance to the teenage girl. It presents this as a totality – and by implication all else is of secondary interest to the 'modern girl'. Romance problems, fashion, beauty and pop mark out the limits of the girl's concern – other possibilities are ignored or dismissed.
>
> (McRobbie 1983: 743)

As McRobbie suggests, however, it is important to question the extent to which teenage readers accept or challenge this reading (see p. 84).

J-17

According to *J-17*, 'For the coolest fashion and hottest gossip, stylish babes read *J-17*'. With a circulation of over 300,000 and a readership of nearly three times that, *J-17* is the most successful of the current 'teen mags'. It is aimed at 'aspirational' females, 'mature for their years', ABC1s in the 12–17 age range.

Research by *J-17* suggests that 'appearance and image are very important' for *J-17* readers and that they are 'the highest spenders on toiletries/cosmetics within the youth market'. *J-17* readers wash their hair on average 4.4 times a week and in 1998 spent £6 a month on hair care and £19.55 a week on clothes, usually bought from places like Top Shop, Tammy, Miss Selfridge and River Island. Also in 1998 they spent on average £48.48 for a pair of trainers and £30 on a new pair of jeans.

Advertising in *J-17* reflects this profile with an emphasis on health and beauty products, fashion and music but also quite a lot of confectionery. Articles include 'how to cope with your parents' as well as fashion tips, star profiles, show-biz gossip and horoscopes, and are all presented on high-gloss full-colour paper.

Most of *J-17*'s readers are under the legal age of consent, and a major part of *J-17*'s attraction is its Problem Pages, where readers can not only 'speak for themselves' but also read about problems and issues that may also feature in their own lives and that they may have difficulty in discussing with their peers or family. The mode of address is personal, friendly and intimate. It is this area of the magazine that is perhaps the most 'reassuring', saying to its readers 'you are not alone, others are having similar problems and fears'. 'Typical' letters might read:

> 'I am not yet 16 and my boyfriend is several years older than me. We have been together for a year and been having sex for several months. He has asked me to take part in a bondage session with him and his friends. I like having sex with him but the thought of being tied up scares me. What should I do?'

> 'Recently I was caught by my mum snogging with my boyfriend. Now she says that she doesn't like us being alone together, and that I'm acting like a slut. But I haven't any plans for sex and I don't understand why my mum doesn't trust me.'

These types of feature have been the focus of a 'moral panic' (see pp. 141–3) over the last few years. There have been accusations that these magazines condone under-age sexual activity and seemingly endorse sexual promiscuity as well as offering a 'guide' to different sexual practices. There have been calls for magazine editors to curb such sexually explicit content, although the editors and publishers have argued that they offer 'responsible' advice that their readers may otherwise not receive.

More!

More! is EMAP's second most profitable title and has a circulation of around 300,000 sales per issue and a readership of 800,000 per issue. The target age of its readership is 16–24, of which 48 per cent are ABC1 and 75 per cent single.

More! describes itself as 'the biggest selling young women's magazine in the UK'. According to the editor, *More!* is aimed at

> every up-for-it young woman, because it's all about fun, flirting and looking gorgeous. With its cheeky humour, hunky men, sex advice and red-hot celebrity gossip, *More!* shoots straight from the hip. And with its glamorous new look and gorgeous fashion and beauty, *More!* is everything a sassy young woman wants from her life in handy magazine form. It's the most fun a girl can have with her clothes on!

They claim that '1% of *More!* readers go out 3–4 nights in an average week. Their ideal night out is round a friend's house for a good natter and make-up session, then to the local warm-up before going to a club to check out the totty.' *More!* readers shop at Top Shop, River Island, Warehouse, Oasis and Miss Selfridge; '47% are working in media, teaching, nursing and secretarial work'. Role models in 1997, when the readership was surveyed, were Anita Roddick, Gaby Roslin and Cindy Crawford.

The style and contents are similar to *J-17,* but the products are perhaps a little more 'up-market' (L'Oreal rather than Cote's Puzzel) and the articles are a little more 'serious' (teenage disappearances rather than parental unfairnesses).

The title itself is quite interesting – *More!* More what – Sex? Fashion? Advice? The *More!* editorial team would probably reply 'more Fun'. What that means is suggested by the strap-line 'Eye-Popping! Pant-Busting! Bed-Busting! The sex that changed YOUR lives' on the cover of the issue of 27 January 1999 and the regular 'Position of the Fortnight' feature.

According to Taylor, magazines like *More!* and *J-17* are offering their readers a positive representation of themselves, 'reassuring the girl she is not alone or unusual'. There is a 'theme of taking control of their lives, and living for themselves' (Taylor 2000: 9–12). It is also a representation that shows that teenage girls are mature, independent, sensible and trustworthy – values that perhaps many of them feel are not recognised by the 'adult' world. Part of the mode of address is to reinforce a sense of belonging and a type of solidarity against the unfairness of the world 'out there', a world that won't let them do want they want. According to Taylor, magazines like *More!* and *J-17* provide a teenage girl with 'a learning experience within the privacy of her own bedroom. Whereby she can see and understand her peers, without feeling embarrassed or ashamed. Quite simply the teenage girl can learn about herself, and grasp the meaning of everything that is happening to her' (Taylor 2000: 14).

It would be interesting to speculate about the extent to which those that work for these magazines and speak the language ('Let *J-17*'s Sarra guide you through her four types of lovin' . . .' [July 1999]) in print actually live out the lifestyles that *J-17* and *More!* represent.

'SHE'S A WOMAN WITH RESPONSIBILITY . . . AND A HANGOVER' – WOMEN'S MAGAZINES

Like McRobbie, Ferguson (1983) analyses women's magazines and the extent to which they are concerned with the practices and beliefs of a 'cult of femininity'. According to Ferguson, these magazines not only reflect the role of woman in society but they also offer guidance and socialisation into that role. Ferguson suggests that women's magazines attempt to 'promote a collective female social "reality", the world of women' (p. 185). Top-selling magazines such as *Woman*, *Woman's Own*, *Bella* and *Woman's Weekly* offer both guidance and membership into this 'cult of femininity'. (See also Ideology and Gender on p. 83.)

> This is a world founded on conformity to a set of shared meanings where a consciously cultivated female bond acts as the social cement of female solidarity. . . . Through the selective perception and interpretation of the wider world from the viewpoint of the 'woman's angle', the editors of these sacred oracles sustain a social 'reality' that is 'forever feminine'.
>
> (Ferguson 1983: 186)

These magazines can be seen to offer a representation of the 'ideal' in terms of the self, home, family, career, relationships and lifestyle.

To gain some idea of how the 'world of women' is represented, it is useful to look through the contents pages of some of the magazines.

Woman's Own	Marie Claire	Red	Nova
Fashion	Fashion	Fashion	Fashion
Features	Features	Features	Features
Beauty	Beauty	Health & Beauty	Beauty
Good Health	Health	–	Health
Offers	Special offers	Special offers	–
Cookery	–	Food	–
Regulars	Regulars	–	–
Showbiz	Ideas	Home & Garden	Outside
–	–	Travel	Backbite
–	–	–	Contagious
–	–	–	Personal Call

Nova, an IPC publication, is one of the newer magazines on the market and is trying to develop a niche for itself in a very competitive market. Its contents pages seem similar enough to be familiar and reassuring but different enough perhaps to be new and exciting and draw readers away from existing publications. However, if it fails to attract readers from other publications, it will not survive.

ACTIVITY

Compare the contents pages of a selection of men's magazines such as *FHM*, *Loaded* or *GQ*.

■ Is there a similar set of accepted subjects?
■ What do the topics in men's or women's magazines suggest about their readers and the reader's role and place in society?
■ How do these topics relate to ideas about stereotyping and ideology?

OR

How far do you think it is possible for audiences to resist the ideological messages of media texts?

Ferguson (1983) suggests that new magazines are launched either to offer competition in an existing market or to try to identify a new 'niche' for women – a particular set of experiences, age or income not as yet targeted. This diversification explains why new magazines are constantly coming on to an already crowded and competitive market.

At the time of writing this book there are several new titles being prepared. The BBC has launched *Eve*, for women 'with attitude'. Condé Nast, publishers of *Vogue, Tatler* and *Vanity Fair*, are launching a UK version of *Glamour*, a magazine that sells over 2 million copies every month in America. The editor of *Glamour* claims that it will be aimed at women 'enjoying their freedom and independence' and will have 'real humour without compromising the wit and intelligence of the reader'. Condé Nast already has an Italian version of *Glamour* and is planning a German edition.

At the same time Time-Life Inc. will launch a UK version of its American magazine *In Style*, which it is claimed will be 'significantly different'. John Brown Publishing, publishers of *Viz*, have launched a new health and beauty title, *Bare*, which they claim is 'hedonistic holistic'. All of these will be in competition with established titles like *Cosmopolitan, Elle, New Woman, Marie Claire, Red, Nova*, etc.

As overall the number of magazine-buying women is not increasing, both new and established titles have to fight to build and maintain their position in the market. One of the main ways of doing this is to try to appear 'different' whilst at the same time offering the same benefits as the competition.

ACTIVITY . . .

Spend some time at a large newsagent's looking through the range of magazines on offer.

- Identify the main categories of magazine type.
- Select one particular genre and list all the various titles.
- Are some newer than others? What (if anything) do the new titles offer that the old ones lacked?
- Look at the checklist at the end of this section (p. 162) and carry out an analysis of one of the magazines.

OR

Monitor the success of the new titles mentioned above.

- Are they all still in production?
- How do their circulation figures compare to their competitors?
- To what extent do they succeed (or fail) in being 'different' from their competitors?

Ferguson suggests that each woman's magazine is targeted at a distinct group such as teenagers, housewives, young single women, mothers, brides or slimmers. There are therefore magazines that specialise in almost every stage of a woman's life, offering a 'step-by-step' guide, tips for survival and of course products to purchase. Originally women's magazines focused on romance, marriage and household management. However, since the 1970s, Ferguson suggests, the 'Independent Woman' has emerged who is 'urged to achieve her full potential outside the home as well as within it'. Frequently this is represented as a sexual independence or, perhaps more recently, as a 'ladette' culture promoted by certain magazines and personalities.

It is interesting to try to 'fit' Maslow's Hierarchy of Needs and the different categories of 'socio-economic values' discussed on pp. 130–1 to the range of titles within particular genres. This is one way to identify the way in which a publisher will target particular 'niches' not only in terms of age and income but also in terms of psychological needs, i.e. security and routine, independence and excitement or status symbols and economic 'success'.

According to Ferguson, this range allows a woman to choose the 'kind' of woman she wants to be:

■ The *New Woman* reader is 'gutsy, glamorous and irreverent, embracing the philosophy that there's no right way to live and no single way to be . . . She's a woman with responsibility . . . and a hangover.'
■ The *Elle* reader is 'spirited, stylish and intelligent, she expects to be successful at everything she does. She takes the lead and breaks the rules.'
■ The *Red* reader 'spends as much time in the morning at Harvey Nichols as she does in the afternoon at the garden centre'.
■ The *Elle Decoration* woman is 'well educated, successful and heavily involved in work, she enjoys life in a diverse and cosmopolitan environment'.

However, as much as these magazines may say 'Get out there and show the world you are someone in your own right', Ferguson suggests that they also say 'Remember you must achieve as a wife and mother too'.

Stereotyping provides media producers with a useful shortcut in representing groups of people. What do you think are the dangers of stereotyping? Support your argument with examples.

OR

EMAP's Elan Glossy range includes titles such as *New Woman, Elle, Elle Decoration, Red, Top Santé* and *Escape Routes*. Look at copies of these magazines and try to categorise them according to 'socio-economic values'. Below are some additional data concerning their readership profiles. What other data could be included?

Title	Circulation	Readership	ABC1 %	Ave. Age	Cost DPS*
New Woman	273,016	570,000	67	28	£20,500
Elle	205,151	872,000	70	28	£18,500
Red	170,101	617,000	70	32	£24,200
Top Santé	170,131	391,000	59	37	£11,680
Elle Decoration	57,591	244,000	70	35	£10,000

*Double page spread

Ultimately these magazines must leave their readers with a positive feeling otherwise they may not return and buy the next edition. The July 2000 edition of *Red* carried articles on the menopause and troubled relationships with mothers, but the final paragraph of the editorial reads:

> We haven't forgotten that it's summer, that the sun is shining and it's the season for feeling good. The rest of this issue is packed with sunshine, lighting up fashion (pure gold), homes (gorgeously shabby, in a very chic way), food (delicious salads), not to mention lighting you up too, with our power-packed nutrition feature 'Eat Yourself Happy'. We hope that you do just that. And, while you're at it, check out the 'Sun Beauty Special' pages for the lowdown on the best fake tans as well as the make-up to give you that authentic sun-kissed glow. Then there's all the latest news on health, fitness and feelgood treatments . . .

This paragraph serves several functions. It reassures the reader that not all the magazine is going to be 'serious' and 'depressing'. It helps to reinforce the sense of 'personal address' ('we', 'you') by the manner in which it is written and the accompanying photograph of the editor smiling. It uses colloquial language (i.e. sufficiently everyday to appear like speech, 'while you're at it' 'gorgeously shabby', etc.). It advertises other features in this month's edition; in fact it manages to mention nearly all the magazine's content.

The editorial in *Woman's Own* (April 1996), written by a man, is perhaps more 'mainstream', although the word 'gorgeous' still turns up:

> Families are special. The letters you send to us here at *Woman's Own* remind us just how important they are.

> Which is why Julie and Mick Seale's story is so heart-warming. The couple were refused IVF on the NHS because Julie was too old at 36. But then a mystery man stepped in and paid for private treatment, and now the Seales have a gorgeous boy to make their family complete. . . . It's good to know there are still some people in this world doing things for purely selfless reasons.

Re-read the section on Genre (p. 55) then choose a genre of magazines, i.e. teenage, women's, 'lad's' etc. Analyse a selection and identify the extent to which they share a common iconography (p. 56) and/or mode of address (p. 51).

'ALL THE GOSS, ALL THE NEWS, EVERY TWO WEEKS' – *INSIDE SOAP*

Increasingly brand names are being used across different media, and magazine 'tie-ins' with popular television programmes, like the *X-Files* or *TOTP*, are seen as a means of cashing in on established names. Other magazines that tie in with television programmes are magazines that focus on the soap operas. The longest-running is *Inside Soap* published by the Australian company Attic Futura. They publish a range of 'teen' magazines such as *TV Hits, Sugar, B* and *Shine,* and in 1999 they introduced another soap-based magazine *All About Soap*. Also competing in the market is *Soap Life*, published by IPC.

Inside Soap describes itself as 'the definitive voice on the nation's favourite shows and their celebrities' and in the 'top 10 fastest growing paid-for magazines in the land' with a circulation of 263,794 and a readership of 742,000. It describes its readers as the 'right type': youthful, keen shoppers, brand aware and responsive to advertising.

Advertising consists of a mixture of consumer items such as soap powder, mobile phones, chocolates, a Celtic pendant, an Elvis Presley music box, catalogue shopping, health and beauty products to help reduce weight, and sanitary towels. A typical edition of about 70 pages will have about 11 full pages of advertising plus another two pages of smaller advertisements. As advertisements cost approximately £3,850 per full page and £2,300 per half page and the cover price is £1.10, it seems that *Inside Soap* produces an income of around £350,000 per edition.

The magazine is produced in a glossy full-colour format with a high proportion of photographs of soap opera stars or scenes from the programmes. The design is made up of small, easy-to-digest pieces, or full-page spreads. Photographs accompany all the features although these vary in size and position on the page. Most of the photographs are 'head-and-shoulder' shots of the actors either in or out of role. There is a lot of colour, with the dominant ones being primary reds and blues. The contents are largely gossip or synopses of the latest storylines. Many of the stories focus on the fictitious lives of the soap characters, discussing them as if they were real people. There is little involvement with the outside world; *Inside Soap* seems to offer information, relaxation and escapism. The overall style suggests something that is accessible, easy to read and understand. It does not require much concentration, the only requirement being a familiarity with television soap operas, their stars and stories.

The magazine also includes photographs of the various *Inside Soap* staff who are responsible for particular features, e.g. 'Let Karen know what you think about the soaps'. Readers therefore have the opportunity to contribute through features like 'Soapbox' where they can write or email in with comments or questions:

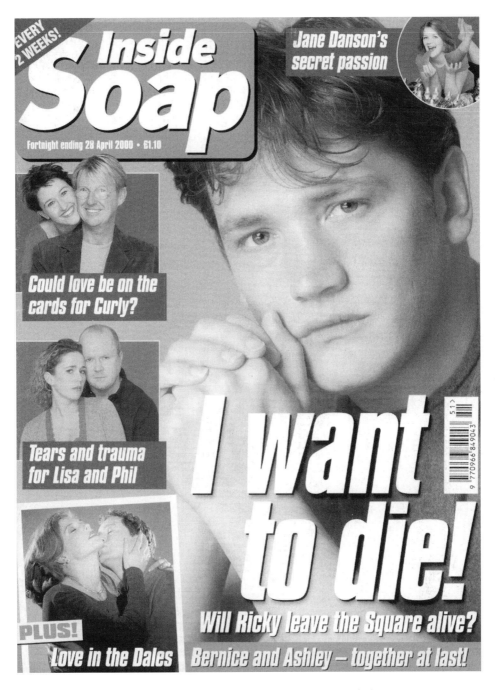

Figure 40

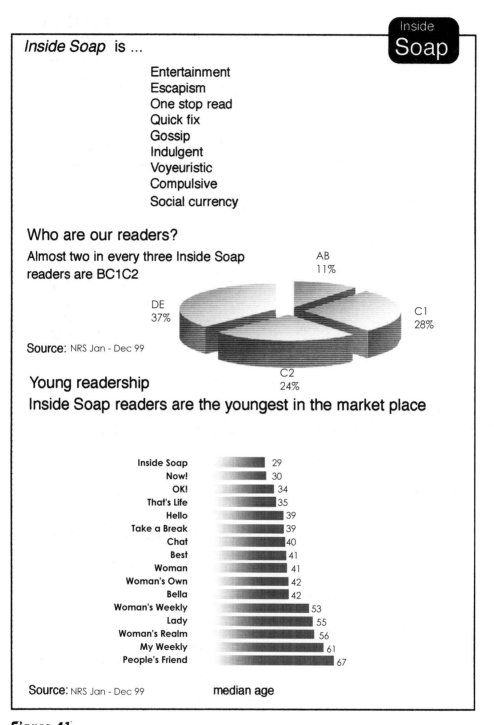

Inside Soap is ...

Entertainment
Escapism
One stop read
Quick fix
Gossip
Indulgent
Voyeuristic
Compulsive
Social currency

Who are our readers?

Almost two in every three Inside Soap
readers are BC1C2

AB
11%

DE
37%

C1
28%

Source: NRS Jan - Dec 99

C2
24%

Young readership

Inside Soap readers are the youngest in the market place

Magazine	median age
Inside Soap	29
Now!	30
OK!	34
That's Life	35
Hello	39
Take a Break	39
Chat	40
Best	41
Woman	41
Woman's Own	42
Bella	42
Woman's Weekly	53
Lady	55
Woman's Realm	56
My Weekly	61
People's Friend	67

Source: NRS Jan - Dec 99   median age

Figure 41

Brand Aware

Inside soap readers are more likely than the aver-age woman to agree that well known brands are better than shop own brands.

They are also more likely to agree that designer labels improve a persons image than the average adult.

Source: TGI Oct-Sep 99

Experimental

Inside Soap's readers are over twice as likely as the average housewife to definitely agree that they often buy new brands to see what they're like. In fact they are more likely to do so than readers of any of the competitive titles in the women's weekly market.

Readers of Inside Soap are more likely than the average housewife to definitely agree that they love buying new gadgets and appliances, more so than readers of any women's weekly magazine.

Source: TGI Sep - Oct 99

Stylish shoppers

Inside Soap readers are twice as likely as the aver-age woman to definitely agree that they like to keep up with the latest fashions. In fact they are more likely than readers of any women's weekly title.

Source: TGI Oct-Sep 99

Aspirational

Over 70% of female Inside Soap readers agree that they sometimes treat themselves to things they don't need and every other reader says she would consider going to Paris for the day.

Source: TGI Oct-Sep 99

'I think it would be lovely if *EastEnders*' Jamie and Sonia got together as a couple. It's about time Sonia found herself a decent bloke, and after Janine, Jamie needs someone nice as well. It would also be great to see Robbie with someone other than Wellard, but I have a feeling finding him a woman could prove more difficult.'

'I am a fan of *Neighbours* and I've noticed that there's one song they always play in the background in the coffee shop. I think it's called *One Good Reason*. Am I right, and can I buy it somewhere?'

(*Inside Soap*, 23 June 2000)

Each issue's star letter wins a prize of £30, and there is a prize crossword and other competitions to enter. Other regular features include horoscopes, recipes, historical moments from soap operas, and television schedules for the various soap operas.

ACTIVITY . . .

Choose two different types of magazine and compare and contrast their contents and the way in which they address the reader. You should consider:

- the amount and style of editorial
- the amount and type of advertising
- the way in which particular lifestyles are represented
- ways in which readers may address the magazine.

You may also wish to carry out a semiotic analysis (p. 41) of the covers to identify the ways in which the magazine is constructed to meet its particular target audience.

You could contact the magazines to see if they will provide you with any information regarding their circulation and/or readership. (Most magazines have a media pack that contains this information.)

You could also carry out a small readership survey. Your findings can be written up as a report or presented to the rest of your group.

WORKSHEET . . .

WORKSHEET FOR ANALYSING MAGAZINES

Consider the title of the magazine:

- Why is it called that?
- What are the significant words?
- What connotations do they have?

The publisher of the magazine:

- Who publishes the magazine?
- What other magazines (if any) does it publish?
- What other media interests (if any) does it have?
- How much does the magazine cost?
- How often is it published?
- What is its circulation/readership?
- Does the magazine have a website?

The target audience for the magazine:

- What type of reader is it targeting?
- How do you know this (i.e. types of articles and advertisements)?
- How does the reader 'interact' with the magazine?

The cover of the magazine:

- Analyse the images on the cover; the types of facial expressions, body language, clothing, etc. used.
- What do they tell us about the target audience for the magazine?
- What else appears on the cover?
- Why are particular items in the magazine featured?
- Explain why particular typefaces, types of graphics, colours, etc. are used.
- Does the cover look similar to other magazines? If so, why? If not, how does it look different?

The 'style' of presentation of the magazine:

- What do you notice about the magazine's presentation?
- Does it look cheap or expensive?
- How does it compare with other similar magazines?
- How does it use colour, print style, artwork, etc. to convey an overall effect?

The 'mode of address' of the magazine:

- How does it address its readers?
- How and when are readers allowed to address the magazine?
- What types of articles/features does it contain?
- What subjects are covered?

The advertisements that appear in the magazine:

- What are the main types of products being advertised?

- What is their price range?
- Who are they aimed at?
- Why are these products featured particularly?
- How do the models featured in the advertisements relate to the target audience?

Representations in the magazine:

- How are men and women represented? (Look at both the images and the text.)
- Are there conflicting representations? If so, why is this?
- How do these representations relate to the readership?
- Is there a limited range of representations for men and women? If so, what are they and why?
- What groups do not appear in the pages of the magazine? Why?
- Are celebrities featured in the magazine? If so, what kinds of celebrities? Why have they been chosen?

The competition for the magazine:

- What other titles are in competition with it?
- What are their circulation/readership figures?
- How much do they cost?
- What are the similarities/differences?

Finally:

- What do you think are the reasons for its popularity (or otherwise)?
- What does the magazine offer its readers?
- What 'values' or ideologies are implicit in the magazine?

The effects that the Internet may have on magazine sales and consumption are not yet clear. Some publishers are concerned that there may be a similar situation to when television became popular in Britain and newspaper sales fell. Internet websites can offer high-quality images, interactivity beyond the pages of the magazines themselves, more buying potential, and a mix of video and audio. Therefore magazine publishers are increasingly looking for ways to offer their particular brand across a range of media – radio, television and new media. They are also looking to the Internet as a new source of revenue. EMAP, for example, has its EMAP Digital division, which is working with both television, C4, and telecommunications, BT. They have formed a consortium that aims to develop magazine brands that can also be developed as online brands. This means more than just putting a (paid for) magazine on to a (free) website. The online version must generate income either through additional advertising revenue or through retail sales of goods and services aimed at the magazine's particular niche 'reader'.

1   You have been commissioned to design a pilot issue of a new magazine aimed at teenagers. The company you are working for is part of a larger group that already has several teenage titles and will need convincing that there is an opportunity to launch a new title, so your magazine must be distinctive but meet readers' needs and expectations. You may wish to work as a group and allocate different tasks to different people as in a 'real' magazine production process.

    ■ You need to decide upon the target audience and, using Hartley's and Fiske's 'subjectivities' (p. 122) draw up a profile of a 'typical reader' that also includes 'lifestyle'. Choose a name and price for the magazine. You could create a 'Media Pack' for your magazine.
    ■ Design a front cover.
    ■ Consider what types of products and brands the readership would be interested in and then make a list of possible advertisers and cross-promotional features. Consider how you would 'sell' the magazine and its readers to potential advertisers.
    ■ Draw up a list of the types of articles and features that should be included in the magazine. For the pilot you may wish to write up one or two of the features and design some advertisements. You could also write an editorial, from the editor to the readers, explaining what the new magazine offers them.
    ■ Produce an advertising campaign for the launch, detailing where the advertisements for the magazine will appear. Again you may wish to produce a finished version of one of the advertisements.
    ■ Consider what else, if anything, you should be doing to convince your company of the viability of the new magazine.

    You will need to work to a deadline and justify all your decisions and choices.

2   Imagine that a new magazine has been developed as a spin-off from a television programme.

    ■ First consider what may be a suitable programme source, who the target audience is and what the content of the magazine may be.
    ■ Then design a page to appear in an existing magazine that advertises the new magazine to its potential audience.
    ■ Detail the reasoning behind your design and content choices.

3   'The most important factor which shapes a publication is its readers.' How does this apply to magazines such as those discussed in this section?

4   There has been a recent expansion in the range of women's and men's magazines available to consumers. Explain how and why this expansion has taken place.

5   Write a review of a magazine (preferably one that you do not normally read) and post your review on the Web. Visit www.smartgirl.com. In their magazine review section you can also fill in a questionnaire on your opinion of *J-17*.

6   Discuss, using examples, the extent to which magazines influence gender identities.

FURTHER READING

Ferguson, M. (1983) *Forever Feminine: Women's Magazines and the Cult of Femininity*, Heinemann.

McRobbie, A. (1983) 'Teenage girls, *Jackie* and the ideology of adolescent femininity' in Waites, B. *et al.* (eds), *Popular Culture: Past and Present*, Croom Helm.

—— (1994) '*More!* New sexualities in girls' and women's magazines' in Curran, J., Morley, D. and Walkerdine, V. (eds) *Cultural Studies and Communications*, Arnold.

Stokes, J. (1999) 'Use it or lose it: sexuality and sexual health in magazines for girls' in Stokes, J. and Reading, A. (eds) *The Media in Britain: Current Debates and Developments*, Macmillan.

Winship, J. (1987) *Inside Women's Magazines*, Pandora.

In this part of the book we:

■ investigate the ownership of media institutions and the power that some of these institutions hold over us as potential consumers of media products

■ look at the way media institutions are regulated and what the future might hold as the media world changes rapidly in the twenty-first century.

Figure 42

Look at the logos in Figure 42.

- How many of the logos do you recognise?
- Which areas of the media do you associate them with?
- Who owns them?
- What country are they primarily based in?

ISSUES OF OWNERSHIP AND CONTROL

As we mentioned in the Introduction, wherever you go in the world it is almost impossible to avoid the media. There are few areas in the world that do not have some kind of newspaper (even if it's only a news-sheet). There is barely a country that does not have a TV station, and if it does not have one of its own, then it is certainly possible to receive pictures broadcast from a neighbouring country (although in some countries this might be considered an offence).

The media have, in many ways, challenged our conventional notions of nationality. We can watch television from many different countries, listen to foreign radio stations, read overseas newspapers and now, with even more ease, access as many websites as we wish from all over the world through the Internet. And of course other countries can consume British media products.

Marshall McLuhan and Quentin Fiore wrote in their book *The Medium is the Massage* (1997) that we live in a 'global village'. They suggested that time and space are vanishing, that people from all over the world can communicate with one another simultaneously, as if they all lived in the same village.

Some say that, because of this, the media have had a profound effect on the politics and culture of the world, although others maintain that this effect is far from positive – that it has in fact made us lazy and perhaps complacent.

The debate about the worldwide political and cultural changes that have occurred as a result of a process known as 'globalisation' is one that is alluded to throughout this book and is an important part of Media Studies.

This process of globalisation involves the idea that the world has shrunk, notably as a result of new technology and the media, and that the populations of virtually every country in the world now have almost instant access to cultures and societies that were once so far away from us that they were just considered 'foreign'. Now we can all see, hear and read about much of what goes on in the world. It is also important to note that part of this process involves the idea that we are now becoming a world audience as well. A successful mass media product often has to have an appeal to worldwide markets if it is to make serious money. But it is important to realise that it is essentially a debate that is still current – the role of the media in the collapse of eastern European communism is a useful example of this ongoing debate.

When the Berlin Wall came down in 1989 many commentators suggested that one of the major factors in the wave of protest that had occurred in Eastern Europe around that time was that a population that had previously been denied access to all things western had, in the previous decade, been able to listen to, and above all, watch western media broadcasts. This meant that they were finally able to see what it was about capitalism and democracy that their political masters had been denying them for decades.

It is suggested that many Eastern Europeans liked what they saw and this was an element in the political struggle that then developed. Of course the issue still remains that what they saw on TV might not have necessarily been a true reflection of the reality of western democracies. Consequently there does seem to be an element of a backlash taking place in some Eastern European countries as we write.

NOTEBOX

The issue of laziness and complacency is another point of debate. Has the 'window on the world' which media globalisation offers opened our eyes or merely overloaded us with information, much of which we don't want or need? Depending on which point of view we adopt, have we as a consequence retreated behind our borders (literal and metaphorical) or have we embraced the world as it is presented to us?

It is important to remember that media texts are not fortunate accidents and that profit is not always the motive in producing them. The vast array of available media artefacts is not simply the product of circumstance and a few altruistic people. It is undoubtedly the case that some media texts are produced by people who feel they have something 'to say' or who anticipate a gap in the market that should be filled.

But, as a general rule, people with money have not announced that a newspaper or magazine is needed because they feel sorry for our lack of awareness of what is going on in the world. Nor are they concerned that we have too much leisure time. In fact the vast majority of media texts are produced by media institutions, who are becoming richer and more powerful by the day as the demand for their products increases.

It is possible to make many generalisations about media institutions. There can be little doubt that there is the potential for enormous profits in the media world. There is equally the potential for financial disaster. But perhaps the most difficult aspect of the media world to come to terms with is the fact that there are no set rules or patterns to follow. There is not a science to running a media institution (nor is there a science to studying a media institution). What may work for one company will probably not work for another. But certain ideas about media institutions remain constant.

On the one hand there is the 'conspiracy theory' of Media Studies. This is the popular, and common, idea that a small group of multi-media tycoons is busy trying to take over or amalgamate with every other media company available, so that in the end this group will end up with the power to control what we know about the world, with all that this implies politically and socially.

Yet there also exist many people in all media fields who remain committed to the notion of choice and independence. They see the wave of deregulation that has taken place, in this country in particular, as not necessarily being in the public interest. They therefore argue strongly for an element of Public Service Broadcasting (PSB) to be preserved.

There is also the perhaps rather more naïve point of view, which sees some parts of the media as a collection of committed and hard-working people who want us to be informed, educated and entertained. This group of people, if they find it difficult to broadcast their products, will set up as independent companies, hopefully beholden to no one but themselves – often in opposition to the media majors.

Neither view is accurate. There are no hard and fast rules that can be applied to the media anywhere in the world, although it is the case that countries do exist where government owns or controls the major mass media (TV and radio in particular). In situations like this the media are often used purely for propaganda and informational purposes. It is interesting to note that when such governments are threatened by public uprising or military coups, one of the first targets for the protesters is these very same radio and TV stations – which demonstrates how important control of the media can be. This was, for instance, the case in Yugoslavia in 2000. When Milosevic refused to accept the result of the election, people took to the streets. Their two targets were the government buildings and the radio and TV stations.

One of the issues that has to be dealt with by those who study or take an interest in the media is the fairly obvious fact that much of the media is largely in the hands of big multinational companies. There are major players on the world media scene (see Figure 43).

The media world undergoes many changes in ownership. For example there are at present:

- only five major record labels in the world
- a rapidly shrinking ownership of mobile phone companies
- domination of the worldwide cinema ticket sales by Hollywood and Bollywood
- only two commercial terrestrial TV companies running most of the ITV network
- heavy competition for ownership of ISPs (Internet Service Providers) on the Internet.

ACTIVITY . . .

All of the information about the ownership and control of media institutions in this book was correct at the time of writing. However, since then there have been many changes. This is very much part of the media world.

- Research the changes in ownership of the institutions outlined in this chapter.
- What were the reasons for the buying and selling (or indeed mergers) that have taken place?
- Are there any media organisations which seem to you particularly aggressive?

MEDIA STUDIES: THE ESSENTIAL INTRODUCTION

- Is it possible at this stage to predict future outcomes?
- Are there any media institutions which now seem particularly vulnerable?
- Is it possible to suggest why this is so?

As has been said elsewhere in this book, it is very important to keep a watchful eye on the machinations that are constantly taking place within the media world. You should keep a scrapbook of all news that seems important to you.

NOTEBOX

It is essential that over the length of your course you monitor what is happening in the world of media institutions. This will involve reading the business news in any of the quality broadsheet newspapers, looking out for articles in magazines about the media, listening to media programmes on radio, watching TV programmes about the media (for example, *Feedback* on Radio 4, occasional items in *The South Bank Show* on ITV). It is important that you monitor as closely as possible who owns what; who sells and who buys. There is a great deal of movement in the ownership of media institutions.

Keep a scrapbook. Cut articles out and file them away carefully. Record the programmes which look as if they will be useful. You may never keep up, but you should develop a fascinating overview.

Not all media companies are large players. But historically a pattern has emerged. Whenever a new technology is invented or discovered, companies have been formed, or existing companies have been forced, to try to take advantage of the benefits and profits that this new technology offers. However, it is often the case that no one is quite sure what those benefits might be, nor that there is any guarantee that profits will be made. This has been true of film, radio and television, and is now very much the case with the Internet.

Each new technology has been hailed as an improvement on existing technology, a boon to consumers and a way for producers to get rich (often fairly quickly). Risks have been taken, some companies have fallen by the wayside, but others have survived and prospered.

Thus, for instance, all the major American film studios started off as small, independent companies. Each found a particular niche for themselves. Warner Brothers, for example, were famous for the realism of many of their films whilst MGM were famous for the escapist nature of their product. Both managed to build on their success. However, there were those film companies who were not able to respond quickly enough to the demands of the audience, or indeed to the threat of new technologies. These companies no longer exist (RKO Radio Pictures to name but one). And what seems to be the most effective way of responding to a new technology? By successfully embracing it.

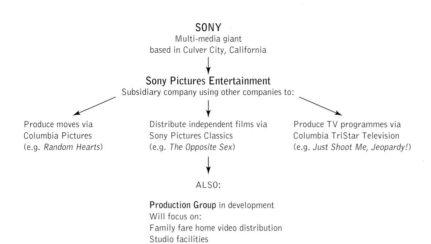

SONY
Multi-media giant
based in Culver City, California

Sony Pictures Entertainment
Subsidiary company using other companies to:

Produce moves via
Columbia Pictures
(e.g. *Random Hearts*)

Distribute independent films via
Sony Pictures Classics
(e.g. *The Opposite Sex*)

Produce TV programmes via
Columbia TriStar Television
(e.g. *Just Shoot Me, Jeopardy!*)

ALSO:

Production Group in development
Will focus on:
Family fare home video distribution
Studio facilities
Interests in international TV networks
Game show network
Loews Cineplex Entertainment (40% of this move theatre chain)

VIACOM INC.
Central office: Broadway, New York

Owns the cable superpower
MTV Networks:
MTV, VH-1, Nickleodeon

Has stakes in:
Comedy Central
United Paramount Network (50%)

Produces and syndicates
TV shows, e.g. *Beverly Hills 90210*

ALSO:
Purchase of CBS will make Viacom the world's
second media firm behind Time Warner.

Owns publisher
Simon & Schuster
Paramount Pictures (e.g. *Titanic*)
19 TV stations
More than 100 theatres in Canada

RANK GROUP PLC
Central office: Connaught Place, London
Leisure and entertainments giant

Hard Rock Café chain
(approx 100 restaurants in major cities worldwide)

Resort and holiday centres under the Haven,
Butlins, Oasis and Warner names

Odeon theatre chain in UK

Film division offers:
Studio and production space at Pinewood Studios, UK
Film processing through Deluxe Laboratories

Gambling interests include:
more than 30 Grosvenor casinos
approx 130 Mecca bingo clubs

Theme Park:
Owns 50% of Seagram's Universal
Studio's Escape theme park in Orlando,
Florida

Figure 43

CABLE AND WIRELESS PLC
Central office: Theobalds Rd, London
International telecommunications holding company

Owns a 54% stake in Cable &
Wireless HKT (formerly
Hong Kong Telecom)

Owns 53% of Cable & Wireless
Communications (UK's largest
cable company and second-largest
phone company behind British
Telecommunications)

Has investments in:
Australia
Caribbean
Middle East
US

GRANADA GROUP PLC
Central office: Cleveland Row, London

TV interests:
Owns a third of ITN network in UK
Owns approx 20% of Scottish Media Group

Restaurant and hotel business:
Owns more than 400 Little Chef roadside
restaurants
Owns more than 50 Burger King
restaurants

ALSO:

Motorway service station operator – the largest
in the UK

Contract catering – one of top four in UK

Trust Houses Forte – hotel division
e.g. Le Meridien, Posthouse, Heritage

CARLTON COMMUNICATIONS PLC
Central office: Knightsbridge, London

TV enterprises:
Producer and broadcaster of
TV programming in the UK
Provides production services
to the film, video and TV industries

Includes stations and cable channels

With Granada Group and Ondigital
owns principal licence for terrestrial
TV in the UK (launched late 1998)

Other interests:
Processes movie film
Delivers prints to cinemas
Provides post-production facilities
Makes editing equipment

Owns CD and digital versatile disk maker,
Technicolor Nimbus

Owns a library of 2,200 films and
15,000 hours of TV programmes

Source: www.hoovers.com

The potential for riches in the media world is enormous, but equally the potential for financial ruin is also rather large. This same phenomenon can now be seen with the advent of the Internet. Suddenly everyone wants to jump on board, particularly large multi-media companies who see some of the benefits which the Internet offers (new channels for advertising, promotion, sales, etc.), but who also want to secure a larger market share than their competitors whilst knowing that future financial benefits might be slow in arriving. The Internet has also become a place for small entrepreneurs to start up companies. If successful, they may make a profit or indeed be bought out by the majors at considerable financial gain to the owners in the first place. The medium has potential and, whilst no one is sure quite where it will go, everyone wants to be on board. However, the collapse of some Internet companies demonstrates there is just as strong a likelihood that the Internet will not end up being the money-making machine that some people hoped it might become.

A reshuffling is taking place – a series of mergers, amalgamations and takeovers – as the major media players tackle the advent of new media technologies and their effect on the global media landscape.

ACTIVITY . . .

During the period of your course you should also keep a watchful eye on the Internet. Yet again the major source of your research should be the business news in the quality broadsheet newspapers. However, it is also important to keep an eye on developments on the Net itself.

■ What are the major ISPs?
■ Who owns the major ISPs?

Keep a close watch on the way that the major ISPs make themselves known to the market. It is not simply done by television and press advertising.

■ What new developments can each ISP offer you as a possible user?
■ What are the drawbacks to using the Net in this country and how are the ISPs trying to get around these problems?
■ How successful do you think they are?

It might also be worthwhile to conduct some market research of your own:

■ Who uses which ISP and why?
■ What are the benefits of each one?
■ What are seen as the drawbacks?
■ How many people use more than one ISP and why?

Keep a scrapbook of developments on the Net.

In the 1950s the American film industry initially dismissed TV as a medium that would not last, then tried to combat it by making films that could only be seen at their best at the cinema. As a consequence, these companies watched their revenues dwindle as audiences decided they preferred to stay at home. It was only later that the successful and more thoughtful film companies (or producers) realised that TV networks, as well as movie theatres, needed product. So they diversified into TV production as well.

Nowadays, almost every TV programme we see, particularly those of American origin, has the logo of a major film *and* TV production/distribution company at the end of the final reel. Thus Fox, Columbia TriStar, Warner Bros and Paramount are all involved in large-scale film production and also involved in the production of product for TV. In the UK the situation is very different. Many TV productions on all channels now increasingly derive from small, independent TV production companies. This is the direct result of a shift from in-house production in the years preceding the late 1980s to the external sourcing of production, which is the direct result of the deregulation of broadcasting which took place under successive Thatcher governments.

Is it just coincidence that a considerable proportion of TV programmes today are spin-offs from successful films (e.g. *Stargate SG* and *Lock Stock and Two Smoking Barrels*), or that there has recently been a trend for producing film versions of successful TV programmes, particularly of the 1950s and 1960s (e.g. *Lost in Space* and *The Avengers*)? (See the section on Genre, p. 55.)

ACTIVITY

It is interesting to note that the four American companies named above – Fox, Columbia TriStar, Warner Brothers and Paramount – are still players in the media world yet have all, at one time or another, had periods when their future might have been in doubt.

Research the history of these companies and try to establish what went wrong at various periods in their existence – and what has gone right for them so that they are now in their present powerful positions. Is it the case that they have simply been lucky? Or have important policy decisions been taken during the past 50 years which have safeguarded their positions?

- How are they now planning to maintain their positions as major players in the media?
- What is threatening their position at present?
- How do you think they will respond to these threats?

NOTEBOX

A word of caution: At the present time the Internet is being looked at as the 'medium of the future' and a possible 'goldmine' for investors and media companies. Yet very much the same was said about radio stations in America in the 1920s. Over-investment in these companies – and a disappointing string of financial results over a period of years – is considered by some economic historians to have been a major contributory factor to the Wall Street Crash and the Great Depression.

It can be fascinating to compare the media industry with another industry such as food commerce. At one time there was a range of grocery shops who all received their products from food wholesalers. Shoppers would go to the high street and visit the grocer that was fractionally cheaper, more friendly, or which stocked goods that the competitors did not.

There was a range of different shops to visit. The grocer for dried, tinned and delicatessen-type goods, the greengrocer for fruit and vegetables, the butcher for meats and the baker for bread, cakes and so on. And then shoppers went to the chemist and the stationer's and the story unfolded.

Shopping at that time was a major time-consuming, but comparatively sociable, event. However, times changed. Work patterns altered, the weekend was no longer sacrosanct, and time started to be of the essence. The supermarket changed all that. Despite initial consumer resistance, the ease of shopping and the fact that prices were often cheaper (because supermarkets could buy in bulk and demand higher discounts from their suppliers) eventually won over the consumer.

The interesting thing about supermarket chains is the fact that initially all they sold were name brands – basically the same products as were being sold in the high-street grocers – but it didn't take long for supermarket chains to discover that, since their sales were large, it made sense to contract out the production of 'own-label' goods. These may well be made by the original manufacturers of the branded goods but both sides ended up happy, because eventually people were still buying the product. Thus the supermarkets paid the producer of the goods but were then able to pocket much more profit, first because the unit cost of the goods was less in the first place and second because all of the profit went into their own tills. Also, the notion of a loss-leader became apparent – if some things are cheap, then people will come in and have a look and be tempted to buy other products whilst there. So in fact this became a three-way advantage to the owners of supermarkets. Though it is now the case that in some supermarkets certain popular goods are only available as own-label goods. Why pay others when you can make and sell the product yourself?

Consider the cinema industry. Why make a film – which has an average cost of around $30 million – and then let another company exhibit the film and make money from a product in which you have invested heavily? It makes fairly obvious business sense to produce the product, distribute the product and then also exhibit the product as well. Not only does it mean that you have control of the product from the very moment of inception to the end of its life-span, but also you are likely to make a far greater profit.

It is not a very large step from here to the idea of multiplex cinemas. A multiplex cinema can have as many as 30 different screens in one building. Immediately there are benefits

MEDIA STUDIES: THE ESSENTIAL INTRODUCTION

to the owner in terms of costs. Only one or two projectionists are needed and a minimum number of staff (note that most staff may well be working on the kiosks anyway). Heating and lighting and cleaning costs can be kept to a minimum, even advertising costs kept low. But the major point is that, if people arrive to see a film and it is sold out, they do not just go away cursing their bad luck. Having made the effort to get to the cinema in the first place, the likelihood is that they will see another film that is showing at that multiplex instead. At the same time they are likely to buy food and drink at vastly inflated prices. This is again very similar to what happens in the supermarket. Few people go into a supermarket and only buy a loaf of bread – even if that is why they entered the shop in the first place.

MULTIPLEX A cinema that contains several screens under one roof – usually with one projection booth servicing all screens. The number of screens can vary; the new Warner Village in Birmingham contains 30 screens.

There are implications here, and they reflect what occurred in the example of the high street. What is happening is that the owners of multiplexes are in danger of suffocating the opposition. What future has a small, locally run and owned cinema when the competition down the road has so much to offer and can also control the product – despite monopoly laws? And consider the element of choice for the consumer.

On one level the multiplex offers a wide choice of films, though a particularly popular film can be shown on several screens at once and only one print of the film is actually needed (there need only be a slight time delay between screenings). But what happens to a film that might not be quite so popular and is perhaps a risk in terms of profitability? It makes sense for the multiplex owner not to bother showing such a film, since the job is to make money, not necessarily to cater for the minority film-goer. There are of course independent cinemas in existence in this and other countries. But even they have to make a profit to continue their existence. It can be argued therefore that a system that appears to offer more choice can often lead to *less* choice.

In terms of issues of ownership, what this implies is that decisions about what is available to media audiences rest in the hands of a few media companies. And they, of course, have to answer to their shareholders and the financial institutions that have invested in them. Film companies, like all media companies, are not altruistic and have never pretended to be. They may take risks, but their responsibilities to investors and the like suggest that they are very unlikely to do so.

It is also interesting to note that some multiplexes have a policy of devoting one screen (from the many available) to foreign-language or minority-interest films. However, the evidence seems to be that the audience does not go to the multiplex to see these films but prefers to go to the local art-house or independent cinema to see them anyway. It is interesting, though, that many multiplex cinemas in cities with a large Asian community are now devoting several screens to the exhibition of films from Asia, with considerable success.

This suggests that the process of distribution and exhibition is rather more complicated than many might like to think. Big is not necessarily bad. Much has to do with the nature of the audience (see the section on Media Audiences and the case study on Cinema).

HORIZONTAL AND VERTICAL INTEGRATION

The principle motivating this process seems to be to take over or merge with those companies who are in the same area as you. This is what is known as horizontal integration. One example of this process is the ITV network where 13 separate television companies are now virtually owned by two companies – Carlton and Granada. While there still remain several smaller network companies, such as Border and Grampian, many of the others have since been swallowed up by the 'big two'.

HORIZONTAL INTEGRATION This involves the acquisition of competitors in the same section of the industry. It might be possible for one company to seek to control all of the market – a monopoly position – but most capitalist countries have laws to prevent this happening.

ACTIVITY . . .

The ownership of newspapers and of radio stations in this country is also one where control is slowly shifting into the hands of fewer companies. Investigate the following:

- Who owns the national daily newspapers?
- Who owns the Sunday national newspapers?
- Who owns all the UK radio stations?
- What are the benefits for companies who own several newspapers or radio stations?
- Do you think consumers are also benefiting?

But what are the advantages and disadvantages of this process (a) to the consumer? and (b) to the producers? If you control exhibition, then it obviously follows that to increase power and profit you should as quickly as possible move into the area of distribution and production.

This has happened in the film business where, in particular, the American film production studios rapidly moved into distribution (thereby gaining control over product made by smaller and less powerful rivals) and then, when legally possible, into exhibition.

This process is nowhere more apparent than in the UK, where the major chains of multiplexes are in fact owned by major American production companies (Warner and UCI to name but two).

MEDIA STUDIES: THE ESSENTIAL INTRODUCTION

However, this is far less the case in TV in the UK where, as mentioned previously, both the BBC and ITV, and particularly satellite and cable channels, now buy in or commission productions made by independent production companies. TV companies can be seen to operate much more like publishing houses, where the commissioning editor has an important role – indeed, C4 creates no in-house programming.

By and large, in certain areas of the media, companies will want to control the three main areas of production, distribution and exhibition. This is called vertical integration. Many companies, given the opportunity, want to maximise potential profits by cutting out the interference of other people. Why produce a product for someone else to sell?

VERTICAL INTEGRATION This involves the ownership of every stage of the production process (production + distribution + exhibition), thereby ensuring complete control of a media product.

Take for example Fox Entertainment Group, Inc. This is an American company that is now 83 per cent owned by Rupert Murdoch's News International. If at one time during the late 1970s and early 1980s Twentieth Century Fox was a Hollywood film company that had perhaps seen better times, it is now (again) one of major mass-media companies worldwide. Famous originally as a film production company, Fox Entertainment now produces, develops and distributes TV and film programming through its Fox Filmed Entertainment and Twentieth Century Fox units. It also owns the Fox Television network in the USA, has interests in cable TV channels and major league sports teams, and owns a chain of cinemas in the US.

But it does not end there. News International is also a worldwide media organisation with part-ownership of many satellite and cable channels across Europe and Asia. The company also owns many newspapers, notably in the USA, Australia and the UK.

The advantages of this global ownership are many. A film produced by Twentieth Century Fox can be shown in Fox-owned cinemas, publicised in News International newspapers, then shown on Fox-owned TV channels. All media associated with Fox can give the product publicity in one shape or form. (It is interesting to note that Fox became joint producers of the film *Titanic* at a point when it was about to become known as the most expensive film ever made – and perhaps a financial disaster. The very fact that it received such notoriety before its release is now seen as very clever 'hype' – it became a film everyone wanted to see, and the rest is history.)

A media product can therefore be sold, publicised and marketed to an audience through many different media, and blanket coverage is possible if a company has ownership of the following media:

- films
- videos
- soundtracks
- TV stations

- Radio stations, newspapers and magazines
- the Internet.

Select a film produced by Twentieth Century Fox for exhibition in this country (you can find a list of these on their website www.foxmovies.com). Research the many different ways it is brought to the attention of an audience through the use of other media companies associated with Fox and News International. Remember, bad publicity is often as useful as good publicity!

OR

As patterns of ownership in the media change and technologies converge, how is this likely to impact on the intertextual nature of promotion across media forms?

So what we have are

1   the majors – international media conglomerates
2   the medium-sized – usually nationally based media companies
3   the independents – those that have established their own niche market, such as small art-house cinemas, independent radio production companies
4   the alternatives.

ALTERNATIVE MEDIA

Alternative media organisations exist as a counterpoint to everything that has been mentioned above. Not everything in the media world is about market domination, large-scale target audiences and possible enormous profit.

Companies and organisations do exist that attempt to make a positive virtue out of being small and, perhaps most importantly, out of being independent. If a typical media organisation is, almost by definition, run on hierarchical grounds, beholden to investors and shareholders, yet organisations do exist that are organised on democratic principles, where all workers have a say in the policy and direction of the company. A primary example of this was the London listings magazine *Time Out*, which originally operated on these grounds. All employees had a stake in the company, and everyone who worked there was essentially paid the same. Of course, a problem surfaced when the magazine started to become very successful – at which point the owner decided to rationalise the pay structure, returning to a more conventional format. This resulted in the formation of an alternative listings magazine in London, called *City Limits*, started by disgruntled ex-members of the *Time Out* staff. This magazine continued to be run on a co-operative basis but foundered within a decade of its formation, essentially because the circulation figures were never high enough to attract serious advertising revenue.

If an organisation is run on essentially democratic grounds, and has a policy of independence, then the genuine voice of an artist or writer is more likely to flourish. This is nowhere more true than in the music industry, particularly in the UK. Here pop music has flourished and with it the creation of, for example, girl and boy bands – many of which seem to follow a well-worn formula. A band or musician/singer who produces material that does not 'fit' the major record companies' notion of what should or should not be released may not get a contract and might never be heard. Thus independent record labels – small, with low budgets and few overheads – have given artists the opportunity to produce material. There might not be such a large publicity machine working for them, nor instant access to radio and TV play, but there is also an audience who have rejected the product of the mass-media organisations and keep a lookout themselves for product to purchase, often through the medium of music fanzines.

KEY TERM

INDEPENDENTS Companies (usually relatively small ones) that maintain a status outside the normal big-business remit and therefore tend to focus on minority-interest products.

This is also true of football fans. For years football fans have paid their money at the gate, supported their team, and developed a sense of ownership. After all, the gate money is vital to the economic stability of a football team. Yet the run-of-the-mill football programme is frequently an anodyne affair – glossy pictures, many advertisements, but rarely any genuine discussion of football, the team, or financial affairs. The increase in the number of football fanzines is very much a phenomenon of the 1990s. It reflects many people's dissatisfaction with the typical football programme or magazine available on the mass market – a product which cannot help but be tied in to the sponsors' and the owners' point of view and is unlikely to rock the boat, or court controversy.

ACTIVITY

Take two media products, one mass market and one significantly alternative – for instance a football magazine and a football fanzine, or a mainstream music paper and a music fanzine.

- What are the differences?
- What are the similarities?

Concentrate particularly on:

- the content
- the style
- the political stance (if any)
- the nature of the editorials
- the nature of the advertisements
- the quality of design and layout
- the target audience.

ISSUES OF CONTROL

We have outlined above the process by which major media conglomerates seemingly have a stranglehold over much that media audiences are consuming. Although the emphasis above is on the film industry, this is also the case in many other media industries. And of course, as has been noted above, few media companies are satisfied with simply sticking to one particular medium, as is demonstrated by the increasingly cross-media composition of many of the very large companies.

For example, the Walt Disney Corporation has interests in TV and film production (ABC Entertainment Television, Buena Vista Motion Pictures Group, and Miramax), theme parks (including Disneyland, Euro-Disney, and the Epcot Center), publishing companies, a cruise line, Internet companies (go.com), and professional sports franchises (the Mighty Ducks NHL team). Division ABC Inc. includes the ABC TV network in the USA, nearly a dozen TV stations, and shares in nine cable companies (including the Disney Channel). We have also noted above the fact that there are certain disadvantages and advantages inherent in this situation, both for producers and audiences.

It is in this area that the works of Noam Chomsky are particularly relevant. Noam Chomsky is an American intellectual who has written many books about the media and is particularly interested in the social and political implications of the mass media and their ownership. The basic premise of much of his writings on the media is as follows:

- Society is made up of two different classes of people.
- There is the top 20 per cent, the professional class, those who feel they have a stake in the decision-making processes in society, such as judges, lawyers, teachers, intellectuals, etc. Many of these people have a genuine interest in politics and the rudiments of power that are associated with their positions. They like to think that they have some influence on the way things are run and governed. It is also the case that this group is (in general) the one with the most financial clout in society.
- Then there are the remaining 80 per cent whose main function is to work and follow orders, usually at the bidding of the top 20 per cent. Their interest in politics tends to be minimal, as long as they are housed, fed and have enough money to finance their leisure time.
- The top 20 per cent, the group with the money and power, is also likely to contain those individuals who are involved with or who actually own the media.

Chomsky argues that the media, especially the large multi-media concerns, have one prevailing motive apart from profit and that is what he calls the 'Manufacture of Consent'. Essentially, Chomsky argues, the media today are involved in a two-pronged process.

First, to keep the top 20 per cent content by maintaining their position as policy-makers, those in control of *some* of the rudiments of power. The issue is one whereby the media help to keep government on a path that keeps this elite content and feeling that their position in society is of some worth, whilst continuing to promulgate the lifestyle and political attachments of this elite. Most of the media are therefore inevitably interested in maintaining the status quo, as frequently is the power elite.

Broadly speaking, this means that much of the time government and the elite are involved in an alliance – but only when it suits them. Obviously issues will and do arise upon which the government and the elite disagree. For instance, towards the end of the Conservative government in the middle of the 1990s, even normally 'friendly' newspapers turned against the Tory party, particularly in the area of personal morality and sleaze. This can be seen as an example of the media acting as the spokesperson for this elite and 'taking on' the government. But by and large the media can wield a considerable amount of power because, certainly since the Second World War, every government has been dependent on the media to get into office. Not for nothing was Rupert Murdoch's *Sun* able to boast that it had won the election in 1992 for the Tories. And indeed the same newspaper certainly helped the Labour party get into power in 1997, too.

But what of the remaining 80 per cent? Chomsky would argue that the function of the media here is to keep them happy – a concept called 'bread and circuses' – with a diet of gossip, sport, soap operas and light entertainment which they can read and watch without too much challenge. This could be seen as a rather cynical view, certainly one that might make us feel rather uncomfortable. On the other hand, the counter-argument would suggest that this is a very generalised view and also shows no understanding of the pressures under which those in the media world work – it also in itself seems quite elitist at times, assuming as it does that the 80 per cent are in fact compliant in every way – which is not always the case.

Thus it can be seen that the media – and the mass media in particular – have vested interests: in broad terms, to maintain the status quo, to link arms with government (whenever possible) and to make money. Chomsky argues that this process is a form of control in a democratic society.

This process can happen in a number of different ways. It is of course not enough simply to feed people a diet of gossip, soap opera and sport. This is necessarily a very simplistic account. There is an underlying assumption here that the audience is a homogeneous group who all consume the media unthinkingly, and believe every word that they read or hear. (Much media effects research would refute this assumption – see the section on Media Audiences.) One particular area that is worth some examination is the news.

As we discuss elsewhere in the book, news doesn't just happen, nor is it readily available to us when and where and how we want it, though we are certainly given the impression that that is the case. The concept of mediation is important to the study of all media, and the news is no exception. A process of news selection takes place in all forms of news media, and this selection is based on the agenda that the particular organisation wishes to follow. While we may well be witnessing the depoliticisation of the news in this country (in the sense that few newspapers now proclaim their political allegiance quite so clearly or boldly as might once have been the case), it is still true that each news organisation has a target audience and an agenda which will appeal to that audience and also appease the owner/shareholders. We cannot therefore automatically accept that what we are told or shown is necessarily what is going on (see also the section on Realism, on p. 87).

Whilst it is easy to accuse Chomsky of paranoia and seeing conspiracy everywhere in the media, the fact remains that the media-spin placed on events is now such that few thinking individuals ever take the news at face value. Chomsky himself cites the example of the genocide which took place under Pol Pot and the Khmer Rouge in Cambodia during 1975–9, events that were heavily reported in the western press, whilst similar genocide taking place in East Timor when Indonesia invaded the island in November 1975 was barely mentioned. Chomsky suggests this is because Indonesia had been armed by many countries in the western world and also because the island of Timor occupies a strategically important place in the south-eastern part of the Pacific Ocean. Equally the Kosovan crisis involved much press vilification of Serbian military activity (but little analysis of the roots of the troubles) and a very sympathetic treatment of the actions of NATO at the same time. Chomsky suggests that there was a series of political and cultural reasons why this was the case.

ACTIVITY

On any given day, you should purchase every daily newspaper, watch as many different news broadcasts as possible on the TV, and also listen to as many radio news broadcasts as you can.

- Analyse the content of each as fully as possible.
- Is there any truth in what Chomsky is suggesting?
- Is there any evidence on one given day to suggest that there is one type of news for those who read the quality press and watch serious news broadcasts, and a different type altogether in the less serious press and broadcasts?
- What stories are present in the first group of media and ignored by the latter?
- To what extent are the media guilty of ignoring 'important' stories in favour of light-hearted gossip and celebrity news?
- Is it indeed possible to avoid the 'serious' news altogether?

REGULATION OF THE MEDIA

There are dangers inherent in a media structure that has no rules. Those dangers are fairly obvious. At a basic level there are laws relating to media which must be obeyed.

But there are also concerns about an unfettered media industry for a variety of reasons:

1 the laws of monopoly
2 worries about media ownership and control
3 the notion of competition
4 the protection of minority interests and notions of fair play
5 the understanding that cross-media ownership can act against the interests of the consumer.

In fact our media industries are more regulated than many in the rest of the world. The burgeoning of new media has had an interesting effect on the rules and regulations that govern media industries in this country.

For example, we might consider governments' attempts to take some kind of a grip on the World Wide Web. For many years now there have been few, if any, regulations affecting the Internet. The content of, and access to, the Internet have, on the whole, been unregulated – something which has caused great concern to many governments. In America, as a result of concern about children having access to unsuitable material, certain sites are now accessible only to people who have signed up to an age certifier/security system, based on credit card details. But, although this system ostensibly protects minors from material of an unsuitable sexual nature, it is still the case that anybody can set up a website and the Net is now so vast that the origin of a site deemed dangerous or unsuitable might be very difficult to trace.

The last few years have seen more and more governments becoming concerned by the fact that political extremist groups, or groups advocating illegal activities, can communicate across the Web without difficulty. In Britain the government has responded to what they see as a genuine threat from political extremist and potential terrorist groups. All Internet Service Providers (ISPs) now have to keep a log of the activities of their subscribers, and the police can now apply to a magistrate to 'tap' into any website address – very much like phone-tapping – to monitor a suspect group or individual. This means that the ordinary email is no more secure than a postcard sent by mail – though the government claims that law-abiding citizens have nothing to fear from such policing of the Internet. Yet it does have implications in terms of freedom of speech.

Much of this concern from government is due to yet another 'media panic' caused, in the main, by the stories that have been published in the press about football hooligans organising acts of violence abroad, particularly during Euro 2000, through the Internet. Equally, the Columbine massacre as it is now called, which occurred in April 1999, is said to have been inspired in part by some sites on the web, though this has yet to be proved and still belongs to the 'folklore of the web'.

But the difficulty is that if we were to look for any logic or repeating pattern in the regulation or control of any particular medium (e.g. film or TV), then we are unlikely to find it. There are various reasons for this:

1 Successive governments have differing policies and attitudes towards the media.
2 There is a basic understanding that governments tend not to undo the work of previous

ones except in special circumstances – and certainly the regulation of media ownership is considered a bit of a political hot potato.

3   There is a PSB organisation (the BBC) which it is clearly in the government's remit to maintain (see below for more details on this). The government has to be seen therefore to be acting even-handedly when dealing with commercial companies.

4   Most media industries are relatively new, and we are finding out more and more about them as they develop. Most governments tend to adopt a 'wait and see' position, preferring to leave things alone unless issues or problems are raised.

Yet, as we mentioned in the Introduction, the fact remains that all media in this country are regulated in one way or another, for the very reasons listed above. What is interesting is that most of the media have in a sense imposed regulatory systems upon themselves. This is particularly true of the newspaper and film/video industries who are regulated by the PCC (Press Complaints Commission) and the BBFC (British Board of Film Classification) respectively. Whilst it is true that this process has in the main been due to government pressure or a groundswell of popular opinion, it nevertheless seems to have beneficial results.

There is of course an (uneasy) relationship between these regulatory bodies and government. The self-regulatory bodies have always tried to keep one step ahead of any legislation (thus the Press Council and the privacy of individuals) whilst even the regulatory bodies set up by governments in the past have frequently been at odds with government over particular issues such as ownership of media industries. This is now becoming so complicated that government is having trouble keeping up with it. As media companies merge, take over and buy into one another, so it becomes harder to know who owns whom. This is happening more now that the ownership of media companies crosses borders.

NOTEBOX

When BSkyB attempted to buy a controlling interest in Manchester United Football Club the government intervened to prevent the takeover on the grounds that there would be a clash of interests when the question of football coverage on TV came up for discussion and auction later on in the year. However, in the past year or two there have been many examples of media organisations buying as many shares in football clubs as they are allowed (Granada buying into Liverpool Football Club, ntl buying into Newcastle United for instance).

ACTIVITY

■   What are the possible advantages that exist for a media company buying into a football club?

There can be little doubt that the regulation of media industries in this country is becoming less and less rigorous. There was once a cosy system in TV broadcasting whereby the BBC and the ITV network transmitted to the whole country. Written into their charters were certain stipulations. The BBC had to broadcast a certain proportion of news and factual programming and even the ITV was forced to do the same. Thus farming programmes were produced in the Anglia region, for example. However, during the late 1980s the Thatcher government sought to shake up broadcasting, believing that deregulation would free up finance, increase competition and, by extension, viewer choice. This resulted in the Broadcasting Act of 1990, and the awarding of TV franchises to the companies who passed a quality threshold with the highest bid. TV in this country is now much freer of government and regulation, but whether the promise of viewer choice has actually been delivered is a matter of continuing debate.

Where there were once 13 different ITV companies across the country, each with its own regional programming (admittedly mostly at off-peak times), now these companies exist in name alone, most having been swallowed up by two major ITV companies, Carlton and Granada. This has been one effect of deregulation. The regional element is very much in danger of disappearing (though lip-service is paid to it) as the ITV network becomes more centralised.

The face of TV in Britain has changed radically in the past decade. Where once there were two channels available, now there are over 100 on the two main English satellite providers, and with a movable dish and a non-generic receiver the list of channels available rises to way above 1,000. Since so many of these channels originate from outside this country, it not possible to regulate them. The only thing a government can do if it objects to the content of a channel is make it an offence to watch it, which involves enforcing legislation that makes it illegal to sell or possess the appropriate viewing cards (essential to watch many channels on cable/satellite TV). Therefore, in many ways, attempts at regulation (or censorship) are futile. It can therefore be argued that the lessening of regulation in this country signals the acceptance of a new way of broadcasting. The government has a vested interest in prolonging the life of the BBC and ITV companies in the same way that they fight to preserve other British industries, for example fishing, in the context of globalisation.

So on the one hand we have the regulation of the industry from without, but equally self-regulation from within.

BRITISH BOARD OF FILM CLASSIFICATION (BBFC)

The BBFC is an interesting case in point. Originally set up by the film industry itself to bring uniformity to standards of film censorship imposed by the many disparate local authorities in 1912, the BBFC has become a regulatory body with an ambiguous relationship with the industry and the audience. This is a pattern that is common to most regulatory bodies.

No entertainment organisation wants to become involved in legal battles because litigation is notoriously expensive and the publicity which court cases attract can backfire. At the same time all entertainment organisations have a genuine sense of what audiences might want and they also have to make a profit. A film, especially one made in the USA, has an average cost of $30m and rising, which is a considerable investment.

The essential role of the BBFC is to classify films and videos, assessing their suitability for public and private viewing across various age ranges. There is a range of certificates which can be given to film and video material. This system is particularly helpful for the exhibitors of films (the cinemas) because they feel safe in showing material without the threat of legal or other action being taken against them in terms of the nature of the material being shown. However, there have been times when this was not the case. *Crash*, a film directed by David Cronenberg and released in 1996, was banned by Westminster City Council, despite being given an 18 certificate by the BBFC. Members of the Licensing Committee decided to ban the film from cinemas in their area because they felt that it was an immoral film that might actually inspire 'corrupt and depraved' behaviour in those who saw it. (It is interesting to note that since that time the film has been shown repeatedly on one of the Sky movie channels without a whisper of protest being heard.) Cinemas within the Council's boundaries simply did not show the film.

Figure 44 BBFC classification symbols

At the heart of all classification undertaken by the BBFC is the attempt to protect children from material which might be harmful to them, and also to protect the public at large from material that might deprave, harm or corrupt. This obviously pertains, in the main, to material of a sexual or violent nature.

Four points of interest:

1   The nature of the classification system has changed over the years. As a result of increasing liberalisation, films such as *The Texas Chainsaw Massacre* (see Figure 60, p. 272), which have been unavailable for decades, have received certificates to be shown at cinemas and released on video. Indeed, *The Texas Chainsaw Massacre* was shown on C4 in October 2000 as part of its horror weekend. In the last few months certain films, which only a year ago would have had to have been censored because of their hard-core sexual nature, have been granted an R18 certificate.

2   The BBFC has often been seen as the mouthpiece of the government, and certainly there is a great deal of communication between the BBFC and the Home Office, though the BBFC maintains that the Home Office has never interfered in its classification of a film or in the creation of guidelines. However, in the light of events highlighted above, there are times when the BBFC takes on the politicians. The Home Secretary Jack Straw is said to be more than upset by the liberalisation of the R18 certificate and may make changes to the Video Recording Act as a result of his concern over the BBFC's classification decisions.

3   Classification is not the only issue. There have been occasions when the BBFC have refused a film or video a certificate because it breaks their guidelines. This in turn has led to a debate about the nature of classification and whether it should be read as a form of censorship. Here one should mention the fact that some films containing hardcore scenes have been passed for exhibition in a foreign language (e.g. *Romance*, *The Idiots*).

4   The nature of the job is such that there are in fact no formal qualifications needed to be a classifier. However, classifiers tend to be well-educated professionals. There is no evidence that any members of the film industry's target audience (for instance 18–25 year olds for a horror film) sit as a classifier. The BBFC says it recruits from the late twenties age group upward because it thinks that the level of maturity required to assess some of the very disturbing material viewed by classifiers has not yet been acquired by a lower age group. However, films are tested, usually by distribution companies, with target audience screenings to see how well they are received.

ACTIVITY . . .

Every major medium in this country has a self-regulatory body protecting the public in one way or another. A list is provided at the end of this section (p. 204).

You should contact each body, either by phone or by entering their website. It is important to find out exactly what each body has been set up to do, who sits on each board, and how they see their remit.

Ultimately there are several important questions:

■ Are audiences protected?
■ From what?
■ Who protects them?
■ Do you consider that the rights and interests of media audiences and the general public are protected satisfactorily?

PUBLIC SERVICE BROADCASTING (PSB)

The concept of Public Service Broadcasting (PSB) was adopted in this country in the 1920s. The most obvious example of a PSB organisation is the British Broadcasting Corporation (BBC) which was founded in 1926, initially as a radio service, though it was later to involve the new medium of television. The fundamental principle behind the PSB was to provide a service for all members of the community, with what Lord Reith, Director General of the BBC in the 1920s, called a duty to 'inform, educate and entertain'. For the payment of a yearly licence fee, the public received a national radio service which was joined by a television service after the Second World War. Originally, all households that owned a radio had to buy a licence. Later, ownership of a television meant the purchase of a TV licence was obligatory as well. Obviously nowadays the two licences have been merged into one – but it is still a legal requirement to have a TV licence if a household owns a television.

What is interesting about the concept of Public Service Broadcasting is the philosophical stance underpinning it. In a media world where often the central concern is profit, shareholders and aggrandisement, there can still exist, and be room for, an organisation created to serve a nation, not to make money from the nation, financed by a licence fee and, in theory, available to all.

It is important to note, however, that the notion of performing a public service is not unique to the BBC. All terrestrial TV organisations have written into their charters an element of public service – usually that they should provide some kind of news programme, and an element of educational programming, although it is important to note that these regulations are very much looser than they were when the first commercial television station started broadcasting in 1956.

It is also important to note that PSB is not unique to this country. It exists in one form or another in most European countries. Even the USA, where television is dominated by powerful networks showing advertisements as often as they can, possesses PSB channels. However, these channels tend to be funded by sponsorship and donations from members of the public, rather than by a general licence fee.

One of the central arguments for the continued existence of PSB channels is that they represent something that is very important – namely that the public are not a homogenised audience who want to watch only what is popular.

Commercial television is bound to its owners and shareholders. It is financed by advertising. Therefore the onus on all commercial TV channels is to gain as large an audience as possible. This then makes their programmes attractive for advertisers who, on the whole, want to show their adverts to as large an audience as possible. A popular programme attracts a large audience who will then see the advertisement. Thus the onus is to make and broadcast popular programmes, especially during peak viewing hours. Of course there are times when audiences are necessarily small, such as the period between lunchtime and tea-time, when most people are at work or indeed at school. However, advertisers have responded to this by targeting audiences quite specifically. It is now the case that adverts on commercial television in the afternoon are aimed directly at the most likely TV audience at this time, namely retired people or mothers and their pre-school infants.

The problem with this is that commercial television ends up beholden to three masters – the audience, the advertisers and the shareholders. The primary concern becomes to produce programmes that will gain the maximum number of viewers. And the evidence suggests that, in order to do this, schedules tend to become full of soap operas, quiz shows and, more recently, the new popular genre, docu-soaps, such as *Airline* and *Holidays from Hell*.

ACTIVITY . . .

Examine the current television schedules and attempt to identify which programmes or segments of programmes come under the heading of Education/Information and which come under the heading of Entertainment.

- Do any patterns emerge?
- Are some channels more educational or entertainment than others?
- Suggest reasons for this.

Underpinning the concept of PSB is the belief that all members of the community have a right to programming that appeals to them. And of course soap operas and game shows do not appeal to everyone. If 18 million people are watching *EastEnders*, then an equal if not larger number are not. This is not to say that popular genres do not have a place in PSB but that a balance needs to be struck between entertaining popular programmes and those that might not have such a direct appeal but that still have a potential audience. Since the PSB channel does not have to gratify advertisers and shareholders, the opportunity arises to make and show programmes that are not necessarily going to be large ratings winners. (Indeed *all* minority interests have to be catered for under the remit of PSB, which is essentially true of BBC1 as well as of BBC2 and C4.)

This then presents a dilemma, which has been highlighted by the arrival of non-terrestrial broadcasters. The choice of television programmes now available to viewers (especially those who have signed up to satellite or cable television) is large, and expected to become even larger. Yet members of the population who possess non-terrestrial television have to pay for the privilege. Many of those people now find that they no longer watch any programmes presented by the BBC. So, not surprisingly, there is a groundswell of opinion that, if they do not watch BBC programmes, why should they continue to pay their licence fee? This has increased pressure on the BBC to produce programmes that will attract a large audience, if only to justify the payment of the licence fee. The conundrum then turns full circle as people who are committed to the notion of public service television start to complain because, they would argue, public service broadcasting is simply becoming a replica (and perhaps not a very good one) of commercial television, which of course is ostensibly free.

It should be noted here that of course commercial television is *not* free. Millions of pounds are spent by companies in this country every year producing and showing adverts on TV. It can be argued that ultimately we, the consumers, pay for those adverts in the cost of the products that we are being enticed to buy.

There are two other debates currently circulating around the notion of public service broadcasting. This concerns 'narrowcasting' and digital channels.

NARROWCASTING

The way we watch television and listen to the radio is changing (see section on Media Audiences, p. 109). There was a time when there was only one TV channel, and even by the end of the 1970s there were only three.

Television was then akin to a community experience, particularly during peak hours. There was an unwritten agreement that if, for example, a serial was showing on one channel, then the other two would show programmes of a very different nature. Interestingly it was the BBC who realised that audiences for different types of programmes tended to be very different and fairly intractable in their choices. Thus the creation of Radios 1, 2, 3 and 4 in 1967, each catering for four very different types of listener. (It could be argued that this was also the first time that middle-aged executives realised that there was a youth market.)

This variation in audience make-up is now very much reflected in the format of British television on the non-terrestrial services. There are few channels on satellite and cable (other than the existing five terrestrial channels which it must be remembered are broadcast on satellite and cable) which attempt to cater for everyone with a varied diet of programming over any given day. Channels are now devoting themselves to particular areas of viewing material. For example, there are channels devoted to sport and channels devoted to films. But it has become even more subject-specific than that. The present diet available on satellite/cable television includes health channels, home shopping channels, sci-fi channels and channels aimed specifically at minority groups such as the Chinese Film Channel and Zee TV.

Whilst none of these channels yet has an audience that can compete with the numbers of viewers that watch the five main terrestrial channels, yet they are very attractive to advertisers because they allow them to target very specific audiences. And, even if some of these audiences are small, they are in the high-income bracket or have a high disposable income, e.g. teenagers.

If audiences know the genre of programme that they want to watch, then a channel that gives them an assortment of programmes is no longer attractive. There is evidence to suggest that in fact the amount of channel-hopping that takes place in one evening is actually quite small. Once you are watching the Sci-Fi channel you are unlikely to change unless there is a specific programme that you want to watch on another channel. This is one reason why BBC audiences are under threat. Viewing habits are becoming more dominated by genre. And as the take-up of digital television increases, and all television will be digital by 2010, so the problem is likely to get worse.

DIGITAL BROADCASTING

As stated above, by 2010 all television broadcasting will be digital (and it is very likely that the date for the switch-off of analogue broadcasting may well be brought forward). Public service broadcasting organisations will have to respond to this fact.

For all the reasons outlined above, it is clear that the BBC in particular will have to change with the times. There is consumer dissatisfaction with its output, and the role of a channel showing a judicious mix of programmes is changing. In August 2000, Greg Dyke, the Director General of the BBC, outlined a series of proposals to see the BBC into the digital age. His proposals suggest seven BBC channels in the future – very much along the generic lines outlined above. Whilst two channels will still broadcast general light entertainment, there will be two specialist channels of rather more 'highbrow' programming, a rolling 24-hour news channel, two children's channels broadcasting during the day and one channel devoted to arts, politics and discussion. It must be pointed out that this is still very much in the planning stage and there may well be alterations to these plans, but already there has been heavy criticism of them. The 'ideals' of public service broadcasting are seen to be under threat. Critics have been quick to point out that the two entertainment channels may simply be replicas of the many entertainment channels already available, whilst the two other more highbrow channels will be watched by few, and perhaps positively avoided by many. Minority-interest programming will be 'ghettoised'.

Others would argue that the proposals are as inevitable as the changes that are taking place in the broadcasting environment. The licence fee does not cover the cost of the BBC's TV and radio programming. Already the shortage of funds has been highlighted by the dramatic loss of several sporting fixtures which up until a few years ago could be watched free of charge on the BBC, such as Test Match cricket and English football international matches. The large investment in TV, particularly by satellite and cable companies, has been reflected by the enormous sums these companies are prepared to pay for sporting fixtures. It seems inevitable that, to pay for this investment, audiences not only will have to subscribe to certain satellite/cable channels but may well soon have to pay an extra amount to watch certain major sporting fixtures.

This is already the case on some digital channels with the advent of pay-per-view TV. At present this mainly occurs for recently released films, but certain sporting fixtures, notably boxing and wrestling, have also been transmitted as PPV events. And digital TV allows for each premiership football club to own and run its own TV channel to show its own

entertainment

Channel number

106	**one**	**Sky One** Our number one channel for family first-run entertainment and award-winning drama. **24hrs**
109	UK GOLD	**UK Gold** A quality selection of British comedy and drama. It's TV you'll want to see again and again. **7am-3am**
110	UK GOLD 2	**UK Gold 2** The chance to catch up with your favourite UK Gold programmes if you missed them earlier in the day. **6pm-2am**
112	*Living	**Living** A vibrant mix of hit dramas, great films, talk shows and pre-school TV. **6am-midnight**
118	Granada plus	**Granada Plus** The very best of classic British television and popular programmes from around the world. **6am-midnight**
121	?	**Challenge TV** The interactive channel that gives you your favourite gameshows plus the chance to win prizes. **6am-midnight**
124	BRAVO	**Bravo** A channel packed full of energy and attitude with movies, action, compelling series and provocative talk. **noon-6am**
127		**Paramount Comedy Channel** With award-winning sitcoms including *Frasier* and *Seinfeld*, plus the best of British series – Comedy is Paramount. **7pm-4am**
130	Sci-Fi	**Sci-Fi** The only UK channel dedicated to the science-fiction genre, Sci-Fi provides stimulating viewing to those prepared to think differently. **7.30am-4am**
133		**Discovery Home & Leisure** Witty, informative and entertaining, bringing 'how to' programmes on DIY, cookery and outdoor activities to life. **6am-midnight**
136	breeze	**Granada Breeze** Presents the ultimate guide to help women look good and feel fantastic. **6am-9pm**
139	men & motors	**Granada Men & Motors** Fast cars, fast bikes and fast women – the channel for men who like all the action. **9pm-2am**
145	SKY travel	**Sky Travel** Great holiday ideas, travel tips and documentary specials. **11am-4pm**
148	UK STYLE	**UK Style** A channel packed with ideas, inspiration and entertainment. A must for people who enjoy their leisure time and home life. **7am-1am**
151	UK DRAMA	**UK Drama** The only British television channel devoted entirely to drama. **7pm-6am**
178	taRa TV	**TARA Television** Great all-round entertainment – live chat, soaps, sport, music and drama from Ireland for Britain. **noon-midnight**
187	rapture	**Rapture** The ultimate channel for clubbers, free sports and film fans. **10am-2am**
190	HALLMARK	**Hallmark Entertainment Network** This channel showcases a wide range of quality original programming, from epic mini-series to award-winning movies and children's entertainment. **24hrs**
196	Health	**Discovery Health** Empowers viewers to take active responsibility for their well-being with up-to-the minute healthcare information. **6am-midnight**

sport

Channel number

401	SKY SPORTS 1	**Sky Sports 1†**	Sky Sports 1, 2 and 3 on Sky digital bring you the very best live
402	SKY SPORTS 2	**Sky Sports 2†**	sports coverage, including all the award-winning coverage you
403	SKY SPORTS 3	**Sky Sports 3†**	have come to expect from Sky Sports' three dedicated sports channels. **Sky Sports 1 & 2, 7am-3am (Mon-Thu), 24hrs (Fri-Sun); Sky Sports 3, noon-11.30pm**
404	SKY SPORTS EXTRA	**Sky Sports Extra** An enhanced sports channel FREE to subscribers to both Sky Sports 1 and Sky Sports 2. **various times**
410	MU tv	**MUTV†** The world's first seven-day channel dedicated to Manchester United football club. Bringing you closer to the players and staff who make the news. **5pm-11pm**
413	skysports.com TV	**skysports.com TV** Europe's first around-the-clock sports news service. **24hrs**
419	EUROSPORT	**British Eurosport** Focusing on British achievement at home and abroad. **7.30am-12.30am**

movies

Channel number

301	PREMIER	**Sky Premier†**	Sky Premier brings you four 24-hour screens
302	PREMIER 2	**Sky Premier 2†**	of box-office hits, award-winning movies and
303	PREMIER 3	**Sky Premier 3†**	originally produced films – plus shows including
304	PREMIER 4	**Sky Premier 4†**	*Barry Norman's Film Night*. **24 hrs**
305	PREMIER WIDESCREEN	**Sky Premier Widescreen†** A widescreen service featuring at least two movies every evening. **8pm-midnight (weekdays), 6pm-midnight (weekends)**
308		**Sky MovieMax†**	Sky MovieMax provides five screens of
309		**Sky MovieMax 2†**	variety, unadulterated fun and non-stop
310		**Sky MovieMax 3†**	entertainment. It's the home for action,
311		**Sky MovieMax 4†**	adventure, hilarious comedy and drama. With up to 30 movie channel premieres a month,
312		**Sky MovieMax 5†**	Sky MovieMax is a must for movie fans. **24 hrs**
315	SKY cinema	**Sky Cinema†**	Sky Cinema is devoted to the classics of the screen. It features the greatest stars and masterpieces of
316	SKY cinema 2	**Sky Cinema 2†**	the greatest directors. **24 hrs**
324	FILM FOUR	**FilmFour†** The film channel from Channel 4 – the best in modern independent cinema. **6pm-6am**
700-761	SKY box office	**Sky Box Office** Recent movie releases at the touch of a button, 24 hours a day, with films starting up to every 15 minutes, plus exclusive live concerts and sporting events – you only pay for what you order. See p66.

news & documentaries

Channel number

501	SKY NEWS	**Sky News** The award-winning 24-hour service, now with Sky News Active, Britain's first interactive television news service. **24 hrs**
504	Bloomberg TELEVISION	**Bloomberg** Keep up to date with business and financial news, 24 hours a day. **24 hrs**
510	CNBC	**CNBC** Live business and financial news from Europe, the US and Asia. **24 hrs**
551	Discovery CHANNEL	**Discovery** Entertaining factual programmes about adventure, science, nature and technology. **8am-2am**
552		**Discovery (+1hr)** Discovery's high-quality programmes shown one hour later. **9am-3am**
553		**Discovery Travel & Adventure** Thrilling programmes which explore our world, letting you experience it first hand. **8am-2am**
554		**Discovery Civilisation** Meet the people and see the crucial events which have shaped our past and present. **8am-2am**
555		**Discovery Sci-Trek** Innovative, fast-paced programming which shows the impact science is having on our lives. **8am-2am**
556		**Discovery Wings** Explore the wonders of flight and thrill to the feats of skybound explorers. **6pm-midnight**
558	NATIONAL GEOGRAPHIC CHANNEL	**National Geographic Channel** The most powerful teller of stories in the world of documentary television. **11am-5am**
559		**National Geographic Channel +1hr** A second chance to see award-winning documentaries from the heart of our planet. **noon-6am**
560	a1 ADVENTURE ONE	**Adventure One** It's extreme life; it's what drives us; it's A1 in every sense. **8am-2am**
561	THE HISTORY CHANNEL	**The History Channel** Informative, intelligent, entertaining and educational, exploring events and people that have shaped the world. **6am-midnight**
562		**The History Channel +1hr** Another chance to see The History Channel programmes one hour later. **From 1 October, 7am-1am**
563	Biography	**The Biography Channel™** The only channel dedicated to profiling famous figures from around the world. **From 1 October at 6pm, then 6am-midnight**
564	UK HORIZONS	**UK Horizons** It's TV that makes life worth watching. Great for science shows and fascinating documentaries. **7am-1am**
567	[.tv]	**[.tv]** IT news, analysis, testing and appraising, games, gadgets and gizmos, practical tutorials, digital culture, the Internet and more! **noon-midnight**
570		**Animal Planet** The first ever channel that's all about animals. Entertaining factual programming, real-life vet stories and animal dramas. **6am-midnight**

Figure 45 *List of television channels on offer.* Sky Customer Magazine (October 2000)

Channel number

601 Cartoon Network Non-stop toon action for everyone who loves cartoons. **24 hrs**
602 Cartoon Network Plus All Cartoon Network's toon action one hour later. **24 hrs**

604 Nickelodeon Award-winning cartoons, comedy and live action, including *Rugrats* and *Kenan & Kel*. **6am-10pm**
605 Nickelodeon Replay Missed out on Nick? Watch it one hour later on Nickelodeon Replay. **7am-11pm**

606 Nick Jr. Nick's popular pre-school section gets its own channel, loads of fun for young 'uns. **6am-7pm**

607 **TROUBLE(T)** Trouble Get into Trouble, the number one channel for teens, with an upfront mix of music, soaps, dramas and celebrity interviews. **6am-midnight**

610 Fox Kids The most entertaining kids channel, packed full of your favourite shows including *Digimon, Dennis And Gnasher* and *The Power Rangers*. **6am-10pm**
611 Fox Kids + Catch all those fantastic Fox Kids programmes – an hour later. **7am-11pm**

613 Disney Channel† The Disney Channel is bursting with comedies, live-action, drama, cartoons and pre-school programmes. **6am-midnight**
614 Disney Channel +1† Disney Channel, an hour later. **From 29 Sep, 7am-1am**
615 Disney Toon† Inspiring cartoons from the home of animation. **From 29 September, 24 hours**

616 Playhouse Disney† Fun for pre-schoolers: learning through imagination and play. **From 29 September, 5am-8.30pm**

618 Discovery Kids A playground for young minds – the place where kids can satisfy their curiosity and learn about life while having fun. **6am-6pm**

Channel number

440 MTV The most famous music TV channel in the world – just for the UK and Ireland. **24 hrs**

441 MTV Extra The perfect companion to MTV UK, offering an alternative choice of programming and a chance to catch up on shows missed first time round. **24 hrs**

442 MTV Base The first music channel dedicated entirely to R&B and dance music. **24 hrs**

443 VH1 The music channel for adults – videos, documentaries, concerts and the biggest exclusives. **24 hrs**

444 VH1 Classic Classic hits from the Sixties, Seventies and Eighties. **24 hrs**

446 MTV2 The cutting-edge music channel from the makers of MTV. **24 hrs**

449 The Box Music television YOU control, 24 hours a day. **24 hrs**

450 **KISS** Kiss 24 hours of hot chart run-downs and fresh new releases. **24 hrs**

452 **UK PLAY** UK Play The UK's only music and comedy channel. Featuring current sounds and the best in cult comedy. **24 hrs**

455 **Q** Q Brand new music channel from the experts behind *Q* magazine. **From 2 October, 24 hrs**

851- Music Choice + 44 channels of digital audio music available 24 hours a day without advertisements or interruptions. Ten channels are included in the Sky Entertainment packages. You can add a further 34 channels with
894 Music Choice Extra, a premium service. **24 hrs**

Radio

With digital satellite, even if you don't subscribe to Sky digital, you can listen to your favourite radio station in digital-quality sound

Channel number

911	BBC Radio 1	918	Talk Sport ‡	927	BBC Radio Scotland
912	BBC Radio 2	919	Classic Gold	928	BBC Radio Wales
913	BBC Radio 3	920	The Mix	929	BBC Radio Ulster
914	BBC Radio 4 FM	921	Planet Rock	930	BBC Asian Network
915	BBC Radio 5 Live	922	Core	934	BBC Radio 4 LW
916	Classic FM	923	Capital Gold	935	Youth FM
917	Virgin Radio	924	XFM	939	Heart
		926	BBC World Service	‡ available as part of the Sky family pack	

Channel number

101 **BBC ONE** BBC ONE* A rich and diverse mix of entertaining programmes, inc: drama, live news, investigative journalism, documentaries, comedy and entertainment. **24 hrs**

102 **BBC TWO** BBC TWO* Diverse, innovative and contemporary programming on specialist subjects which captivate, inspire and stimulate. **24 hrs**

104 **4** Channel 4 Viewers in Wales should select Skyguide channel 184 for Channel 4. **24 hrs**

105 **⑤** Channel 5 No Channel 5 transmitter in your area? Don't worry: you can tune in on Sky digital. **24 hrs**

160 **BBC CHOICE** BBC Choice*# A mix of entertainment, music and sport. **7pm-2am** CBBC on BBC Choice: programmes for pre-school children. **6am-7pm**

184 **S4C~** S4C Welsh language channel with news, documentaries, sport, music and drama. Viewers in Wales should select Skyguide channel 104 for S4C. **9am-midnight**

507 **BBC NEWS 24** BBC News 24* Full news bulletins on the hour, with headlines every 15 minutes, 24 hours a day. **24 hrs**

508 **BBC PARLIAMENT** BBC Parliament* Live, uninterrupted coverage of the House of Commons and recorded-as-live coverage of the House of Lords. **5.30am-midnight**

513 **CNN** CNN International The world's leading television news channel providing up-to-the-minute news coverage. **24 hrs**

516 Money Channel A channel dedicated to money, which aims to demystify the world of finance. **24 hrs (weekdays), selected service (weekends)**

573 **BBC KNOWLEDGE** BBC Knowledge* A stimulating mix of factual content, both on-screen and online. **9am-3am with three-hour loops of programmes**

655 Community Channel See the work done by charities and community groups, and find out how you can get involved either by volunteering or through buying products on the UK's only charity channel. **From 18 September, 1pm-4pm**

BBC services * All BBC services are non-subscription and funded by the licence fee.
Dedicated versions of BBC CHOICE are available for Scotland, Wales and Northern Ireland.

Channel number

630 QVC The Shopping Channel At your service 24 hours a day. Just call free on 0800 50 40 30 to order any item. **24 hrs**

Channel number

998 An introduction to Skyguide for new customers. **24 hrs**
999 News and highlights this month across Sky's digital services. **24 hrs**

USEFUL INFORMATION

To upgrade your package...
† These are Sky's premium channels. If you wish to add one or more premium channels to your existing Sky digital package, call 08702 415555.

To register for Skytalk...
Skytalk is a service that is available to Sky digital customers who have a BT line connected to a digital exchange. It's free, and it can save you up to 40 per cent on BT basic rates. To register call the hotline: 08702 40 40 40.

Sky's website
Go to sky.com for all the latest information about your favourite Sky programmes, movies, sports and news, as well as on-line shopping from SkyBuy.

Technical helpline
If you have problems with your Sky digital viewing or equipment, call the technical helpline on 08702 435 000.

Customer services
For all other queries, call customer services on 08702 40 40 40.
(In Rep of Ireland call 01 475 1787.)

fixtures. Sport on Sky has had a great deal of investment money put into it by News Corporation (Rupert Murdoch's holding company) and is seen as a loss leader to get audiences to subscribe to Sky channels. Once we could watch the occasional game on the BBC for nothing – now we have to pay £28 a month for the privilege and so we have a dish or cable fitted and suddenly there is a welter of choice – the supermarket principle yet again. Certainly when it first started there was a slow take-up for satellite TV, but the sports channels have been cited as a reason why subscribers signed up, and the satellite industry now seems to have taken off with a vengeance.

ACTIVITY...

- What are the advantages of PSB?
- What do you see as the disadvantages of PSB?
- Are there alternatives to the TV licence fee as a means of financing the BBC?
- Should the BBC become a subscription channel?

NEW TECHNOLOGY

There can be little doubt that changes in communications technology in the past decade have taken many by surprise. Ten years ago some people might have owned a cordless phone at home and used a computer at work. Nowadays mobile phones are everywhere and computers rule the office. Most communication now takes place by email, and the five terrestrial TV channels have numerous competitors.

CONVERGENCE

Convergence means that the new media technologies are all coming together. However, not so very long ago, a typical home would have one TV, a radio and a telephone. It is very unlikely that they were even in the same room – the commonest scenario being a TV in the sitting-room, radio in the kitchen and telephone in the hall. People who spent a long time on the phone were considered slightly eccentric (usually women, as a stereotype, talking to their friends). The radio was still really a source of information and the TV was watched when there was a good programme on. Things are now very different.

Most hardware is now multi-functional. The TV is now digital and interactive. There is the potential to have over 1,000 channels beaming into your sitting-room, or more if you possess a movable satellite dish. This is very different from the era when the choice was between four (later five) terrestrial channels. Pay-per-view television is already in existence, at present featuring mainly films and sporting events, but it is likely that the menu will widen considerably over the next few years.

More interesting is the interactive aspect of media technology. TV has now become a medium through which one can shop, bank, and even send and receive emails through a telephone cable link-up. This works both ways. The phone has become a piece of hardware through which one can still talk but also send text-messages, voicemail, emails and connect to the Internet. The radio is still a radio, but few units are simply just radios – most are again multi-functional, including cassette decks and CD players, or at the very least alarm clocks that wake you to a radio programme.

Thus hardware has become another example of vertical and horizontal integration. If you own the hardware, or make it as multi-functional as possible, then the audience can gain access to your product with greater ease. And if it is accessible, then it is much more likely to be so accessed.

But the implications are far greater than this. The computer, accessed by wide-band-width telephone cables, is very much at the centre of the new technological revolution. To put it another way, we are now living in the digital age, which of course springs from the computer.

FUTURE DEVELOPMENTS

■ It is foreseeable that soon you will be able to download a film from the Internet at home and then play it back to yourself on a virtual reality headset, played through your phone, whilst on a train journey for instance.

■ The technology exists now to download music from the Net. Some musicians have used this technology to allow interested audiences to download their music (either as a taster or because they believe in providing free public access to media products), and there is a movement which supports the idea that the Net should belong to the people and freedom of access is their right.

■ However, there are several test cases currently taking place about copyright laws and the Net, since it is becoming easier by the day to download music which would otherwise cost you money if you were to buy it at a record shop. Obviously the artists and record companies involved are concerned at the loss of revenue such downloading represents. Are we looking at a total sea change both in conditions of consumption and the nature of that which we consume?

■ The technology now exists for programmes to be downloaded into your TV through phone lines. This means that viewers are able to watch whatever they like when they like. This technology is still in its infancy.

■ In the Introduction we mentioned TiVo. TiVo is yet another black box which sits on the television. This piece of equipment will enable viewers to skip over adverts and even pause 'live TV'. It has the capacity to record over 30 hours of television from a maximum of 90 channels. But more interesting is the fact that viewers can key in certain words and the box will then automatically watch out for programmes featuring these words. Thus viewers can select programmes they want recorded or search for different types of programmes, or indeed particular actors or genres (Figure 46).

What all of this means is that the nature of our consumption of the media – and of television in particular – will change. If viewers felt overwhelmed by choice at the outset of digital technology, it now seems as though it is the consumers who are potentially about to take control. From being initially overwhelmed in the first instance by the wealth of

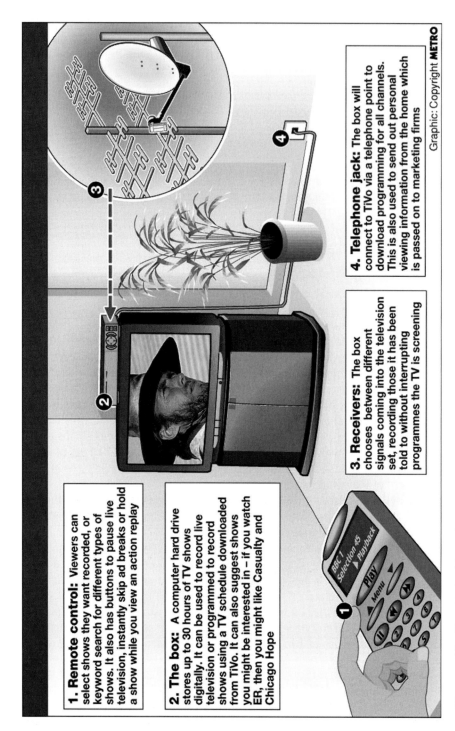

1. Remote control: Viewers can select shows they want recorded, or keyword search for different types of shows. It also has buttons to pause live television, instantly skip ad breaks or hold a show while you view an action replay

2. The box: A computer hard drive stores up to 30 hours of TV shows digitally. It can be used to record live television or programmed to record shows using a TV schedule downloaded from TiVo. It can also suggest shows you might be interested in – if you watch ER, then you might like Casualty and Chicago Hope

3. Receivers: The box chooses between different signals coming into the television set, recording those it has been told to without interrupting programmes the TV is screening

4. Telephone jack: The box will connect to TiVo via a telephone point to download programming for all channels. This is also used to send out personal viewing information from the home which is passed on to marketing firms

Graphic: Copyright **METRO**

Figure 46 *The TiVo black box*

choice, the shoe is now firmly on the other foot and it is viewers who are about to take control.

- What are the possible effects of the digital age in terms of our viewing habits?
- Is TV as a community activity a thing of the past?
- How will scheduling differ in the future?

So far we have only looked at TV, but it is not only in this area that things are changing.

The phone is now ubiquitous and no longer simply a mechanism for trying to contact friends or colleagues. The most recent generation of mobile phones are known as WAP (Wireless Application Protocol) phones, with as yet limited connection to the Internet, but the future of the mobile phone shows an as yet untapped potential.

Research the possible technological developments that are on the horizon.

You should pay particular attention to:

TV	Computers
Radio	Internet
Digital technology	Mobile phones

This of course explains why so many major media organisations are at present juggling with their future. Many see their future to be based on the Internet because one prediction is that eventually every form of media text will be accessed through the Internet.

However, it is still early days. Governments are seeking to control Internet activity and investors in Internet companies cannot yet feel secure. Even though there is still a great deal of uncertainty surrounding future technologies, what is certain is that what we consume and how we consume may be radically different in ten years' time.

GLOBAL MEDIA ECONOMY

There are very few homes without a television in the majority of countries in the world. (Of course in countries like the USA and now Britain it is not uncommon for homes to have at least two TVs – and often one in each bedroom.) Even in countries where televisions are rare, the main local meeting place will often possess a TV that everyone can watch as a communal activity.

The communications technology available in the world today is partly responsible for this sense of global shrinkage, although there are still areas of the world where the technology barely exists. It is still very much the case that the use of most media technologies is confined to developed nations and certain elites within developing nations.

Satellite and digital technology allows us to see instantly live events taking place on the other side of the globe. The Internet has made it possible to communicate directly and cheaply across the world, if access to a telephone line is available. But it is not technology alone that has created this 'global village'.

The demand for information about news and events is now more global than it ever used to be. This is a demand for information not only about news and politics but also about other areas of human activity such as sport and entertainment. The world of the domestic or parochial TV or radio station is changing very rapidly as media institutions, in order to deal with worldwide audience demands, have discovered that they need to look beyond their own borders.

Again money plays a big part. Take, for example, US TV and film production. An American film or television series is made for an American audience on what often amounts to a tremendously well-organised and efficient conveyor belt/studio system production line, after much money has been spent on research and testing audience satisfaction with the product. Test audiences tell the producers whether they like, or even understand, the product. Characters are removed if test plays suggest they are not popular. It is not uncommon for the ending of a film to be changed after testing. Yet the majority of American film and TV products make their money on the domestic front. It is important to remember that the production costs, based on what in many cases amounts to a factory system, are relatively cheap – *relatively* considering the size of the American audience in the first place.

However, a TV company in any other part of the world will often find it cheaper to buy American ready-made programmes than to make them themselves. Again the notion of the loss leader comes into play here. In the first instance these non-American companies can purchase the product relatively cheaply, especially if it is an old programme (*Star Trek* and *I Love Lucy* are perennial favourites). However, should that programme prove to be popular, then the next series will not be quite so cheap (a striking example of this is the escalating price of the TV series *Friends*).

It is also worth noting that nowadays many products come in packages. If the TV company in question wants to purchase a very popular American series that all its rival networks are also interested in buying, then they will often have to purchase other less successful or less popular series made by the same producers at the same time. Naturally, once a TV company has bought a series, then they will show it anyway. If it is not a great ratings winner, then it can be used as early-afternoon or late-night filler material.

There are two reasons why some governments are worried by this trend. On one level this process can have a retrograde effect on the home market in terms of developing domestic production, talent and culture. On another level there can be social and cultural consequences – an issue in Media Studies which is called 'media imperialism'.

MEDIA IMPERIALISM The idea that powerful and wealthy countries can exercise economic, cultural and social control over others through control of media industries.

ACTIVITY . . .

First of all, monitor closely the programming on British terrestrial TV in one week and where possible note the nationality of the programmes. Then do the same for a collection of channels on cable or satellite TV.

■ How many programmes in one week on British television are produced in this country?
■ Of the rest of the programmes on TV, how many are made in Europe and how many are American product?

It is interesting to repeat the process with films showing at cinemas in your local area. Do the results of your research surprise you? Are the results of your survey a matter for concern?

MEDIA IMPERIALISM

Media imperialism is a very important issue in Media Studies. It is very easy to say that American media products are the best because they are what audiences want to watch.

But if *I Love Lucy* can be seen on a television screen somewhere in the world at any given time of day – and the same can be said of *Star Trek* – then this can be seen to have serious cultural and social effects, particularly in countries where there is next to no home-produced material being read, seen or listened to by the indigenous population (see section on Media Audiences).

Both socially and politically there are problems with a diet of media programming which is predominantly American, or indeed from any country other than one's own. If the indigenous population consume nothing but a diet of American media – be it film, TV, music or whatever – then there is a grave danger that they may well buy into an image of America and a way of life which on the surface seems very attractive (a realisation of the American dream) but which encompasses a version of history and culture that is often inaccurate and politically deceitful.

ACTIVITY . . .

■ Why should an audience outside the Americas or Europe watch a diet of American war films and not believe that the Americans won the war single-handed?

- A diet of American rock videos gives what sort of impression of the American way of life?
- Can you think of some American media products which are directly critical or questioning of the American dream and the American way of doing things?

Some media thinkers suggest that the inability of the Soviet leadership to prevent the ordinary population from consuming a media diet that was becoming more western every year was an important contributing factor to the collapse of many Eastern-bloc governments. (Although it is important to add here that for years the Soviet bloc was fed a diet of political, social and cultural propaganda that suited its own regime.)

What the audiences saw and heard showed them things they could not even dream about under the communist system. Unfortunately the collapse of communism has had very traumatic consequences for many in Eastern Europe, since the reality of a free-market capitalist system is often very different from how it appears on TV and in the cinema.

If there are political and social concerns about the spread of media imperialism, there are also very profound *cultural* concerns. In fact the French are so worried about the cultural effects of the dominance of American, and other non-indigenous, media products that they have actually produced legislation to protect their own culture and language which they saw disappearing under the influx of foreign cinema, music and other products. Thus French radio stations have to play a fixed percentage of French material in every hour of broadcast, and French cinemas have to show a fixed quota of home-produced films every year as well.

If the major concern has been historically that of American culture dominating the world, then it is interesting to note a new development in the media world. This is the merger between multinational media companies to form giant media conglomerates.

ACTIVITY . . .

The Universal/Vivendi/Seagram/Canal Plus Merger

Initially Universal – a large American TV and film company – was taken over by Seagram, which was once one of the largest drinks companies in the world. Media analysts were unsure of the motive behind the purchase at the time – and many people were unaware of the fact that Universal was also a large player in the music world.

Early in 2000, Vivendi, a French media company, stepped in and merged with Universal-Seagram. Then in December 2000 it merged again, this time with the French TV and film group Canal Plus, to form Universal Vivendi. This then became the world's number 2 in the communications sector after the merger between AOL and Time-Warner in February 2000.

You should investigate this merger. Look carefully at what each company in the merger has on its books. Now look at what the combined company owns and possesses.

■ In what way do the various strands complement one another?
■ Is the merger part of a disturbing trend towards large multinational media companies?

Or should it be welcomed?

■ What are the advantages for a company as large and as diverse as this on the media stage?
■ What, if any, are the possible pitfalls?
■ Is this perhaps a case of Europe hitting back?
■ Which of the four major parts of the merger do you think are the winners in the merger? And the losers?

What is most interesting about this particular deal between Universal/Vivendi/Seagram announced in the last week of June 2000 is that it should happen at all.

On one level we are looking at the global economy writ large, except that in this instance it is not the American company that is trying to expand and develop, but a European company which was once a small-time player but is now expanding and, in the opinion of some experts, biting off more than it can chew.

This is no longer a case of cultural and media imperialism – there is no way that French culture will suddenly make inroads into American. It is an example of a European company looking outside the confines of Europe, at trends in the media world, and also anticipating the likely needs of the consumer over the next decade or so.

FURTHER WORK . . .

1   Three questions follow which involve research and analysis:

   ■ Do we have reasons to be concerned by the increasing trend towards multi-national media institutions?

   ■ Technology continues to move faster than we can keep up with it. Suggest where we might be in 20 years' time.

   ■ Is the notion of a mass audience, viewing the same text at the same time, becoming outdated?

2   Consider the impact of legislation and equal opportunities policies on media representations.

FURTHER READING

As has been noted several times above, probably the best source of information about media institutions remains the quality broadsheet newspapers. All of them have business sections, which is where you will find regular, and frequent reference to media institutions. Many of the Sunday newspapers also have a media section which always contains valuable information. It is vital however that you file the information in some shape or form.

Websites

There follows a list of important websites, which are regularly updated and will keep you abreast of what is happening in the world of media institutions:

www.mediauk.com/directory
Details the media scene with links to websites of all the main TV and radio stations, magazines and newspapers.

www.bfi.org.uk
Website of the British Film Institute – contains invaluable information.

http://uk.imdb.com/
Virtually everything you want to know about film.

www.raynet.mcmail.com/
Essential information on marketing

www.TheStandard.com
This is essentially an economic website but with a very large media section.

www.mediachannel.org
This has an American flavour but fascinating analyses of contemporary media issues. Many links to other sites as well.

There are many, many more sites available – far too numerous to mention – but part of the enjoyment of the Internet is discovery. Virtually every media organisation now has a website. The easiest way to find them is to type the name in the search section of your search engine and see what happens!

www.google.com
This is undoubtedly the fastest and most rewarding search engine to date.

Further information on regulation from:

The Independent Television Commission (www.itc.org.uk)

British Board of Film Classification (www.bbfc.co.uk)

BBC (Producers' guidelines) (www.bbc.co.uk/info/editorial/prodgl/chapter6.shtml)

British Video Association (www.bva.org.uk)

Advertising Standards Authority (www.asa.co.uk)

Press Complaints Commission (www.pcc.org.uk)

▼ EXAMPLE: CINEMA

In this section we consider:

- the status of cinema as a business and as a cultural pursuit
- the UK's top 20 films
- the current state of the UK film industry
- foreign films.

The ability to project moving images on to a large screen changed the way many people viewed the world. In the late 1890s French audiences queued up to watch a very short film (just a few minutes' duration) of a train entering a station, made by the early pioneers of the cinema, Auguste and Louis Lumière. The camera did not move, there were no edits, it was in jerky black and white, and there was no soundtrack to heighten the impact. Yet, the story goes, as the train neared the camera, so people in the audience would duck their heads for fear of being hit. This may well be an apocryphal tale, but it demonstrates the power that the moving image has over us, a power that still exists today.

Just over a century later there are still occasions when people will queue around the block to see a particular film, yet now the visual and aural impact of sitting in a cinema has changed dramatically. The screen occupies the whole width of one wall, the film has usually been made in colour, the camera moves, and the images have been edited so that the point of view is no longer static. The soundtrack will include music, dialogue and sound effects, broadcast in stereo and Dolby sound through several speakers, some of which are situated behind the screen and others on the remaining three walls of the cinema so that the audience is surrounded by sound.

Yet, essentially, the technology remains the same. It has been improved and modified, but an audience still sits in a darkened auditorium and watches larger-than-life moving images projected on to a screen in front of them.

THE STATUS OF THE CINEMA AS A BUSINESS
AND AS A CULTURAL PURSUIT

No longer is the cinema attended simply for its novelty value. It has become big business, part of the mass media and part of our culture. If the cinema failed to respond particularly well to the competition of TV in the 1950s, and indeed the early 1960s, yet it has now fought its way back into the consciousness of the public. Attendances in the UK have risen dramatically in the past decade. Multiplex cinemas are being built outside most inner cities and large towns, usually with spacious car parks and with restaurants, bars, discotheques and other leisure activities in close proximity. Going to the cinema on a regular weekly basis has again become a habit – particularly for the audience range of 15 to 25 year olds.

Greg Dyke, Director General of the BBC, gave a keynote speech at the Edinburgh Festival in the summer of 2000, where he highlighted an interesting trend. It would appear that the teenage and young adult audience is turning away from watching TV as a leisure activity. What he was unable to clarify was whether this problem was because the programmes shown on national TV simply did not appeal to younger audiences, or whether in fact the alternatives were just more attractive.

NOTEBOX

As the younger audience seems to be turning away from the TV, so they are going to the cinema. The cinema attendance figures in the UK since the 1940s are revealing:

    1946 –1,635 million
    1984 – 53   million
    1998 –135.5 million

(see Figure 28, p. 117)

ACTIVITY

- Why do you think so many people visited the cinema in 1946?
- How would you explain the dramatic rise in cinema attendance figures over the past decade?
- Do you think the arrival of the multiplex cinemas is responsible for this?
- In what ways is the experience of going to a multiplex cinema different from that of going to one of the older, one-screen cinemas?
- Which would you rather see a film in – a multiplex or an older cinema? Why?
- What is the difference in the experience between the two for an audience?
- Could it be that the nature of the films showing at the cinema has changed in the last decade?

- What of TV? Do you think fewer people in the age group 15–25 are watching TV? If so, why do you think it is?
- Has the boom in video rentals helped or hindered the cinema?

What is interesting to note is that although the multiplex cinema is seen as a phenomenon of the 1990s – and as the saviour of the cinema in this country by many observers – yet the fact remains that there are still over 1,000 screens in the country which are not part of a multiplex site (see Figure 47). Obviously some of the cinemas have more than one screen. There was, for instance, a trend in the 1970s to convert the typical, large, one-screened picture palace into three-screen buildings – one largish screen and two smaller screens – but the fact remains that there are still a considerable number of non-multiplex sites in the UK.

Figure 47 UK box office breakdown 1998

Admissions	135.5 million	Total Multiplex Screens	1488
Total Cinema Sites	759	Box Office Gross	£514.73 million
Total Cinema Screens	2564	Average Ticket Price	£3.83
Total Multiplex Sites	167		

Source: Screen Finance/X25
Partnership/CAA/ACNielsen EDI/Media Salles

Let us look closely at the top 20 films at the UK box office in 1998 (Figure 48).

Referring to Figure 48, prepare an analysis of the top 20 grossing films of 1998 in the UK. Answering the following questions should help you:

- What, if anything, do the films in the top 20 have in common?
- What type of audience do you think each one was aimed at? How would you support your assumption?
- What certificate was each film given?
- How many of the top 20 films are British in origin?
- Are there any films in the list that surprise you by being there?
- Were there any other films released in 1998 that you expected to see in this list?
- Did you actually see most of these films?
- If so, did you see them at the cinema, on video or on TV? If not, it would be interesting to explain why you didn't.

Figure 48 Top 20 films at the UK box office 1998

	Film	Distributor	Country of Origin	Box Office Gross (£m)
1	Titanic	20thC Fox	US	68,971,532
2	Doctor Dolittle	20thC Fox	US	19,854,598
3	Saving Private Ryan	UIP	US	17,875,260
4	Armageddon	BVI	US	16,506,605
5	Godzilla	Columbia Tristar	US	15,974,736
6	There's Something About Mary	20thC Fox	US	15,665,386
7	Sliding Doors	UIP	US/UK	12,434,715
8	Lock Stock and Two Smoking Barrels	Polygram	UK	11,520,069
9	Flubber	BVI	US	10,891,774
10	Lost In Space	Entertainment	US/UK	10,664,453
11	Deep Impact	UIP	US/UK	10,199,634
12	The Truman Show	UIP	US	9,929,680
13	Antz	UIP	US	9,672,036
14	As Good As It Gets	Columbia Tristar	US	9,613,181
15	The Wedding Singer	Entertainment	US	9,256,114
16	Mulan	BVI	US	8,902,296
17	The X-Files Movie	20thC Fox	US	8,426,489
18	Scream 2	BVI	US	8,280,725
19	Mouse Hunt	UIP	US	8,218,817
20	Good Will Hunting	UIP	US	7,806,051

Source: Screen International/Screen Finance/X25 Partnership

NOTEBOX

Titanic has in fact become one of the largest-grossing films of all time. Interestingly, it became what is known in the trade as an 'event' movie. This means that every now and then there appears at the cinema a film that everyone feels that they ought to go and see – in particular those members of the potential cinema audience who perhaps only visit the cinema once or twice a year. There are a couple of films in the list of top 20 films which the producers had hoped would also become 'event' movies (*Godzilla,* to name but one of them), but although they did respectable business they hardly set the box-office alight.

It is interesting to note how much more popular *Titanic* was than any other film released in the UK during 1998.

■ Attempt to explain the overwhelming popularity of this film. You should consider, where possible, the pre-publicity for the film, the advertising campaign that was used to sell the film in this country, and also the marketing devices that were used to maintain the interest of its potential audience.
■ Does the fact that it was produced and distributed by Twentieth Century Fox have any significance?

From being the most expensive film ever made, the film then went on to break box-office records worldwide.

■ Find out how well the film performed when it was finally released on video.
■ What were the spin-offs, if any?

THE CURRENT STATE OF THE BRITISH FILM INDUSTRY

When you go to the cinema at the start of your course, or indeed when you next watch a video, you will probably see a teaser – a sort mini-trailer for a film that is due in the cinemas some time in the future – usually a summer or Xmas blockbuster. It will be short, often being merely a short sequence from the film (which may well not have been edited properly yet anyway).

Once you have noted the teaser, you should then monitor as closely as possible the way in which the film is advertised, leading up to its release in this country. This will involve watching out for trailers, posters, articles in newspapers and magazines, features in programmes on TV or the radio about cinema, indeed even the websites of the company which is handling the film. A worksheet is provided below.

WORKSHEET

WORKSHEET FOR ANALYSING THE MARKETING OF FILMS

- How is the film first brought to our attention?
- Do you, at an early stage, feel that it is a film that you might want to see when it is finally released? Why?
- What sort of publicity does the pre-release activity engender?
- Is the film sold on its genre, stars or director?
- Does it remind you of anything else you have seen or have heard about?
- What other media texts are associated with the film – e.g. theme song released as a single, soundtrack album?
- Where are the posters and other publicity material found?
- Does the positioning of the publicity tell you anything about the likely audience for the film?

And, finally, when the film does get released:

- What sort of release pattern does it receive?
- Does it simply arrive at your local cinema or is there some kind of localised campaign to announce its arrival?
- Do local radio stations, record shops, etc. get involved in the marketing of the film?
- How much publicity is available in the newspapers both national and local?
- And how much of the pre-release activity is created simply by word of mouth – perhaps a free preview to an invited audience who will then tell all their friends about it (hopefully)?

As you will have noticed, the majority of the films screened in this country are American. The British film industry is enjoying a renaissance at the present time, helped by investment funds from TV companies and lottery money as well as the conventional production companies, such as Working Title. This accounts for most of the rest of the films which are exhibited on our cinema screens. The British film industry has never really been able to compete with America in terms of the finance available, and so this affects the types of films we are able to finance and make. The blockbuster film, laden with special effects and a multi-million dollar budget, remains predominantly an American concern. Yet, with varied success, the British film industry has increased output over the past 10 years. If the films produced are smaller in scale, yet the possibilities for large cinema audiences and profit are substantial.

Figure 49 Top 20 UK films at UK box office 1998

	Film	Distributor	Country of origin	Box Office Gross (£m)
1	Sliding Doors (15)	UIP	US/UK	12,434,715
2	Lock Stock and Two Smoking Barrels (18)	PolyGram	UK	11,520,069
3	Lost in Space (PG)	Entertainment	US/UK	10,664,453
4	Elizabeth (15)	PolyGram	UK	4,497,977
5	Up'n'Under (12)	Entertainment	UK	3,206,994
6	Paws (PG)	PolyGram	AU/UK	2,175,278
7	The Wings Of The Dove (15)	BVI	US/UK	2,142,932
8	The Big Lebowski (18)	PolyGram	US/UK	1,893,347
9	The General (15)	Warner Bros.	IE/UK	1,694,028
10	Land Girls (12)	Film Four	UK/FR	1,463,805
11	Martha – Meet Frank, Daniel and Laurence (15)	Film Four	UK	1,365,704
12	The Boxer (15)	UIP	US/UK/IE	1,343,129
13	Hard Rain (15)	PolyGram	US/UK/JP/DL/DK	1,077,387
14	Still Crazy (15)	Columbia TriStar	UK/US	896,325
15	Dancing at Lughnasa (PG)	Film Four	UK/US/IE	801,009
16	My Name Is Joe (15)	Film Four	UK/DL/FR/IT/ES	785,594
17	Girls Night (15)	Granada	UK/US	717,673
18	Divorcing Jack (15)	Mosaic	UK/FR	469,961
19	Velvet Goldmine (18)	Film Four	UK/US	454,263
20	Love And Death On Long Island (15)	Pathé	UK/CA	394,372

Source: Screen Finance/X25 Partnership/EDI

MEDIA STUDIES: THE ESSENTIAL INTRODUCTION

Referring to Figure 49, prepare an analysis of the top 20 grossing UK films of 1998 in the UK. Answering the following questions should help you:

■   What, if anything, do the films in the top 20 have in common?
■   What type of audience do you think each one was aimed at? How would you support your assumption?
■   What certificate was each film given?
■   How many of the top 20 films are solely British in origin?
■   How many films are co-productions? Companies from which other countries are involved in co-productions of British films?
■   Are there any films in the list that surprise you by being there?
■   Were there any other UK films released in 1998 that you expected to see in this list?
■   Did you see most of these films?
■   If so, did you see them at the cinema, on video or on TV? If not, it would be interesting to explain why you didn't.

A study of the box office gross is also of interest. Only the top three UK films managed to get into the list of top 20 films, and two of these are co-productions, made jointly with US companies. Equally, as you get to the lower reaches of the list, it is surprising to see how little money these films seem to make. The bottom seven films in the list make less than £1 million each at the box office in the UK. But what must be borne in mind is that their money-making potential does not end there – what follows after cinema exhibition is a video release, and then TV.

So far we have really only looked at mainstream popular cinema.

Try to obtain a listings magazine for your area, something like *Time Out* in London. If your area does not possess a listings magazine, then the Saturday edition of most national broadsheet newspapers will supply the information that you need.

Look closely at the cinema listings. Obviously the vast majority of the cinemas are all owned by one of the major cinema chains – UCI, Warner Village, UGC, Odeon, ABC. However, there will be a few cinemas in your area which are not owned by one of the major cinema chains.

Examine the information you are given about the films they are showing – preferably over a period of about one month. You will probably find that these cinemas break down into two types:

1   those that show very much the same as the other major cinema chains in your area
2   those that show minority interest and foreign language films.

FOREIGN FILMS

It is important to recognise that all cinema-goers are not necessarily *only* interested in mainstream Hollywood/UK cinema – indeed there are those who are actually quite uninterested in mainstream product but are keen to see independent films and those of a more non-populist nature from the rest of Europe, Asia, etc. Luckily for them, there are still some cinemas which cater for this audience, though it has to be pointed out that many of the so-called art-house cinemas are finding it difficult to stay open at present. There are a number of factors which contribute to this:

1   Many foreign films are in fact very expensive to distribute and exhibit, making it very difficult for a small independent cinema to make a profit from a film which might not attract a sufficiently large audience.
2   The multiplex cinemas have made life very difficult for the smaller cinemas, which find it hard to compete with the comfort and facilities available at such modern cinemas.
3   Many of the 15 to 25-year-old audience are simply not aware that such art-house cinemas (and films) exist and show reluctance to experiment with the unknown.
4   Advertising costs for small-scale films are relatively expensive.
5   Many of the films shown by such cinemas appear much more quickly on dedicated film channels on cable and satellite TV or indeed on video.

Many of these cinemas now survive by occasionally showing mainstream popular movies every once in a while. This boosts their profits and attracts an audience who might be unfamiliar with the cinema, but who might enjoy the experience and consequently come again.

ACTIVITY

- Suggest other ways for small art-house cinemas to stabilise and then increase their audiences over a sustained period of time.
- Try programming 6 months' worth of film which you think might generate enough interest in an audience who are otherwise unfamiliar with your cinema.
- Suggest a variety of advertising and marketing techniques which would draw attention to your cinema.

What is undeniable is that, at the moment, the cinema industry in this country is riding on the crest of a wave. However, it is also a fact that audiences in the USA are falling, which is causing some concern amongst the majors. Whether this is a trend that will be replicated here remains to be seen. But multiplexes continue to be built (the new 30-screen Warner Village multiplex in Birmingham is a case in point), so confidence is still apparently high.

▼ CASE STUDY 1: NEWS

In this section we:

- consider the nature of news and its sources

- look at the role of news in the output of television, radio and print media, and the competition that exists between and within these media forms

- consider issues of representation in the news and examine what powers exist to control and regulate news output

- look at how technology influences news output and examine the future of current news output in light of new media technologies.

WHAT IS NEWS?

News is information about contemporary events. It informs us about what is going on in the world at large. In the media it is an important commodity as it is a way of attracting an audience of people keen to be informed about the events taking place in the world in which they live.

News, it can be argued, also performs the important function of helping people make sense of the world they live in. Not only do the media tell people what is going on, they also seek to interpret these events in such a way that they make sense to people. As we will see, this gives media producers an important power in relation to the audience. Not only the selection of events that are reported but also the way in which these events are presented can have a powerful impact on the attitudes of both individuals and of society as a whole.

NOTEBOX

On 23 July 2000, the front page of the *News of the World* alleged under the headline NAMED SHAMED that there were 110,000 child sex offenders in Britain, one for each square mile. Alongside a photograph of the recently murdered schoolgirl, Sarah Payne, the paper stated that the police monitoring of 'these perverts' was inadequate and announced it was revealing 'WHO they are and WHERE they are . . . starting today'.

News also has an important regulating function in the lives of an audience. News is presented by the media at regular intervals. News bulletins on the radio are hourly, national newspapers are published each morning, and television news on the terrestrial channels is broadcast at specific established time slots. When unexpected and 'important' news events occur, these may disrupt and replace existing broadcasting schedules in order to focus exclusively on an important event and the world reaction to it. The death of Diana, Princess of Wales in a car crash in Paris in 1997 is an example of the media focusing almost exclusively on a single event. As we have seen, it led commentators to ask how far the media were reporting a spontaneous outpouring of national grief and how far the saturation coverage by the media had engineered this response.

This regularity of news dissemination, occupying prime-time TV slots, and the idea that other media events can be displaced by it reinforce to us the important role of news in the media. The very nature of the way in which it is used by the media signifies that we, the audience, must be aware of its importance and take it seriously.

ACTIVITY . . .

Consider the role of television news in the evening television schedules.

■   Why in the past have the major terrestrial channels avoided showing the news at the same time as each other?
■   Why are the two major terrestrials now competing for the same time slot?
■   How might an audience be influenced by news bulletins in planning an evening of family viewing?
■   What sort of events do you think are considered important enough for broadcasting schedules to be disrupted to report them? Suggest two or three examples of such events.

NOTEBOX . . .

If you consider television news, there are a number of other prompts that suggest the news is important and has to be taken seriously. Consider, for example, the type of music that introduces news bulletins, the nature and status of news readers and the way in which the studio has been designed. Notice also the way in which news readers use phrases like 'that's the way it is' to conclude the news bulletin, suggesting that the representation of the world we have been shown is the only way in which it can be seen.

SOURCES OF NEWS

Part of the mythology that surrounds the news is that news is always unexpected. In many ways the media are happy to nurture this myth by implying that the job of a reporter is to rush to the scene of an event that has just happened and find out the facts to tell the audience. On occasions this may be the case; events do happen without warning. Such incidents as accidents on the roads, railways or at airports cannot be predicted. Similarly, natural disasters such as floods or earthquakes often happen with little warning.

The vast majority of items that are reported as news, however, are predictable events that the news media know about in advance. This enables them to ensure that a journalist is in place ready to cover an event in advance of its happening. A royal visit is a good example of such an event. Generally royal visits, for example to open a new public building, are planned many months in advance. The news media have prior warning and put the visit into their diary of upcoming news events. In some sectors of the industry, reporters call such events 'diary jobs'. There is obviously plenty of opportunity for pre-planning the news coverage of such events. Television cameras can be positioned ready to ensure the optimum visual advantage is obtained. In the same way press photographers can ensure they are well placed to get a photograph of the action.

Indeed, some events are so well prepared for in advance that they even become stage-managed. The major political parties ensure that the news media have access to their annual conferences to ensure that the messages given to the party faithful who attend the conferences also reach the wider electorate in the country as a whole. In political terms, a party may go to some lengths to ensure that positive aspects of its policies are reported in detail, while unpopular policies or political gaffes are given much less prominent coverage. Ensuring that coverage is of the type the party wants is the job of the spin doctors, who are basically public relations (PR) officers whose job is to ensure a positive public image.

PR and spin are not limited to politics. Increasingly, commercial organisations and even individuals such as celebrities are employing people to ensure that a positive image of them is promoted in the media. The PR guru Max Clifford, for example, looks after the media profile of a number of major and minor celebrities and openly admits to manufacturing stories that will gain publicity for his clients.

ACTIVITY . . .

Examine an edition of a newspaper or news bulletin on the radio or television. Make a note of each story and decide whether the news media had advanced warning of the story or whether it happened unexpectedly. Explain how you are able to differentiate.

A number of devices are used by the PR industry to ensure that organisations and individuals get their point across to the media. The most popular and probably the most economical is the press release. Press releases are sheets of information, often written in the form of a news story, that are sent to news media. They usually give details of newsworthy events, such as the launch of a new campaign, often with either a photograph or the opportunity for the press to take a picture. A well-written press release can often be used with little rewriting by a journalist, especially in a small local newspaper.

Most large organisations provide access to their press releases through their websites. It is a useful exercise to visit a site such as Virgin to look at the press releases it has issued to publicise the activities of the organisation to the media.

Another weapon in the armoury of the PR office is the news conference. News conferences are often called by organisations such as the police when they want to publicise a major criminal investigation. Often news conference are screened directly on to television news bulletins with TV, print and radio journalists all seen being briefed and asking questions. In a similar way, the lobby system in Parliament is used by reporters to receive briefings about the activities of different government departments. The press secretaries of ministers have become powerful figures in the manipulation of the news media, especially the Prime Minister's own press secretary, Alistair Campbell.

Manipulating and even setting the news agenda in this way is called news management. For many people who rely on public recognition for their success, keeping a high media profile is important. In fact, it has been argued that there is no such thing as bad publicity. Even negative stories in the press are a way of keeping celebrities in the public eye, even if this involves revealing intimate details of their private lives.

NEWS AS A COMMODITY

Every day we need news, and the news media need to supply us with it. News, however, has to fit into packages, the size of which is usually predetermined. News bulletins run for a fixed length of time, and newspapers generally have a similar number of pages each day. Obviously the amount of news available is likely to vary from day to day. Some days there will be more news than can be used, and items may have to be discarded. On other days, events that might not normally warrant much attention will be reported prominently to make up for the absence of news.

Linking food with sex may well have been done before, but never in such an original, witty, intelligent and downright *erotic* way.

`The overriding point is that eating is both pleasurable and painful, boring and stimulating, a luxury and a necessity.'

Elspeth Probyn, in her deliciously-titled **Carnal Appetites**, has written a stunning work that deserved as wide a readership as Jamie Oliver's latest offering. In entering Probyn's world, the reader is instantly captivated by her sharp prose and devastating scholarship - she draws one in, offering a board laden with fine fare. From musing over the way breakfast for her has changed (from coffee'n' fags to the dutiful imbibing of `fortified' cereals whose packaging gushs with the promise of health): `It's all a bit much first thing in the morning when the promise of long life seems like a threat', to queering the Two Fat Ladies, Probyn interrogates the connections between food and sex, between sensuousness and satiation.

`I had never quite honestly thought of double-peeling broad beans but it soon becomes addictive: popping alien green little beans from their blanched coats stills time while the mind wanders to other revealing acts of exposure.'

In an exploration into eating and food, Probyn investigates the hitherto hidden areas of identity politics, shame and disgust: `From the shadows of shame, the politics of pride has extended these efforts to unequivocally posit that there is nothing to be ashamed of if your body is gay, black, disabled, fat or old.' Controversially she suggests the end-point of representation politics *as a place where there is no place for a politic.*

`On the one hand, the disgusting is pushed underground as it were – it is still there but cannot be spoken. And on the other, the chances of shame being transferred to the interlocutor are slight...In this model it seems inevitable that shame will be displaced into guilt.'

Probyn asks whether eating food commonly held to be disgusting takes one onto another plane, a place where the complex dance between desire, disgust, shame and bodies continues. Having herself partaken (out of `ingrained politeness') of delicacies as wondrous as sheep's eyeballs and `the wonders of a cheese buried until it is ripe and ready with cheese-fed larvae that quiver slightly upon the tongue', Probyn is more than adequately armed for such a questioning.

From Divine's infamous shit-eating grin to the sexing of food, from rare steaks cosseted in crotches to the economics of cannibalism, Probyn offers a generous helping of theory slathered with lashings of insight and wit!

Carnal Appetites
FoodSexIdentities
Elspeth Probyn

Published by Routledge, September 2000: 234x156: 176pp
Hb: 0-415-22304-0: £45.00 Pb: 0-415-22305-9: £12.99

For further information or to interview Professor Probyn, please contact Áine Duffy on 020 7842 2117

***Figure 50** Example of a press release for a Routledge book*

Figure 51 Richard Branson publicity photo

Weekends and holidays are times when limited amounts of news are available. This is due in part to the fact that such sources of news as Parliament and the law courts are not sitting or people are away on holiday. In fact, the summer holiday is known in news circles as 'the silly season', as the lack of more serious news often permits the reporting of trivial or silly stories.

Consider the output of news on a particular day.

■ How would you rate it as a 'news day'?
■ Were there lots of stories available or a limited number?
■ What evidence do you have for your answer?

One of the issues prompted by the need to decide on the content of newspapers and news bulletins is the idea of what constitutes news. Why are some events considered more important than others? The idea of news values is important here. News values not only determine whether a story is to be included, they also determine how high up the list of items it comes, or what position it occupies in a newspaper.

In a newspaper the most important, or lead, story makes front-page headlines. In TV and radio bulletins the most important story is given priority by being first in the running order. Compare two newspapers and two news bulletins for the same day.

■ Do they all give priority to the same story or do some favour one story rather than another?
■ What reasons can you think of for different stories being prioritised by different news media?

In 1973 Galtung and Ruge undertook a study of news stories. They identified that certain items of news are more likely to be reported than other items and, similarly, some items of news are likely to be given more prominence than others. A full list of factors they identify can be found in *Understanding News* (Hartley 1982), in a chapter in which the selection and construction of news are given detailed consideration.

It is useful to look at some key factors that can determine if an event is considered newsworthy. Events that take place close to home or are culturally relevant are more likely to be reported than events that happen in remote parts of the world (Galtung and Ruge call this 'meaningfulness'). A train crash involving a few injuries that happens in this country may well be given more prominent coverage than a disaster involving injury or even death to many hundreds of people in Asia, for example. Similarly, events that happen to important people will be reported in much greater detail than events that occur in the lives of ordinary people. For example, a story about a cabinet minister caught speeding will be given much greater prominence than a story about a media student (unless he or she is a close relative of a cabinet minister).

Another important factor that determines whether a story is reported or not is the element of surprise or unexpectedness it contains. Consider a news bulletin and decide which stories have been included because of the element of surprise that they contain.

Many of the key decisions about what gets reported relate to the way in which the news-gathering operation is organised and to the professional working practices of workers employed in this branch of the media industries. A key figure in the news-gathering operation is the news editor. News editors are common to both print and broadcast media. Their function is to take charge of the news desk and to act as a filter or gatekeeper in determining which stories will be reported. They have to decide, for example, which diary jobs to despatch reporters (and film crews or photographers) to cover. They also decide which of the many hundreds of press releases which the organisation receives is worthy of being used or followed up. Pictures and stories from freelances and news agencies will also be vying for attention. A news editor needs to have a good news sense to decide how best to use the resources at his or her disposal.

Look at an early evening news bulletin on either BBC or ITV. Consider what thinking may have been behind the decision to cover different stories. Most reporters and film crews are based in London. Do you think this is reflected in the coverage of events in the bulletin you looked at?

In making the decision about what stories to cover, the news editor will need to employ his or her own professional judgement and experience. However, there will be other factors and pressures that will influence the decision that is made. These will include an awareness of what competitors might be doing. It will not look good if a story given extensive coverage in one newspaper or one news bulletin is wholly omitted by another. Similarly there may be pressures from a newspaper proprietor either to include or omit a particular item for political, business or even personal reasons.

Where a newspaper has obtained a particular story that no other paper has reported, this is labelled with the tag 'exclusive'. In order to protect an exclusive story, a newspaper may omit it from the very early edition, in order to prevent rivals seeing and using it in their later editions.

The desire for an exclusive is just one example of the competition that exists between news media. On television, for example, news bulletins play a key role in the scheduling of prime-time evening viewing. The fact that news bulletins have regular slots means that they act as important regulating factors in establishing viewing patterns. Audiences tuning in to an early evening news bulletin may well continue to watch a particular channel. Similarly, the main evening news fulfils an important function in dividing the evening between family viewing and more adult viewing possible after the watershed.

It has been argued that this function of news in terms of scheduling means that there is pressure on producers of news programmes to make them entertaining so as to attract and retain viewers. This has led to charges that the presentation of news has been 'dumbed down' to make it appeal to as wide an audience as possible. Indeed it has been suggested that television news has become increasingly more 'tabloid', with shorter news items on Channel 5, for example, appealing to a youth audience supposedly with a limited attention span.

The word 'tabloid' comes from the print news media and refers to the downmarket newspapers such as the *Sun*, the *Mirror* and the *Star*.

These papers are also referred to as the 'red top' newspapers owing to the colour of their mastheads, where the title of the newspaper is displayed. This distinguishes them from other newspapers with a tabloid shape, such as the *Daily Mail* and *Daily Express* which are considered to appeal to a more sophisticated readership.

The red-top newspapers are identifiable by a number of features:

■   They are generally easy to read and require a short attention span featuring lots of short stories with small amounts of text.

■   They rely heavily on pictures and illustration to support the text.

■   The stories they contain tend to be trivial and rely heavily on information about celebrities.

■   They tend to sensationalise news stories by exaggerating what has taken place.

■   They pander to populist opinion, for example by encouraging xenophobic attitudes to foreign countries and their peoples.

■   They are responsible for the creation of moral panics, for example by stirring up public outrage over such issues as paedophiles.

TABLOID   A compact newspaper, half the size of a broadsheet, designed to appeal to a mass audience. Tabloids, particularly at the lower end of the market, are associated with sensationalising trivial events rather than with comprehensive coverage of national and international news.

KEY TERM

ACTIVITY

Look in detail at one tabloid newspaper.

■   How far do you think the above qualities are evident in the paper? Find examples that either do or do not support each of the above assertions.

■   How far do you think it is true to say that television news bulletins exhibit similar qualities?

■   Do any radio stations have bulletins that can be called tabloid?

Figure 52

It is also interesting to note that competition exists not only within media forms but also between media forms. Television, radio and print media all compete to supply audiences with the commodity of news. This competition is further intensified by the arrival of other means of delivering news, such as the Internet.

A key quality of news is that it is contemporaneous. This means that it is reported soon after it has happened. Clearly, for television and radio, which have several bulletins a day, it is far easier to be contemporaneous than a newspaper which tends to be limited to a single daily edition. If news is important enough, broadcast media can interrupt existing programmes to bring it to the audience. Print media cannot currently compete with this, although as many newspapers develop their own websites they now have an electronic means of their own to ensure audiences are up to date with the latest or 'breaking news'.

It is interesting to consider how newspapers have responded to the challenge of competing with broadcast and electronic media for audiences for the news. Had they simply been content to report what had been broadcasted on television the day before, their sales would have declined sharply. Instead, newspapers seek to engage their audiences with other strategies in order to ensure that sales remain buoyant.

KEY TERM

BROADSHEET A large rectangular newspaper, such as the *Daily Telegraph* or *The Times*. Broadsheets are usually associated with serious journalism, reporting important events at home and abroad. They are targeted at an upmarket, professional readership.

ACTIVITY...

Outline what content other than news you are likely to find in a national newspaper. Consider both broadsheet and tabloid newspapers. What items do they have in common? What are the major differences?

News is often categorised into different types of story. What we normally think of as 'news' is probably more accurately called 'hard news'.

KEY TERM

HARD NEWS This is news that is important and happening at the time it is reported. A rescue attempt on a cross-Channel ferry, or the death of an important national figure, or a rise in mortgage interest rates could all be classified as hard news.

Human interest stories are another popular type of news story. It can be argued that most stories that are reported involve people and therefore have an element of human interest. A human interest story is one that has a particular appeal because of our interest in other people and the way in which they live their lives. Stories about the adventures of lottery winners are a good example of a human interest story. Much of the appeal of these stories is that the audience may like to imagine how they might behave in a similar situation.

KEY TERM

BREAKING NEWS A news story, the details of which are unfolding as the news is being reported.

The arrival of 24-hour news broadcasting in the form of Sky News and BBC News 24 has also made 'breaking news' an important phenomenon. With a news channel on the air 24 hours a day, there are likely to be many instances of this, and it is interesting to watch a news story develop as more details become available to reporters.

Many types of news form a category in their own right. Sports, political or business news are typical examples. These categories usually have their own section in a newspaper or news bulletin. Similarly, broadsheet newspapers often break news down into sections according to its geographical location: home news, European news, or world news, for example.

ACTIVITY

Why do you think that sports news occupies a position at the back of both newspapers and news bulletins? What impact do you think the positioning of sports news in this way has on the audience consuming the text?

KEY TERM

FEATURE In newspapers, this is generally an article that concerns itself with a topical issue, whilst not having any hard news content.

Newspapers also make use of their format to include features as part of their news content. Features often provide the public with the opportunity to read in greater depth about the background to a topical news event or issue.

ANATOMY OF A NEWS STORY

Like all media texts, news stories are invariably constructed according to established conventions. These vary between media forms, but it is interesting to note that certain conventions exist in all the media. You may find it useful to look back at the section on Narrative, where we suggested that narrative was an equally important aspect of non-fiction texts as of fictional ones.

A news story relies on a narrator controlling the flow of information to the audience in much the same way as in a fictional narrative. Most news stories begin with a hook designed to grab the attention of the audience and make them want to know more about what is to follow. Headlines are used in both print and broadcast media to do just this. They create an enigma which the audience is required to resolve by consuming the information that the remainder of the text will provide. A good headline will provide just enough information to attract an audience but leave them wanting more information, e.g. POP STAR IN DRUGS SCANDAL.

The narrative conventions of news reporting require a hierarchical structure to the story itself. By this we mean that the most important point generally comes first. The first paragraph (or intro) by convention offers the most important piece of information. Indeed, some journalists would argue that the first paragraph should sum up what the story is about and that subsequent paragraphs exist simply to elaborate on this information. A good intro, therefore, might almost be considered a complete news item in its own right. In a print news item, the intro is often given visual priority by the use of a larger point size, or bold text, or both.

Another quality that is common to news items across media forms is the way in which information is broken down into manageable portions. In a print news story, the paragraphing is generally much shorter than in an academic essay, for example. This means that the reader is able to digest the information easily as it is provided in manageable portions.

SOUNDBITE A snappy and memorable quotation that can be easily assimilated into a broadcast news story.

NOTEBOX

Notice the use of quotations in newspaper stories and how these are set out. Each newspaper has its own style book that provide journalists with a list of rules about what is acceptable in terms of how stories are written. Quotations are especially important to news stories because they both provide an authentic voice that supports what the story is saying and at the same time provide an element of human interest. On radio and television, interviews are used as a means of providing quotes to support the story.

The importance of good quotes is clear from the concept of the soundbite. Politicians are keen to use effective soundbites in their speeches as they know that the news media will want to include these in their reports. Tony Blair's 'education, education, education' soundbite in one of his election speeches is a good example.

Pictures are an important aspect of news stories, except in the medium of radio, of course. A good picture can often mean that a news story may well have far more prominent coverage than a similar story with no pictures. This is especially true with television news, where often stories that do not have good visual support are placed in a much lower place in the running order.

Watch a television news bulletin and consider its use of images.

■ How far do you think the availability of visuals has influenced the running order of the items?

■ Do you think any stories would have been given greater prominence if there had been better visual support?

OR

The radio equivalent of pictures is called actuality and consists of sound recordings of events taking place. Consider how important to a radio news bulletin is this use of actuality.

KEY TERM

ACTUALITY Recordings of images and sounds of events made on location as they actually happen for inclusion in news reports or documentaries.

An important issue in the study of news coverage is the extent to which the news media give us an impartial view of the events they report. For many people, television and radio news are seen as being objective media. This may be due in part to the requirement in the BBC and IBA charters, which define the public service responsibilities of television broadcasters to maintain balance and impartiality. The idea of balance implies that both sides of an argument should be represented. So in the reporting of a parliamentary debate, for example, both the government's view and that of the opposition should be included. Indeed, this notion of debate is central to the way in which broadcast media report most issues that involve controversy. Similarly, the media should not be seen to favour one particular viewpoint, especially in terms of the major political parties.

No such requirement to maintain neutrality in the coverage of political events exists for the press. The *Sun* newspaper, for example, openly instructs its readers how to vote in general elections. In fact, the support of Rupert Murdoch's News International papers was seen as essential by the Labour party if they were to win the general election in 1997. Famously, at the previous election, Neil Kinnock's Labour party lost partly on the strength of a damning headline in the *Sun*, suggesting that, if Labour won, the last person to leave the country should turn out the lights. A newspaper like the *Daily Mail* makes little secret of its support for the Conservative party. However, the change in the political landscape, with the Labour party increasingly representing the interests of the centre ground of British politics, has meant a good deal of realignment of traditional allegiances. In consequence it is dangerous to offer a simplistic view of a Tory press opposed to everything a Labour government may seek to do.

ACTIVITY

Look at two tabloids and two broadsheets.

- Can you determine which political parties these papers support?
- Who owns each newspaper? Do they own any other newspaper?
- Look at a recent issue of each paper. Can you find any particular stories relating to the main British political parties or political figures which you think reveal political bias?
- Examine closely the choice of vocabulary and note any particular words or adjectives that are positive/approving and any that are negative/pejorative.

NOTEBOX

An organisation that has done a lot of research into the concept of bias in news reporting is the Glasgow Media Group. In 1976 they published *Bad News*, which suggested that the reporting of such issues as industrial relations was not unbiased. They argued that such reporting very much favoured the employers rather than the striking workers. They published another study in 1980, entitled *More Bad News*, which further supported this view.

REGULATION AND CONTROL

As we have seen, the news media are a powerful way of disseminating information. Television news is for a large proportion of the population the main way they find out what is going on in the world. One in four of the population looks at a copy of the *Sun* newspaper daily. Clearly the news media can exert a considerable influence over the way in which people view the world and the opinions that they hold. It follows, therefore, that there needs to be some accountability or even control over what is published or broadcast. Balanced with this need, however, is the importance of media free from government control, which are able to play a key role in the democratic process. At times, it may seem that these two requirements are difficult to reconcile.

It is important to realise that there are restrictions and controls over what the news media can report. Some of these are enforced by law and are called legal or statutory constraints; others are voluntary constraints set up by the industry itself. The latter is an example of what is known as self-regulation.

One important form of statutory control is the law of libel. Libel covers any form of media that can be considered permanent, for example print, television or radio, as opposed to a transitory medium like the unrecorded spoken voice. If anyone publishes information that can be considered to be untrue and damaging to the reputation of another person, then that person can take out an action for libel. One of the main defences in a libel action is to demonstrate that the information stated is in fact true. The onus, however, is on the defence to prove this.

Unfortunately for most people, taking a libel action against another individual is too costly even to contemplate. Doing so for most people against a large and powerful media institution would be financial suicide. The reason for this is that in a libel case the losing side is usually required to pay the costs of both parties to the action. With legal costs easily running into many thousands of pounds, a libel action cannot be readily contemplated by any but the wealthiest.

NOTEBOX

Elton John v. the *Sun*

There have been many famous libel actions over the years. Probably one of the best known was when the singer Elton John took out an action against the *Sun* newspaper, which made a series of allegations about his personal life. Elton John was eventually awarded damages of £1 million and received a front-page apology in the newspaper. The *Sun* printed front-page allegations on 25 February 1987 which smeared the character of Elton John. When challenged by Elton John's lawyers for a retraction and an apology, the paper doubled the pressure with a headline on 27 February which said 'You're a liar, Elton'. Once it was proved that the stories printed were uncorroborated allegations contributed by a rent-boy paid by the *Sun*, and who told the *Independent Magazine* 'I would give the *Sun* a line and they would print it up. It was a manufactured story', the newspaper was forced to pay damages. Their printed apology was the headline: 'Sorry Elton'. (Source: Hansard)

Fortunately for the less affluent, it may not always be necessary to have recourse to law in order to obtain justice from the news media. A good example of the regulation of the media is the Press Complaints Commission. The PCC was set up in 1991, formed on the basis of the old Press Council. It was the result of an enquiry into the press conducted by Sir David Calcutt. The newspaper industry was required to set up the Commission, the function of which is to deal with complaints by members of the public into what is published in newspapers and the conduct of journalists. The PCC published a code of conduct which has been subsequently updated and consists of 16 points. Any complaint made to the Commission must relate to one of the points in this code of conduct.

Complaints made to the Commission are investigated, where appropriate, by the 16 members of the PCC. These members are both representatives of the newspaper industry

MEDIA STUDIES: THE ESSENTIAL INTRODUCTION

and members of the public. The members of the Commission issue an adjudication and, if they feel that a newspaper is at fault, they can order the publication of the adjudication in the newspaper.

What they cannot do is to hand out any other kind of punishment, such as a fine, to the offending publication. In consequence, the PCC has been described as a toothless tiger that does little more than pander to the interests of the newspaper industry. Many people argue that proper controls are needed if the newspaper industry is to behave responsibly. Arguments have been put forward, for example, for a privacy law that would protect people from unwanted media intrusion. This would prevent members of the Paparazzi stalking people in order to obtain photographs without their consent. Another legal change that has been mooted is the introduction of a law giving people the right to reply when they have been attacked in a newspaper. Such a law would confer on people an opportunity to reply to comments and criticisms made against them in the press.

Governments, however, are understandably reluctant to curb the freedom of the press by introducing such legislation. Antagonising the press unnecessarily may not be in their best interests. Many would argue that, despite its inadequacies, self-regulation may be the most effective system to ensure a press which, whilst free to pursue matters of public interest, will behave ethically and responsibly towards the public.

ACTIVITY . . .

How far do you feel there are arguments for regulating the media's coverage of news? For example, do you think that celebrities, such as pop stars, football players or members of the royal family have a right to prevent their photograph being taken when they are engaged in private activities, such as eating out or going to clubs?

NOTEBOX . . .

All of the bodies responsible for media regulation have their own websites, a list of which is given in the Resources section at the end of this book. It is useful to visit these sites, not only for background information, but also to look at some of the adjudications, or decisions they have made about issues raised by the public.

An organisation called the Campaign for Press and Broadcasting Freedom (CPBF) also has some useful information about topics relating to media freedom and regulation, as well as issues of ownership and control. They have a useful website (details in the Resources section) and also publish a newsletter (also available online), called Free Press, which contains news and comment on media-related issues.

CODE OF PRACTICE

Ratified by the Press Complaints Commission – 1 December 1999

All members of the press have a duty to maintain the highest professional standards. This code sets the benchmarks for those standards. It both protects the rights of the individual and upholds the public's right to know.

The code is the cornerstone of the system of self-regulation to which the industry has made a binding commitment. Editors and publishers must ensure that the code is observed rigorously not only by their staff but also by anyone who contributes to their publications.

It is essential to the workings of an agreed code that it be honoured not only to the letter but in the full spirit. The code should not be interpreted so narrowly as to compromise its commitment to respect the rights of the individual, nor so broadly that it prevents publication in the public interest.

It is the responsibility of editors to co-operate with the PCC as swiftly as possible in the resolution of the complaints.

Any publication which is criticised by the PCC under one of the following clauses must print the adjudication which follows in full and with due prominence.

The Public Interest

1. The public interest includes:
   i)   Detecting or exposing crime or a serious misdemeanour
   ii) Protecting public health and safety
   iii) Preventing the public from being misled by some statement or action of an individual or organisation
2. In any case where the public interest is invoked, the Press Complaints Commission will require a full explanation by the editor demonstrating how the public interest was served.
3. There is a public interest in freedom of expression itself. The Commission will therefore have regard to the extent to which material has, or is about to, become available to the public.
4. In cases involving children editors must demonstrate an exceptional public interest to over-ride the normally paramount interest of the child. . . .

1. Accuracy
   i)   Newspapers and periodicals should take care not to publish inaccurate, misleading or distorted material including pictures.
   ii) Whenever it is recognised that a significant inaccuracy, misleading statement or distorted report has been published, it should be corrected promptly and with due prominence
   iii) An apology must be published whenever appropriate.
   iv) Newspapers, whilst free to be partisan, must distinguish clearly between comment, conjecture and fact
   v)   A newspaper or periodical must report fairly and accurately the outcome of an action for defamation to which it has been a party.

(Press Complaints Commission 1999)

Other categories of the code of practice include:

Opportunity to reply	Reporting of crime
Privacy	Misrepresentation
Harassment	Victims of sexual assault
Intrusion into grief or shock	Discrimination
Children	Financial journalism
Children in sex cases	Confidential sources
Listening devices	Payment for articles
Hospitals	

The full text of the code can be found at www.pcc.org.uk

Figure 53

THE FUTURE OF NEWS

In recent years the way in which news is delivered to audiences has undergone considerable change. We now have dedicated 24-hour news channels, making television news available on tap for audiences. No longer do we have to wait for a news bulletin broadcast at a specific time to catch up with the day's events. The advent of Channel 5 with its youth-oriented programming has had an impact on the way in which news is presented to us, with a much more informal and relaxed approach to presentation.

Perhaps one of the most fundamental changes that is taking place, however, concerns the influence of technology on the way in which we access information. As we noted in the Introduction, society is now very much divided between groups of people who are information-rich and those who do not have ready access to information technology. One of the basic divides is access to the Internet. People who are able to access the Internet not only have news available to them on demand, but are also able to choose the news that they want to consume. This can be achieved in several ways, including the simple custom-ising of a browser to provide specific categories of news, for example, sport, financial, or showbiz. Similarly, it is possible to obtain news direct from the source by accessing celebrity websites to find information about what the stars are up to. Footballers involved in transfers have taken to breaking the news on their own personal websites. By setting up their own websites, celebrities seek to control the way news about them is presented.

As technology develops or converges so that access to the Internet is readily available through television sets, so the way in which we will consume news is likely to develop further. It looks certain that the mass audience for news, along with the mass audience for such programmes as soaps, is set to decline. In its place we may well see the development of individualised and perhaps even interactive sites in which people are able to call up the news that they want to hear and avoid the news that they don't. One of the categories that Galtung and Ruge suggested for news values was negativity, i.e. the idea that bad news is good news. With the growth of customised news media, it may well be that many people will wish to screen from their lives any suggestion of the bad things that happen in the world. On digital satellite television, the Sky News service already allows viewers to gain access to 'news on demand', a sub-menu that provides the audience with the opportunity to tune in to a range of live events, such as conferences or major 'happening' news stories.

FURTHER WORK . . .

1   Collect press stories about a celebrity who has been negatively reported in the tabloids. Create the mock-up of a website for that celebrity which would present a more positive representation.

2   What information is provided by the British press other than news? Provide examples from a range of newspapers.

3   How far is it fair to say that most newspapers no longer consistently support either of the two main political parties?

VIDEO REPORTS

📹	**News**	**Play**
📹	**Sport**	**Play**
📹	**Entertainment**	**Play**

Need help playing video?

BREAKING NEWS: *Two north London sisters have been jailed for a total of 18 years for kicking to death an 87-year-old woman at her home.* Full story

UK at a glance

Straw's brother convicted of molesting 16-year-old
Sisters jailed for 18 years after kicking OAP to death
French-style fuel protests spread across Britain
Body undiscovered for 12 hours in hospital toilet
Pet food poultry sold for human consumption
Hit films 'glamorise gangsters'
Latest UK stories

Sign up for e-mail alerts on...

Nevada bus crash
Fuel prices
Omagh bombing inquest
Big Brother
Olympics latest
Funny old world
Amazing science

ALERTS BY E-MAIL:

● First-time users
● News
● Entertainment
● Business
● Leisure
● Sport
● Olympics
● Politics
● Science and technology

 Weather
Ananova brings you the
details for your
area. **more**

NEWS CHOICE:

● Entertainment
● Funny old world
● Business
● Health
● Technology
● The internet
● The papers

Figure 53 *Example of virtual news on demand – Ananova.com*

4   In what ways has the presentation of television news changed in recent years? How do you account for such changes?

5   'Radio news is just television news without pictures.' Discuss with reference to the news output of at least two radio stations.

6   What do you understand by the term 'dumbing down'? Is this an accurate description of recent developments in television news coverage?

7   'The tabloid press are concerned only with sensationalism at the expense of reporting real news.' How far do you agree with this statement?

8   Most newspapers, both national and local, now have their own website. (For examples see the Resources section.) By carefully comparing an edition of a newspaper with the website, consider the relationship between the two. Consider what advantages each might have for:

■ the newspaper industry
■ the audience.

Do you think that one day websites will replace newsprint?

FURTHER READING

Allen, S. (2000) *News Culture*, Open University Press.

Hartley, J. (1982) *Understanding News*, Routledge.

Keeble, R. (1998) *The Newspapers Handbook*, 2nd edn, Routledge.

Schlesinger, P. (1987) *Putting Reality Together – BBC News*, Methuen.

Selby, K. and Cowdery, R. (1995) *How to Study Television*, Macmillan.

▼   CASE STUDY 2: ADVERTISING

In this section we look at:

- the historical context of advertising
- the process of advertising
- audience targeting, products and brands
- regulation and sponsorship
- the effects of advertising.

INTRODUCTION

In 1997 over £13 billion was spent in Britain on advertising, either on buying 'space' to show the advertisements or on their production. This money not only financed a wide range of media texts (magazines, radio and television, websites, newspapers, etc.) but it also meant that a vast amount of advertisements were made and then seen by people in Britain. Advertising is therefore an important part of the media, not only in terms of what it finances and the effect that this may have on the content of other media products but also in its own right in terms of the advertising texts themselves, their content and their possible effect on audiences.

ADVERTISING: INSTITUTION AND HISTORY

Advertising is considered to be one of the oldest forms of media. There is, for example, evidence of professional advertising at Pompeii, the Roman city that was destroyed in AD 79 by an eruption of Mount Vesuvius. Pub and inn signs, which date back to the Middle Ages, are a means of advertising their wares and attracting customers.

The series of advertisements for Pears Soap (Figure 56) is interesting not only in that they represent some of the most successful nineteenth-century advertisements but also because they show that advertising techniques have not significantly changed over the last 100 years. Like advertisements today, the Pears campaigns show that advertising is largely about image and association rather than providing clear information about the products themselves.

Figure 55 Advertising expenditure by media

	1989	1993	1995	1997
Total press	5,131	5,085	5,979	6,967
Press classified	2,143	2,078	2,515	3,860
Press display	2,987	3,008	3,463	3,860
Television	2,288	2,604	3,125	3,651
Outdoor	271	300	378	500
Radio	159	194	296	393
Cinema	35	49	69	88
Direct mail	758	907	1,135	1,540
Total display	6,498	7,061	8,466	10,032
TOTAL	£8.6b	£9.2b	£12b	£13.1b

Source: *Advertising Statistics Yearbook*

For instance, part of the Pears success was based on their catch-phrase 'Good morning! Have you used Pears soap?' which became an automatic response to the phrase 'Good Morning'. Most of the Pears advertisements use images of children to represent traits such as innocence, youthfulness, freshness and cleanliness. This connotation of children is still prominent in advertisements today, particularly in those advertisements to do with cleaning products such as soap and washing-up liquid.

The exception in the series is the advert with the (male) shopkeeper/chemist apparently 'recommending' Pears. Today the (male) expert is still a popular advertising ploy, although it is sometimes used in a humorous (or ironic) way. The fact that Pears soap won a prize is also featured in one of the adverts. The advert with the boy blowing bubbles was in fact originally an oil-painting, 'Bubbles', that became very popular and was purchased by Pears to use in their advertisements.

ACTIVITY ...

Try to research 'old' advertisements, perhaps from the 1940s or 1950s, and identify ways in which advertising has (or has not) changed over time.

■ What do you think are the reasons for any changes that you have identified?
■ What similarities can you identify?

Talk to people of different ages to see what advertisements (if any) they remember and why they remember them.

■ How effective are catch-phrases, theme tunes or jingles in helping people remember particular advertisements or products?

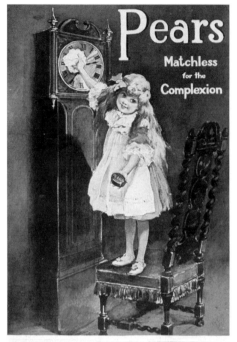

Mamma says it is good for the face and hands

Figure 56

THE ADVERTISING PROCESS

The advertising process involves a lot of people working at different stages of production. There is a great demand for research into consumer habits, needs and desires as well as the development of particular products and brands. Increasingly, this is a worldwide process, especially for companies like Gap which have a global market and therefore try to create a global advertising strategy.

Advertising agencies are used to carry out research, and to design and create the advertisements, possibly using actors, television studios, editing facilities, etc.

NOTEBOX

When Gap introduced a new range of clothes in the spring of 2000 the advertising campaign was created in America. Gap decided to use as a theme the musical *West Side Story*, what they called 'an American classic', for its 'energy and passion' which they claimed was 'the perfect way to tell the story of these vibrant new clothes'. Called the 'Jean and Khakis Trilogy' they shot three different scenes, the first called 'Jeans', the second called 'Khakis' and the third, called 'Mambo', where 'the Jeans and Khakis collide in a dance-off to ultimately ask, "Are you a jean or a khaki?" '

The manner in which Gap used the rivalry between the two gangs (the Sharks and the Jets) in *West Side Story* as a way of promoting its clothes is an interesting example of intertextuality (see p. 72). The target audience for the campaign is probably much too young to remember the film when it was first released in 1961 yet the campaign's reference to the film seemed to be successful.

The next stage in any campaign is to 'buy' advertising space on television, in magazines, newspapers or wherever the advert needs to appear. The Gap advertisements appeared worldwide but in Britain appeared on Channels 4 and 5, on some regional and national digital television and in magazines such as *Vanity Fair*, *Vogue*, *Elle* and *FHM* and on billboards. Presumably Gap use Channel 4 and 5 because they have the correct viewer 'profile' for Gap merchandising. (You might like to speculate as to which national digital television channels Gap used.)

Research amongst advertising companies suggests that it is not only important to have advertisements placed in the correct commercial break or publication but also that it is its positioning in the particular commercial break or publication that is as, if not more, important. Most magazines and newspapers have higher rates for particular spots such as the inside covers or back pages but will also have different rates for right- and left-hand pages or different sections of the publication. On radio and television, being the first in a sequence of advertisements in a commercial break is often viewed as being more effective. Increasingly on television, particular advertisements will appear at both the beginning and end of the commercial break to try to create more 'impact'.

The final stage in the advertising process is to carry out some kind of research to check how successful the advertising campaign has been and to see if it is getting the correct message across to the target group in the most effective (and economical) way. One of the best indicators of this is, of course, increased sales. Gold Blend claim that the sales of their coffee rose by 40 per cent over the five years of their romantic soap opera series of advertisements.

It is claimed that sales of the Renault Clio rose by 300 per cent over the three years that the 'Papa and Nicole' series of advertisements ran. Some 23 million people are supposed to have watched the first broadcast of the final advertisement where Nicole runs off with Bob Mortimer. This example of intertextuality (see p. 72) is a direct copy of the ending of the film *The Graduate*, ironically a film (like the *West Side Story* example earlier) that many of those 23 million would have been too young to have seen in the cinema. These advertisements were shown only in Britain because they played on British ideas of 'Frenchness'. They seem to have become part of our popular culture as well as an interesting example of representation (see p. 63).

We tend only to hear about the successful campaigns like those mentioned above (and others such as Levi 501s, Guinness, etc.). The failures are usually kept very quiet.

Another measurement of the 'success' of an advertisement is to measure its 'impact'. This is often done by asking viewers and listeners what advertisements they can recall having recently seen or heard.

In 1981 Saatchi & Saatchi carried out the 'Ironing Board Study', where they asked 300 housewives to bring their ironing to the researchers' homes. The housewives thought that they were trying out a new starch, but the advertising agency played a radio tape in the background during the 15 minutes that they were asked to iron. The radio tape was specially created and contained a mixture of advertisements and programming. At the end of the session the housewives were questioned about the starch but then also 'spontaneously' asked questions about what they remember hearing on the radio. The most successful advertisements were recalled by about a third of the housewives, the least successful by about a tenth. This and other research suggests that listeners do 'take in' messages from the radio even when concentrating on other activities. However, in general television is seen as the most effective in terms of recall.

Choose a company like Gap, or one that is currently running a particular campaign. Try to 'deconstruct' the campaign:

- Using the categories identified earlier in the chapter, try to identify who the target audience is and what the 'theme' or message behind the campaign is.
- List all the media where the campaign appears (apart from the more obvious media sources, this may include billboards, the cinema and websites).
- Explain why the advertisements appear where they do.
- If possible, visit the shops and see what 'point-of-sale' advertising is taking place, i.e. displays in the shop, leaflets by the check-outs, etc.
- Perhaps the company will send you some information if you contact them.
- You may be able to estimate approximately the amount of money they have spent (although this can be difficult because rates tend to be commercially sensitive).
- Carry out a survey amongst the target audience to see how effective this campaign has been. You may want to consider the audience's awareness of the campaign and products as well as their intention to purchase any of the products.

NOTEBOX

It is worth spending some time thinking about the criteria for 'successful' advertisements. In a television poll held in 2000 of the 'greatest' television advertisements, the Guinness 'Surfing' advertisement came top. It is interesting to speculate why so many people thought that it was 'great'. It certainly caused a lot of comment, but many people seemed unable to explain fully what the advert was about. Perhaps this is the key to its success – the polysemic nature of its message (see p. 35). Second in the same poll were the Smash 'Martians' adverts. It is worth speculating as to the extent to which the success of either of these adverts will have significantly increased the sales of their respective products.

Some adverts win awards but do not increase sales. The 'Talking Creatures' ('Creature Comforts') advertisements that made Aardman Animation so popular in the 1980s were advertisements for electricity but, according to Aardman, are frequently referred to as 'those gas advertisements'. There are very few advertisements that are totally successful in the sense that they are liked by members of the advertising industry, win awards, catch the popular imagination and increase the sales of the product. Jack Dee's 'widget' advertisements with the penguins for John Smith's beer is one such example as it won awards as well as increased the sales of the beer.

Increasingly advertising is not just aimed at boosting sales but also at maintaining public awareness of existing brands in the face of increasing competition from new products and services.

Find examples of what you consider to be 'effective' advertising and 'non-effective' advertising.

■ Explain why you think one particular campaign has been successful and another unsuccessful.

■ What are your criteria for 'successful'?

■ Carry out some research to see if other people share your criteria or have their own.

ADVERTISING AND AUDIENCE

Much of the success of advertising depends upon getting the right advertisement in front of the right audience. Much of the research discussed in Part 2 on Media Audiences reflects advertisers' concerns to target the correct audience.

In Media Audiences we looked at some of the ways in which advertisers try to identify or categorise audiences. In the advertising world there are new methods being developed constantly as advertisers try to become more sophisticated and accurate in their targeting.

Direct mail advertisers spend a lot of time trying to target the correct people. In addition to buying lists from other organisations, they also categorise people by their postcodes, making assumptions about income level, social grade, etc. by the street, road, or avenue in which people live and the type of housing found there. Britain's postcodes are divided into 11 groups varying from Higher Income to Poor Council estates.

You can see a description of your own postcode by accessing www.upmystreet.com

Direct mail advertisers can also use people's names to make assumptions about age. For instance people called Violet, Ethel, Arthur or Cyril are assumed to be old-age pensioners whilst those called Sharon, Tracey, Gavin or Daniel are probably in their late teens/early twenties. Names will also provide clues as to the social grade and disposable income of people.

The cinema is a good source of effective advertising because the advertisers will have an idea of the age make-up of the audience by the type of film being shown – whether it is a certificate 15 comedy like *There's Something about Mary* or an 18 certificate like *American Beauty*.

Contact an advertising agency and ask for details of their organisation and some of their campaigns.

Part of the difficulty advertisers face is that quite often we, the audience, are trying to avoid advertisements. We may do this by throwing away direct mail without opening it, by arriving late at the cinema before the main film has started but after the advertisements have been shown, by 'zapping' through advertisements on videos or between television programmes, or by 'skimming' through newspapers and magazines. The Radio Advertising Bureau claims that radio is the one medium where we do not actively avoid the advertisements. We may not like them and may get bored with them, but they suggest that the advertisements are treated largely like the rest of the radio output. This may, however, mean that we are not concentrating on *any* of it, whether it be advertisements, music or news, but just drifting in and out of the output as we carry out other tasks.

Radio, according to the Radio Advertising Bureau, is a good 'auxiliary' medium to complement campaigns running in other 'primary' media like television.

KEY TERMS

PRIMARY MEDIA Where we pay close attention to the media text, for instance, in the close reading of a magazine or newspaper, or in the cinema where we concentrate on the film in front of us.

SECONDARY MEDIA Where the medium or text is there in the background and we are aware it is there but are not concentrating on it. This is likely with music-based radio; also when the TV is on but we are not really watching it.

PRODUCTS/BRANDS

Most advertising is concerned with selling something – a product – although usually it is the brand rather than the product that is being sold. Brands are different from products. A product may be instant coffee, but within the product there is a range of different brands – Gold Blend, Kenco, etc. – all of which try to have a separate image and identity to distinguish one brand of instant coffee from another. Generally, particular brands are aimed at particular groups of consumers. Often one company, like Nestlé, will have a range of different brands of the same product that look as if they are in competition with each other but are in fact trying to target different segments or 'niches' of the instant coffee market. Increasingly advertisers talk of giving different brands different 'personalities'.

NICHE MARKET A small target audience with specific interests.

ACTIVITY . . .

Advertisers often try to sell the same products to different people in different ways. Choose a particular product (cars, instant coffee, shampoo, washing powder etc.) and then select four particular brands of that product (e.g. for instant coffee these might be Gold Blend, Kenco, Café Hag and Nescafé; for washing powders they might be Ariel, OMO, Bold and Radion). Then analyse the different ways each particular brand is targeted towards its particular audience segment.

Consider:

- How each brand has its own 'unique' or special image.
- The particular audience profile for each brand and how it is different from the other brands.
- Select individual advertisements and using semiotic analysis (see p. 41) identify how their target audience determines the construction of the advertisements.
- Identify how each advertisement is placed in the media to reach particular target groups.

ADVERTISING AND REGULATION

The degree to which advertising is regulated and controlled gives some idea of the importance, and potential influence, that it is considered to have. There is a range of organisations whose role is to make sure advertisements are not causing offence or breaking the rules. Many parts of the industry also have their own 'advisory' codes on what is acceptable in terms of advertising. The BACC (Broadcast Advertising Clearance Centre), for instance, is a non-statutory body that takes responsibility for 'checking' all radio advertisements, although it is the Radio Authority that has the legal responsibility for regulating all commercial radio advertising.

The ITC (Independent Television Commission) regulates advertising on commercial terrestrial television, and cable and satellite. Terrestrial television advertising is limited to an average of 7 minutes per hour during the day and 7.5 minutes per hour during the evening peak time. On satellite and cable channels the average is 9 minutes per hour. On some types of programming, for example religious services, currently no advertising is allowed.

There have been strict controls on the advertising of health products, medicines and medical services since commercial television was introduced in 1955. However, over the years there has been a gradual loosening of the restrictions. As a result of concerns over AIDS (Acquired Immune Deficiency Syndrome) in the 1980s advertisements for condoms became acceptable. In the 1990s the restrictions on sanitary towel advertisements were relaxed although the advertisements seem to have become rather clichéd and a source of humour.

The ITC is proposing that some of the restrictions on the types of product that can be advertised should be lifted. These include escort agencies, private detectives, treatments for hair loss, pregnancy testing services and hypnotists. They are also considering allowing more 'authoritative' celebrities, like newscasters, to endorse products and for doctors to endorse drugs.

The BSC (Broadcasting Standards Commission) is the only organisation that covers all television and radio, including the BBC, as well as cable, satellite and digital services. Set up by the 1996 Broadcasting Act its aims are

- to produce codes of practice relating to standards and fairness
- to consider and adjudicate on complaints
- to monitor, research and report on standards and fairness in broadcasting.

The ASA (Advertising Standards Authority) regulates advertising in magazines, the cinema, posters and direct mail. It is the organisation responsible for the 'Legal, Decent, Honest & Truthful' campaign.

BENETTON

Any discussion of advertising has to acknowledge the impact that the campaigns of Benetton have had over the years, whether it is its images of a newborn baby, a dying AIDS patient or Mafia victims.

The AIDS patient advert was refused by several magazines including *Marie Claire*, *Woman's Journal* and *Elle* as well as *J-17* and *19*. This advert, like many others, was referred to the ASA, which recommended that this, like many of Benetton's other advertisements, be withdrawn. However, the controversy itself gave Benetton plenty of publicity.

These campaigns have succeeded in making Benetton a household name, which was the intention of Luciano Benetton and Oliviero Toscani, the founders of the campaigns. Their advertisements have generated a lot of debate, and you can make your own contribution to this debate via the Benetton website (www.benetton.com).

CHILDREN

One of the most tightly regulated areas of advertising concerns children. There are many restrictions on the content of advertising aimed at children, the types of advertising that can be seen by children, as well as guidelines on how children can be portrayed in advertisements.

The ITC stipulates that advertisements should not mislead, particularly in relation to games and toys. Advertisements must not make 'direct exhortations' to children to ask their parents to buy products for them and should not imply that a child will be 'inferior in some way or liable to be held in contempt or ridicule' if they do not own the product.

Many of these rules are the result of parents complaining about 'pester power', the amount of pressure put upon them as a result of advertising aimed at children, particularly in the run-up to Christmas. Toys may be demonstrated 'in action' on television but in real life often require additional components or perhaps need expensive batteries to operate in the manner shown on television.

There are restrictions on the types of advertisements which can be transmitted around children's programmes. Products that cannot be advertised at these times include alcohol, liqueur chocolates, matches, medicines, lotteries, and 15 and 18 certificate films. The ITC code also stipulates that 'children in advertisements should be reasonably well-mannered and well-behaved'.

In October 1999 Barnardo's launched a newspaper campaign that caused some controversy. Figure 57 shows one of two advertisements featured in the campaign that were referred to the ASA. The other one, 'Martin Ward', featured a boy on top of a high-rise block of flats about to jump off.

According to Barnardo's website at the time,

> the current communications campaign challenges outdated views of Britain's biggest children's charity. It positions the organisation in the forefront of the fight to build better futures for disadvantaged, abused and troubled children. Though the advertisements are hard-hitting, the message is one of hope – that Barnardo's can help children overcome childhood deprivation and avoid futures like these. While Barnardo's work has evolved to encompass all the key issues affecting the lives of disadvantaged children, young people and their families, the public image of the organisation has not kept pace with this development. Research shows that the majority of people in the UK retain an essentially historical view of Barnardo's. They continue to see it as a charity running 'orphanages', or large-scale residential childcare facilities. The image of the organisation remains rooted in its past, epitomised by the 'cottage collecting boxes' once a feature of millions of homes.
>
> (www.barnardos.org.uk)

NOTEBOX

This is the ASA's adjudication of the Barnardo's ad shown in Figure 57:

Media: national press
Agency: Bartle Bogle Hegarty
Sector: Non-commercial
Complaints from: Nationwide (28)

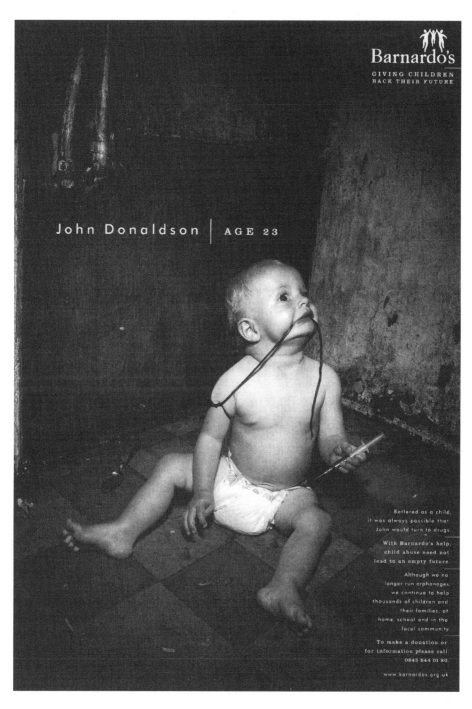

Figure 57

Complaint: Objections to an advertisement in *The Guardian, The Independent, The Independent on Sunday, The Observer, The Scotsman, Scotland on Sunday* and *The Times* for a children's charity. It featured a baby sitting alone in squalid surroundings. Dirt covered the floor and walls; in his teeth the baby held a cord, which was tightened round his right arm to make a tourniquet; in his left hand he held a syringe as if to inject heroin. The headline stated 'John Donaldson Age 23'; the body copy stated 'Battered as a child, it was always possible that John would turn to drugs. With Barnardo's help, child abuse need not lead to an empty future. Although we no longer run orphanages, we continue to help thousands of children and their families at home, school and in the local community'. The complainants objected that the advertisement was shocking and offensive.

The advertisers believed the advertisement complied with the Codes. They said it was part of a campaign to raise awareness of their preventative work with children and young people; the campaign was designed to make people reconsider their opinions about Barnardo's work and the subjects depicted in each advertisement. The advertisers argued that they had not intended merely to shock. They said they had taken the precaution of researching the campaign twice among their target audience of ABC1 adults aged 35 to 55 and their supporters, staff and service users. They submitted the research findings, which they believed showed most people understood the advertisement's message and found its approach effective in changing opinions about Barnardo's work. The advertisers maintained that, because the consequences of drug addiction were potentially devastating, the stark image was justified as a means of raising public awareness of the potential dangers for disadvantaged children; they believed it was an effective way of making the point that Barnardo's could help keep them safe. Their consumer research acknowledged that some people found images of alcoholism or drug abuse upsetting. They nevertheless maintained that an image based on the innocence of a child and potential pain in adult life communicated the message that Barnardo's was a contemporary charity with modern perspectives on child development. The advertisers submitted extracts from published research, which showed that disadvantaged and abused children were particularly vulnerable to emotional and behavioural problems in later life; they provided recent survey results that showed that parents and children found drugs worrying and frightening. They asserted that the child depicted had not been put at risk and that the advertisement was made with full parental awareness and consent. The advertisers said they had monitored public responses to their advertisement; they had received more supportive responses than complaints. *The Independent* said they had received less than five complaints and considered that the advertisement would not cause serious or widespread offence to their readers. *The Guardian* said they believed their readers would understand the advertisers' message and they had received no complaints. The *Scotland on Sunday* said they regarded drugs very seriously but considered that Barnardo's advertisement was compelling and justified. They said they had received no complaints. *The Times, The Scotsman, The Independent on Sunday* and *The Observer* did not respond. The Authority noted the advertisement had offended or distressed some readers. It nevertheless acknowledged that the advertisers had intended to convey a serious and important message. The Authority considered that they had acted responsibly by conducting research among their target audience to ensure the message was understood and unlikely to shock or offend. The Authority noted the picture of drug abuse was directly related to the advertisers' preventative work with children and considered that the target audience was likely to interpret the image in the context of the accompanying text. The Authority accepted the advertisers' argument that they had not intended merely to shock. It considered that, because the advertisers had used the image to raise public awareness of the seriousness of drug abuse and the action that could be taken to prevent it, the advertisement was unlikely to cause either serious or widespread offence or undue distress and was acceptable.

Adjudication: Complaints not upheld.

ACTIVITY...

Access the BSC website www.bsc.org.uk and look through the BSC's code of practice. You can then look at some of the recent cases reported to the BSC and the decisions reached by the BSC.

PRODUCT PLACEMENT

This term deals with the placement of particular brands of products in high-profile situations, for example the character Rachel from *Friends* working for Ralph Lauren and Ralph Lauren himself appearing in episodes of the show. One of the best-known examples is the accessories that feature in *James Bond* films (Omega watch, Aston Martin or BMW cars, Smirnoff vodka, etc.). Companies will pay film producers to have their products featured in films. It is now an established part of the financing of Hollywood films, and there are companies whose 'job' it is to guarantee product placement in films for particular brands.

Product placement on British television is supposed to be banned, but the days are gone when the BBC covered brand labels with sticky tape to hide the real name of the product. There have been suggestions that certain brands do appear in programmes. It could be argued, however, that if a programme like *EastEnders* is to appear realistic, then perhaps a packet of Kellogg's cornflakes should be seen on the kitchen table at breakfast time.

SPONSORSHIP

Sponsorship of television programmes has been allowed in Britain only since the 1990 Broadcasting Act. It is the role of the ITC to ensure that sponsors do not exert too much influence on the editorial content of the programmes they sponsor and that the sponsorship is clearly signalled to viewers. There are certain types of programme that cannot be sponsored, for instance the news. The most popular programmes for sponsors are, not surprisingly, those programmes that attract the biggest audience, for example Cadbury's sponsorship of *Coronation Street* or Ford's sponsorship of Premier Football on Sky. Other sponsorship deals may target specific groups, for example Orangina presumably sponsors *Eurotrash* because of the programme's audience profile.

ADVERTISING EFFECTS

One of the most important debates surrounding advertising is the influence that advertisements may have on both us, the audience, and on those who rely on advertising for their income, namely the media producers.

It is very difficult to assess the effect of advertising and the extent to which people are affected by the advertisements to which they are exposed. In the section on Media Audiences we looked at some of the difficulties that arise in the case of moral panics and in trying to isolate the effect the media may have from other influences on us – such as parents, education, peer groups or religion. This is perhaps even more difficult in the case of advertising, as we often are not consciously aware of advertisements – they are often a tertiary medium that we may skim past in a magazine or newspaper or fast forward through on a video.

KEY TERM

TERTIARY MEDIA Where the medium is present but we are not at all aware of it. The most obvious examples are advertising hoardings or placards that we pass but do not register.

One of the pieces of evidence to suggest that advertising works is the fact that companies spend so much money on advertising. According to some commentators up to one-third of the cost of a bar of soap or up to 40 per cent of the price of a tube of toothpaste may represent advertising costs. Remember that, for example, £13 billion was spent in 1997 on advertising.

ARGUMENTS IN SUPPORT OF ADVERTISING

- It finances a whole range of media (see section on Media Audiences) and provides us with a wide range of choice in terms of the media available to us.
- It can be seen as an essential part of a modern-day, consumerist society and is a very effective way of informing us about new products.
- It stimulates consumption, which benefits industry, increases employment and leads to economic growth.

- Over the years advertising has been a very effective way for government and its various agencies to provide public information about safe sex and the use of condoms, the dangers of drinking and driving or, more mundanely, changing telephone codes. The government is one of the major advertisers in this country.
- Sponsorship is an important source of funding for many sporting and artistic events.
- The advertising industry provides many people with employment.

ACTIVITY . . .

Identify and analyse one particular public information campaign that is currently taking place. How successful is it? Who is it targeting?

ARGUMENTS USED TO CRITICISE ADVERTISING

These are perhaps a little more subtle and complicated, as the following list suggests:

- Advertising creates false hopes and expectations.
- It works on our insecurities.
- It promotes unrealistic and dangerous role models.
- It can influence the content of media texts.
- Advertising revenue can direct programming.
- It can limit the range of media texts available to audiences.

Let us examine each of these allegations in turn.

'Advertising creates false hopes and expectations'

Commentators like C. Wright Mills in the 1950s (see p. 132) and organisations like Adbusters (www.adbusters.org) today are critical of the consumerist nature of our society for this reason. They suggest that advertising excludes the less wealthy and creates a 'must-have' society (advertising on children's television is often cited as one of the main examples of this). Advertising, combined with easily available credit, means that some people may buy products they cannot afford. This then may lead them into debt or criminal action to try to obtain those goods that are made desirable to us through advertising (ram-raiding is cited as an example).

The purpose of publicity is to make the spectator marginally dissatisfied with his present way of life. Not with the way of society, but with his own life within it. It suggests that if he buys what it is offering, his life will become better. It offers him an improved alternative to what he is.

All publicity works upon anxiety. The sum of everything is money, to get money is to overcome anxiety.

(Berger 1972)

'Advertising works on our insecurities'

The work of John Berger (1972) has been used by many people to explain the way in which advertising works upon the individual. Berger suggests that advertising works upon our insecurities and our need to feel 'esteemed' in the eyes of others by implying we are less than perfect if we do not own a particular product or look like the models in the advertisements. The advertisement implies that if we buy that product we will look like the models or lead the type of life shown in the advertisements. Advertising is always working on our insecurities and making us constantly aspire to something new.

'Advertising promotes unrealistic and dangerous role models'

There has been a considerable amount of debate in recent years over the effects of 'super-waif' and 'heroin-chic' images of models in glossy magazines. It is claimed that the constant representation of ultra-thin models in both fashion spreads and advertisements has led to an undermining of girls' self-esteem and to eating disorders. An article published in the *British Medical Journal* in 2000 by Jones and Smith suggests that between 1 and 2 per cent of women between the ages of 15 and 30 suffer from some kind of eating disorder and that this is directly attributable to the images that appear in fashion and 'lifestyle' magazines. (See also p. 63 on Representation and p. 148 on Lifestyle Magazines.)

As a result of this 'moral panic' (see p. 141) in June 2000 a Body Image Seminar was held at 10 Downing Street with the Prime Minister, chaired by Tessa Jowell. A committee of magazine editors and stylists was set up to monitor advertisements, editorial pages and articles for 'unrealistic' or unhealthy images of young women. The group is supposed to say what an 'acceptable minimum body size' is, and magazine editors and other people with influence over the representation of women and young girls, such as advertisers, are supposed to encourage self-regulation in terms of presenting a wider range of body types in their publications. The BSC will also monitor media images to evaluate whether a diverse enough range of women is being shown on television. (It will be interesting to monitor how successful this group will be and the extent to which we notice a greater variety in the types of models being used.)

(We had wanted to show an illustration of an advert for Kellogg's Cornflakes that used a 'super-waif' type of model and suggested that eating Kellogg's cornflakes was a way of staying slim but also remaining healthy. However, perhaps because of criticism that Kellogg's received as a result of this advertisement and because of the sensitivity of the whole issue, they would not grant permission for us to use the advertisement.)

ACTIVITY . . .

Look through back copies of newspapers and magazines and collect examples of these types of advertisements and articles about the issue of female representation.

■ Can you identify any change in the portrayal of women over the last few years?

Advertisements are selling us something more than consumer goods. In providing us with a structure in which we and those goods are interchangeable, they are selling us ourselves.

(Williamson 1978)

ACTIVITY...

Choose one particular product or service and illustrate the range of ways in which advertisers have attempted to make it desirable for consumers.

'Advertising can influence the content of media texts'

Some commentators suggest that advertisers can influence the content of media texts, although there is very little direct evidence that this takes place in the British media. One notable example is from the 1960s when the *Sunday Times* Insight team were investigating the links between cigarettes and cancer. Tobacco companies threatened to cancel their advertising with the *Sunday Times* if the investigations were published. The then editor, Harold Evans, published the investigations and the cigarette companies did pull their advertising (a considerable amount in those days) but eventually returned to the *Sunday Times* because it was a particularly effective means of targeting their desired group.

What is perhaps of more concern is the relationship between programme content and sponsors of programmes. This is an acknowledged issue in America but generally has not been seen to be an issue in this country.

It is undeniable that advertisers do have considerable power over the media in which their advertising appears. In the 1980s the *Sport* and the *Star* ran a joint newspaper (see Figure 58) but the *Star*'s main advertisers, household names like Tesco and Sainsbury's, were unhappy at being associated with the types of stories, features and pictures that appeared in the *Sport*. They threatened to cancel their advertising if the joint venture continued. The *Star* then pulled out of the venture with the *Sport* to safeguard its advertising revenue.

'Advertising revenue can direct programming'

Many commentators feel that C4 has become less radical and adventurous over the years and suggest that this may be the influence of advertising revenue. When C4 started broadcasting it had a number of quite (for the time) radical programmes, some with fairly small audiences and could not fill all its advertising space. Gaps would appear on the screen in the commercial breaks with a notice saying that 'Programmes will continue shortly'. Since C4 has been allowed to keep all its advertising revenue instead of having to pass it on to the other commercial television companies, some commentators suggest that there has been a general shift towards more popular, younger programmes that attract younger audiences and so raise advertising income.

ACTIVITY

Look at the schedules for C4. Can you identify the way in which different audience 'segments' are packaged together? To what extent do you think that the present C4 schedules offer something that is 'innovative'?

Most commercial radio stations tend to offer the same mix of music and presenter 'chat' because they know that this will attract the largest number of the 15 to 25 year olds that advertisers want to target. A commercial station that initially attempts to offer something different, as did London's X-FM or Kiss, often quickly changes its format to reach a more popular market.

ACTIVITY

Carry out a survey of the radio stations that are available in your area.

- Group them under particular types of programming and the audiences that they are aimed at.
- Think about which groups (if any) are not represented by these radio stations. Why do you think this is?

MEDIA STUDIES: THE ESSENTIAL INTRODUCTION

Figure 58

OR

Carry out a survey at your local newsagent's on the magazines that are available.

- Group them under particular types and audiences.
- Are there any groups missing? If so, why?

'Advertising revenue is the foundation of new newspapers'

Newspapers like *Today*, the *Post* and the *Sunday Correspondent* all started up in the 1980s but folded in the 1990s because they could not attract sufficient income from advertising. This may have been as a result of fierce competition in the newspaper market or because the products were not good enough to attract high circulation figures, but in the case of the *Sunday Correspondent*, a left-wing newspaper founded in 1989 and lasting less than one year, it is possible to argue that there was a conspiracy behind its demise, which happened after advertisers withdrew their support. Other radical magazines such as *Red Pepper* or the *Big Issue* struggle to survive because of the lack of advertisers willing to spend their money in these publications.

In the section on Media Audiences (pp. 128–9) we looked at the case of *News at Ten*, where the need to increase audience ratings and thereby advertising revenue was an issue.

ACTIVITY . . .

Carry out research asking people what effects they think advertising has on our society.

- Do different groups of people have different views?
- To what extent do people feel that advertising helps consumer choice?
- Do people think that advertising is 'legal, decent, honest & truthful'?

FURTHER WORK . . .

1   Using your own examples, consider the extent to which advertisers in magazines and television use and manipulate the self-image of potential customers.

2   Carry out content analysis of two different newspapers or magazines (e.g. the *Sun* and the *Daily Telegraph* or *Loaded* and *Cosmopolitan*). Identify the range of advertisements that appear in each of them and then compare and contrast the two publications. What differences do you identify and how do you account for these differences? Draw up an 'imagined audience' profile (see p. 121) for each publication.

3   Consider the consequences, both positive and negative, of the BBC taking advertising.

4   Read the section on the *Wiltshire Times* (p. 123) and then look through your local newspaper and 'measure' the amount of space that is taken up with advertising. Identify different types of advertising, i.e. classified, block advertisements and 'advertorial' that looks like editorial but is in fact advertising.

     Look in *Benn's Media* (see p. 123) or contact the newspaper and see if they will give you some idea of their advertising rates. You can then work out the approximate income that the newspaper receives through advertising revenue.

5   Look through the regulation and controls of advertising. Do you think there is too much, or not enough, control and regulation of advertising? How would you change it?

6   How has advertising changed in the last ten years? What are the main reasons for these changes?

7   Evaluate the success of a particular advertising campaign.

8   Imagine you are creating a marketing campaign for a film, television series, radio station, or magazine shortly to be launched. Decide on what you think would be appropriate promotional material. Which media would you use for advertising and promotion?

FURTHER READING

Berger, J. (1970) *Ways of Seeing*, Penguin.

Dyer, G. (1982) *Advertising as Communication*, Methuen.

Myers, G. (1985) *Understains: The Sense and Seduction of Advertising*, Comedia.

Packard, V. (1979) *The Hidden Persuaders*, Penguin.

Williamson, J. (1978) *Decoding Advertisements: Ideology and Meaning in Advertisements*, Boyars.

Other resources

www.adbusters.org (the organisation responsible for 'Turn Off TV Week').

Advertising Standards Authority publishes a monthly report (see Resources, p. 309).

▼ CASE STUDY 3: POP MUSIC

The music industry is perhaps the most difficult area to study within the remit of Media Studies. The aim of this case study is to help you to obtain an overview of the area. We look at:

■ the historical context of recorded sound

■ formats for sound recordings available now

■ the importance of the charts in determining successful sales

■ pop music and the video.

The music business is an area that is the most difficult to get concrete information about. It is also the area where the output every year around the world is huge. It is important to remember that in this country we tend to listen to European music, and popular music that is predominantly sung in English. Yet any journey abroad will show you that the indigenous music industry still thrives. We no longer need to go abroad to understand this. Many large music retailers now have a world music section in their shops, which just proves how much variety of music is available. You should also try investigating the classical music department of a specialist record shop. Again, the variety of music available seems to grow and grow.

ACTIVITY

The next time you visit a record shop, try to note down the different sections under which the CDs (compact discs) are compartmentalised. Begin with the popular music department. Then have a look at the classical music department.

■ Are there any other departments in the store?
■ How many different sections are available within each department?
■ Does this make any particular piece of music easier to find, or harder?

- What do you do if the CD you want to buy is not easily classifiable?
- Does this breaking down of music into types or genres help the CD buyer? Or is it more likely to help the CD seller? Why do you think this is so?
- And do you think it helps the artist?
- What might be the problems for artists in breaking music down into genres?

BEGINNINGS

'If music be the food of love, play on . . .'

If music is still predominantly the food of love, for which we need simply witness the singles charts every week, it also now represents a multi-million pound industry.

Once there was simply live music. If we wanted to listen to music, it was necessary to find a venue where it was being played by live musicians. The more fortunate, who were rich, were able to hire a singer or musicians to perform for them at home. Now, of course, since the advent of recorded sound, music has become available to most of us in many different formats. It is also obtainable at all times of the day, virtually wherever we happen to be. There is now no reason to go without music since the hardware has become very transportable, and the software seems to get smaller and smaller, too.

NOTEBOX

The most important date when studying the music industry must be 1877 when Thomas Alva Edison invented the world's first recording and playback machine. Twelve years later commercial recordings were made available for public consumption. The primary objective in early recordings was to try and reproduce as faithfully as possible the natural acoustic balance of the performance. Thus recordings were made 'live' – the instrumentalists would be recorded in one take and the idea was for listeners to feel that they had been transported to the concert hall or studio.

Another breakthrough came in the 1940s when Les Paul began to experiment with sound-on-sound recording, what we now call 'multi-tracking'. This involved laying down a basic track and then adding further tracks one after the other. This obviously made it possible for one person literally to produce a multi-instrumental performance.

MULTI-TRACKING The process whereby different instruments and voices are recorded separately and then mixed together in a recording studio.

This technique has now become incredibly sophisticated, and multi-tracking is now used virtually all the time on both popular and classical music recordings. In fact many purists find that the experience of listening to a piece of classical music is now rather a false one since it is so easy for recording engineers to manipulate the tracks and alter the sound so that the recording is no longer a true representation of what was being played in the recording studio – rather it is as close as possible to the notion of perfect sound and performance. Interestingly this has led to an increasing number of classical performances being recorded live, thereby removing the criticism and also adding a sense of the non-mediated sound reproduction which includes the odd mistake and indeed the occasional cough from the audience.

FORMATS

Music is available to us in many different formats. Some are much more accessible than others. It is possible to spend thousands of pounds on a state-of-the-art home reproduction system – CD/DVD-player, pre-amplifier, amplifier and speakers – at the very least. Yet we can also listen to music on the smallest of portable radios which we carry around with us and listen to with the help of headphones if we so wish.

Music can be listened to with our fullest attention but can also be used as background or ambient sound to help us concentrate or perhaps because we just do not like silence.

ACTIVITY

Make a list of all the different places where you hear music in any given week. You should include those times when you deliberately set out to listen to music and those when it exists in the background, even though its existence is not necessarily your choice.

As in all the mass media, the technology is unrecognisable from what was available 50 years ago. The quality of sound reproduction has improved almost beyond recognition. (Note that all improvements in the cinema over the last decade or so are actually to do with the reproduction of sound – the picture quality remains virtually the same.)

We are now used to nearly 80 minutes of sound being contained on a CD or minidisc that we can literally slip into our pocket. There was a time when if you wanted to listen to a symphony it was contained on a series of brittle 78rpm discs, 12 inches in diameter, which had to be changed every 5 minutes or so. Listening was never a continuous experience.

MEDIA STUDIES: THE ESSENTIAL INTRODUCTION

Originally the player was a clockwork mechanism which had to be wound up before any 78rpm disc was played. Reproduction took place through a steel needle which wore down very rapidly and also had to be changed regularly. For this reason it was the radio that people turned to when they wanted to listen to music while working or doing something else.

It was the invention of the 45rpm disc and the 33rpm disc, manufactured out of vinyl, which began the revolution in the music business. Accessibility became the name of the game. Extended play facilities changed the way that we consumed music and also changed the hardware upon which we played it. There are now many different formats available to the consumer.

ACTIVITY...

Make a list of the different formats in which music is now available for us to purchase and play.

- What are the advantages and disadvantages of each?
- Which formats do you own?
- Why did you make that decision?
- Was it a matter of cost?
- What is likely to be the next format that you buy, if any?
- What are the advantages to the listener of the digital formats now available?
- And what do you think that the future has to offer?

There are several issues that are connected with the increase in the technological changes taking place at the moment. The impact of the Internet is seen as considerable. It is now possible to download music from the Web and utilise an MP3 player to listen to it when away from the computer. It is also now possible to create your own CDs using a CD writer linked to the computer. Thus it is possible to envisage a time when everyone will be able to create their own individualised CDs.

The record industry is still in the process of negotiating with the companies that own sites for downloading music. Some media forecasters are suggesting that the future is very precarious for record and music companies since the ability to download music from the Web threatens sales of singles and albums. Others suggest that in fact this new technology will stimulate interest in the products available and consequently it is good for the industry as a whole, and could well contribute to an increase in sales.

ACTIVITY...

Investigate the variety of formats now available to consumers for listening to and recording music.

- Are they all compatible with one another?
- Is it easy to work out the differences between each format?
- Which one would you choose and why?
- Is it possible to discover how long before each format will become outdated and therefore obsolete?
- Which, at present, is the most popular format for the music-buying public?
- Is this simply through choice or are there other reasons for its popularity?
- To what extent is the average music-buyer able to differentiate between the sound quality of each individual format?
- What, then, are the other advantages and disadvantages of each format?
- Are the public particularly well informed about technological advances in sound reproduction and playback?
- Does this matter if all we want to listen to is some music?

It is interesting to note that the new DVD-players are able to reproduce sound and vision as well as playing the old CD format. But what is the difference between the old vinyl discs and the new digital technology?

Research the shortcomings of the 33 rpm vinyl disc.

- What are the advantages of converting to the CD format, or indeed DVD?
- Why is some music still released on 12-inch vinyl disc?
- What are the arguments against CD digital technology?
- Is there still a market for music released on cassette?
- Is the future looking bleak for cassette tape or will it continue, perhaps, as the medium for home taping?

When you have finished the activity above then it might be interesting to examine why the industry decided to go down the digital route. Certainly vinyl records disappeared from mainstream shops very quickly. It is also very interesting to note the increasing popularity of second-hand record shops. Despite the fact that the hardware is becoming more expensive to maintain, because the cost of a stylus for a turntable seems to increase every year, an audience still exists for albums. And their increasing rarity value means that people are discovering that the record that they kept for 25 years is actually worth a great deal of money as a collector's piece.

MEDIA STUDIES: THE ESSENTIAL INTRODUCTION

It seems that records do have as long a shelflife as CDs (if looked after properly) and CDs are not as damage-proof as we once liked to think. A cynical view might be that the very rapid changeover from records to CDs was, in fact, industry-led. The reason for this being the notion that the real music fan would feel obliged to purchase the new hardware necessary for the playing of digital technology – and would also want to replace their records with CDs. Because there is little doubt that if a technology is branded as 'new', then there are those who will feel that they should buy it almost without thinking.

An interesting example of this is the videotaping system. When first heralded, there were in fact three systems fighting it out to win the home market – VHS, Betamax and 2000. Over a short period of time first the 2000 system fell by the wayside, swiftly followed by the Betamax system, even though the picture quality is demonstrably better than VHS, and the video cassettes are smaller. But what of the homes that had bought the Betamax system, for no film is now released on that format any more?

ACTIVITY . . .

Is there any evidence that an obsolescence factor is built into the production of music hardware and technological systems?

THE CHARTS

The charts have become an essential part of the pop music business. Every week, almost everywhere in the world, charts are published, naming the best-selling singles and albums. Although there have been a few controversies in the past about the way the charts are compiled, this has died down of late. Yet, no matter what statistical analysis is used, no one in the industry can deny the importance of these charts.

On the face of it, all that is published is a list of the best-selling singles and albums in any given week. The position of any record in that week assumes tremendous importance once it has been published. It is seen as a barometer of the popularity of an artist or band but, more importantly, once a record has gained a place in the top 20 singles or albums charts, then as a general rule the likelihood is that it will then continue to go on and sell more copies. The reason for this is that far more records are released in a week than anyone, other than a radio station, could possibly afford to buy. By getting a record into the charts, it is bringing it to the attention of the potential record-buying public. A record in the charts gets automatic air-play on the radio, at clubs and pubs and at all the other different types of venue where music is played. It is then heard by other people who, if they like it, will go out and buy it. The important thing is to get it heard in the first place. There will always be a hard core of fans who will buy the product of an artist without bothering to hear it in the first place. Getting the record into the charts is a sure way of capturing this market. The essence of pop music is the word 'popular'. And curiously it is often the case that once a product is seen to be popular, then it will be purchased by others as well – simply, it seems, because it is popular. This explains the enormous investment in marketing activity by recording companies in terms of advertising and reviewing before the release of a pop record.

Keep a look-out for the imminent release of a new single by a relatively well-known artist or band. The pre-release activity may take the form of fly-posters (particularly common in cities or large towns), and references made on TV and the radio, in magazines and newspapers. You should then track the progress of this pre-release activity.

- Do the artists appear on TV to herald the arrival of the record?
- How much further coverage do they receive in the press and on the radio?
- At what stage does the music press pick up on the release?
- What other publicity takes place?
- Is the new record linked in any way with another media product (e.g. does the record happen to feature in a forthcoming film)?

Once the record has been released it is then an interesting exercise to track its progress in the charts. These are published every week in some of the daily newspapers, several magazines and the music press.

What becomes particularly interesting is the phenomenon called the 'battle of the bands'. This is when several very popular artists have records released in the same week. The press corps will often go into overdrive on this occasion – 'Who will win the battle of the bands?' Yet, interestingly, the real winners will often be *all* of the artists involved because they may well find that their record sales have all increased because of this publicity campaign.

It is important to remember that pop music is not just about pop music. It is about fans, loyalty, adolescence, image and many other factors as well.

Take a look at the information given in Figure 59 about the best-selling albums of all time. Many of these records and artists may well be unknown to you. As a group you should divide up the list into manageable sections and attempt to find out as much as you can about each of the artists or groups mentioned and the albums.

- Does it surprise you that there are so few contemporary artists appearing in this list?
- Does the list reflect sales over a long period of time or are there perhaps other reasons why these albums have sold so well?

Figure 59 Top 100 Albums

Level	Title	Artist	Format	Label
26	EAGLES/THEIR GREATEST HITS 1971 –1975	EAGLES	ALBUM	ELEKTRA
25	THRILLER	JACKSON, MICHAEL	ALBUM	EPIC
23	THE WALL	PINK FLOYD	ALBUM	COLUMBIA
22	LED ZEPPELIN IV	LED ZEPPELIN	ALBUM	SWAN SONG
20	GREATEST HITS VOLUME I & VOLUME II	JOEL, BILLY	ALBUM	COLUMBIA
18	RUMOURS	FLEETWOOD MAC	ALBUM	WARNER BR
17	THE BEATLES	BEATLES, THE	ALBUM	CAPITOL
17	THE BODYGUARD (SOUNDTRACK)	HOUSTON, WHITNEY	ALBUM	ARISTA
16	BACK IN BLACK	AC/DC	ALBUM	ATCO
16	BOSTON	BOSTON	ALBUM	EPIC
16	NO FENCES	BROOKS, GARTH	ALBUM	CAPITOL NAS
16	CRACKED REAR VIEW	HOOTIE & THE BLOWFISH	ALBUM	ATLANTIC
16	JAGGED LITTLE PILL	MORISSETTE, ALANIS	ALBUM	MAVERICK
15	SATURDAY NIGHT FEVER (SOUNDTRACK)	BEE GEES	ALBUM	POLYDOR/AT
15	HOTEL CALIFORNIA	EAGLES	ALBUM	ELEKTRA
15	APPETITE FOR DESTRUCTION	GUNS 'N ROSES	ALBUM	GEFFEN
15	GREATEST HITS	JOHN, ELTON	ALBUM	ROCKET
15	PHYSICAL GRAFFITI	LED ZEPPELIN	ALBUM	SWAN SONG
15	DARK SIDE OF THE MOON	PINK FLOYD	ALBUM	CAPITOL
15	BORN IN THE U.S.A.	SPRINGSTEEN, BRUCE	ALBUM	COLUMBIA
14	THE BEATLES 1967–1970	BEATLES, THE	ALBUM	CAPITOL
14	ROPIN' THE WIND	BROOKS, GARTH	ALBUM	CAPITOL NAS
14	COME ON OVER	TWAIN, SHANIA	ALBUM	MERCURY NA
13	THE BEATLES 1962 – 1966	BEATLES, THE	ALBUM	CAPITOL
13	WHITNEY HOUSTON	HOUSTON, WHITNEY	ALBUM	ARISTA
13	BAT OUT OF HELL	MEAT LOAF	ALBUM	EPIC
13	PURPLE RAIN (SOUNDTRACK)	PRINCE & THE REVOLUTION	ALBUM	WARNER BR
13	BRUCE SPRINGSTEEN & E STREET BAND LIVE 1975 – '85	SPRINGSTEEN, BRUCE	ALBUM	COLUMBIA
12	SLIPPERY WHEN WET	BON JOVI	ALBUM	MERCURY
12	II	BOYZ II MEN	ALBUM	MOTOWN
12	HYSTERIA	DEF LEPPARD	ALBUM	MERCURY
12	BREATHLESS	KENNY G	ALBUM	ARISTA
12	LED ZEPPELIN II	LED ZEPPELIN	ALBUM	ATLANTIC
12	KENNY ROGERS' GREATEST HITS	ROGERS, KENNY	ALBUM	CAPITOL NAS
12	DOUBLE LIVE	BROOKS, GARTH	ALBUM	CAPITOL NAS
11	ABBEY ROAD	BEATLES, THE	ALBUM	CAPITOL
11	SGT. PEPPER'S LONELY HEARTS CLUB BAND	BEATLES, THE	ALBUM	CAPITOL
11	HOUSES OF THE HOLY	LED ZEPPELIN	ALBUM	ATLANTIC
11	METALLICA	METALLICA	ALBUM	ELEKTRA
11	TEN	PEARL JAM	ALBUM	EPIC
11	DIRTY DANCING	SOUNDTRACK	ALBUM	RCA
11	JAMES TAYLOR'S GREATEST HITS	TAYLOR, JAMES	ALBUM	WARNER BR
11	CRAZYSEXYCOOL	TLC	ALBUM	LAFACE
11	THE WOMAN IN ME	TWAIN, SHANIA	ALBUM	MERCURY NA
11	PIECES OF YOU	JEWEL	ALBUM	ATLANTIC
11	BACKSTREET BOYS	BACKSTREET BOYS	ALBUM	JIVE
11	CANDLE IN THE WIND 1997/ SOMETHING. YOU LOOK TONIGHT	JOHN, ELTON	SINGLE	ROCKET
10	THE HITS	BROOKS, GARTH	ALBUM	CAPITOL NAS

265

10	MUSIC BOX	CAREY, MARIAH	ALBUM	COLUMBIA
10	UNPLUGGED	CLAPTON, ERIC	ALBUM	REPRISE
10	NO JACKET REQUIRED	COLLINS, PHIL	ALBUM	ATLANTIC
10	BEST OF THE DOOBIES	DOOBIE BROTHERS	ALBUM	WARNER BR
10	DOOKIE	GREEN DAY	ALBUM	REPRISE
10	PLEASE HAMMER DON'T HURT 'EM	HAMMER	ALBUM	CAPITOL
10	GREATEST HITS	JOURNEY	ALBUM	COLUMBIA
10	TAPESTRY	KING, CAROLE	ALBUM	ODE
10	LIKE A VIRGIN	MADONNA	ALBUM	SIRE
10	LEGEND	MARLEY, BOB & THE WAILERS	ALBUM	ISLAND
10	FAITH	MICHAEL, GEORGE	ALBUM	COLUMBIA
10	NEVERMIND	NIRVANA	ALBUM	DGC
10	CAN'T SLOW DOWN	RICHIE, LIONEL	ALBUM	MOTOWN
10	THE LION KING	SOUNDTRACK	ALBUM	WALT DISNEY
10	THE JOSHUA TREE	U2	ALBUM	ISLAND
10	1984 (MCMLXXXIV)	VAN HALEN	ALBUM	WARNER BR
10	VAN HALEN	VAN HALEN	ALBUM	WARNER BR
10	ELIMINATOR	ZZ TOP	ALBUM	WARNER BR
10	DAYDREAM	CAREY, MARIAH	ALBUM	COLUMBIA
10	FALLING INTO YOU	DION, CELINE	ALBUM	550 MUSIC
10	TRAGIC KINGDOM	NO DOUBT	ALBUM	TRAUMA/INT
10	YOURSELF OR SOMEONE LIKE YOU	MATCHBOX 20	ALBUM	ATLANTIC
10	TITANIC	SOUNDTRACK	ALBUM	SONY CLASSI
10	LET'S TALK ABOUT LOVE	DION, CELINE	ALBUM	550 MUSIC/E
9	THE SIGN	ACE OF BASE	ALBUM	ARISTA
9	AEROSMITH'S GREATEST HITS	AEROSMITH	ALBUM	COLUMBIA
9	COOLEY HIGH HARMONY	BOYZ II MEN	ALBUM	MOTOWN
9	GARTH BROOKS	BROOKS, GARTH	ALBUM	CAPITOL NAS
9	SOME GAVE ALL	CYRUS, BILLY RAY	ALBUM	MERCURY
9	PYROMANIA	DEF LEPPARD	ALBUM	MERCURY
9	BROTHERS IN ARMS	DIRE STRAITS	ALBUM	WARNER BR
9	EAGLES GREATEST HITS VOLUME	EAGLES	ALBUM	ELEKTRA
9	WHITNEY	HOUSTON, WHITNEY	ALBUM	ARISTA
9	THE STRANGER	JOEL, BILLY	ALBUM	COLUMBIA
9	ESCAPE	JOURNEY	ALBUM	COLUMBIA
9	HI INFIDELITY	R.E.O. SPEEDWAGON	ALBUM	EPIC
9	ALL EYEZ ON ME	2 PAC	ALBUM	DEATH ROW/
9	GREAT BAND ERA	VARIOUS	ALBUM	READER'S DIGEST
9	[.] BABY ONE MORE TIME	SPEARS, BRITNEY	ALBUM	JIVE
9	MILLENNIUM	BACKSTREET BOYS	ALBUM	JIVE
8	LICENSED TO KILL	BEASTIE BOYS	ALBUM	DEF JAM/POL
8	TIME, LOVE & TENDERNESS	BOLTON, MICHAEL	ALBUM	COLUMBIA
8	TONI BRAXTON	BRAXTON, TONI	ALBUM	LAFACE
8	IN PIECES	BROOKS, GARTH	ALBUM	CAPITOL NAS
8	THE CHASE	BROOKS, GARTH	ALBUM	CAPITOL NAS
8	MARIAH CAREY	CAREY, MARIAH	ALBUM	COLUMBIA
8	GREATEST HITS	CLINE, PATSY	ALBUM	MCA
8	BAD	JACKSON, MICHAEL	ALBUM	EPIC
8	MIRACLES: THE HOLIDAY ALBUM	KENNY G	ALBUM	ARISTA
8	LED ZEPPELIN I	LED ZEPPELIN	ALBUM	ATLANTIC
8	GREATEST HITS 1974–1978	MILLER, STEVE, BAND	ALBUM	CAPITOL
8	HANGIN' TOUGH	NEW KIDS ON THE BLOCK	ALBUM	COLUMBIA

- What genre does each album represent?
- Try to find out how well albums sell in the 2000s when compared to album sales in previous decades.
- Is it possible to draw any conclusions about the music industry today?
- How has it changed?
- Is it now an industry that deals with more disposable products than in the past?
- Or has perhaps the type of audience changed?

Certainly there can be little doubt that the main purchasers of singles at present are teen and pre-teen girls.

ACTIVITY...

Take a look at the present singles chart.

- Try to analyse the typical audience and purchasers of each of the singles in the chart.
- How many of the singles are taken from a new album rather than standing alone?
- Is it possibly now the case that the single has become the loss leader for new albums – or, if not the loss leader, then a form of advertising for a new album?
- What are the various genres of singles in the chart?
- Which genres seem currently the most popular?
- What is the typical audience for each genre?
- What does this tell you about the pop music industry at present?

VIDEOS

There are now 10 pop music video channels on digital television. Each one is slightly different from the other.

ACTIVITY...

What are the music channels currently available on digital TV? Try to look at each one over as long a period of time as possible. For each channel answer the following questions:

- What sort of music does it specialise in?
- Are there any other music channels which seem to cater for the same musical taste?

Certainly much current thinking in the pop music business would suggest that a hit single is not going to be possible without a video to accompany it. And the video has to do far more than simply act as a vehicle for the song. It is now vitally important for the video to make some kind of impact. This might mean that it has to be sensational, or just witty, but the important thing is that it is remembered by the audience and can be viewed over and over again, in the same way that the song can be heard over and over again. The video must also help establish the image of the artist.

ACTIVITY

Watch the top 20 videos programme on MTV.

- For each video shown, attempt to analyse what the video is trying to tell you about the artist(s).
- What is it saying about their lifestyle, their image, what they stand for, whether they are serious or amused by what they are doing?
- How important do you think image is for a pop musician?
- How much notice do their fans take of a musician's or group's image?

NOTEBOX

The pop music industry is an industry in a permanent state of flux. No one can ever predict what will be popular, nor how long the career of a particular artist will last. There are pop stars whose careers span decades. Equally there are those who can only be labelled 'one-hit wonders'. Somewhere in between these two lie the majority of musicians and singers who enter the industry. But what is fascinating is to examine the way these careers are handled by the industry itself, because the most notable survivors are the companies who market and distribute the product (see section on Media Institutions, p. 167).

1   Why is it considered impossible to make a hit single without a pop video? Consider the variety of different ways that the pop music industry advertises and markets pop singles.

2   Investigate the five major record companies.

■ Who are they?
■ Which labels do they own?
■ Do you think it is possible to produce a best-selling single or album and not be connected in some way to one of these major companies?

3   Why is it now so important for films targeted at teenage audiences to have contemporary pop music soundtracks?

4   You have been asked to devise a compilation album of songs, aimed at teenagers, to be released at Christmas. To make life difficult, you have been told to try to make your compilation as unique as possible while still maintaining an element of popular appeal.

■ List the tracks, giving reasons for your choices.
■ Design the front cover of the CD.
■ Explain why your compilation CD will be a better seller than all the others that are due for release at the same time.

FURTHER READING

The most valuable source of information about the music industry remains the music press. In particular *Melody Maker* and *New Musical Express* are still worth reading on a regular weekly basis. There are many glossy monthly magazines available at present – *Q* and *MOJO* are recommended.

As ever, there is a wealth of information available on the Internet. Many of the sites mentioned in the section on Media Institutions have links to information about the industry. However, it is important to define your terms very closely when using a search engine. For instance the phrase 'CD charts' will give you thousands of sites to look at – but the usefulness of the charts from a chain of Polish record shops is doubtful.

Other resources

If you are lucky enough to have an independent record shop in your area, then this is the place to visit. Such shops tend to be owned and run by real music enthusiasts who often have an encyclopaedic knowledge of all things music, and they are often very happy to talk to fellow enthusiasts. And who knows? They may well introduce you to some interesting music while you are in there.

▼ **RESEARCH SKILLS**

In this section we:

■ look at what is meant by research in the context of Media Studies

■ offer some guidelines about what you need to do to carry out effective research

■ look at different types of research, some of the difficulties that you may encounter, and offer advice on how to carry out your own original research

■ suggest where you may be able to access the results of other people's research.

WHAT IS RESEARCH?

There is a considerable amount of media-related research carried out in this country. This research is undertaken for academic purposes, mainly by universities, and for commercial purposes by many commercial media organisations.

In the section on Media Audiences much of the material that we looked at was produced as a result of research carried out by a wide range of different researchers over long periods of time. Although they may have been looking at different things, all these researchers were generally interested in one thing – how audiences interact with the media that they consume. Many of their results have been widely discussed and used to help shape policy either by media organisations themselves, by governments or other media-based trade and industry bodies who set up codes of practice. In the subsection on 'the "effects" debate' (p. 141) we looked at some of the criticisms that have been levelled at some of this research. We can see that it can be a difficult and complex task to carry out research that will stand up to close scrutiny.

As the media become more fragmented and competitive, commercial organisations – from media producers to advertisers – increasingly try to monitor consumption and anticipate our interests and desires. They all therefore undertake a large amount of research, or commission others to do the research on their behalf. This research is perhaps less academic or policy-based but has great commercial value. It will help producers and advertisers target their products more effectively and help identify new niche markets.

Figure 60 The Texas Chainsaw Massacre *(1974)*

Research is usually trying to 'test' a hypothesis. For example, 'Does the advertising of alcoholic drinks on television reinforce images of male superiority?' or 'Is the idea of Public Service Broadcasting out of date in the age of digital radio?' Getting your hypothesis right is important and requires a considerable amount of thought and discussion.

HYPOTHESIS   is an assumption or question about something that the research will investigate and hopefully either prove or disprove.

WHY UNDERTAKE RESEARCH?

One reason is to pass exams as most Media Studies examinations have a requirement that you should undertake some kind of independent research activity. However, there are other, more positive reasons for undertaking research:

- You will gain a greater in-depth knowledge and understanding of the topic that you are researching.
- You will develop your research skills and learn about the processes and methodologies of research. These skills will be useful to you if you go on to higher education or in many work situations.
- The more research you carry out, and with your developing understanding of how research works, the more able you will be to criticise and evaluate research carried out by other people.
- There is a sense of excitement and achievement in the knowledge that you are carrying out original research, doing something that no one else has done before, and actually creating 'new' knowledge.

ACTIVITY...

Look at the credits on a range of television broadcasts and see how often the role of researcher comes up. Suggest reasons why particular programmes may need researchers. What sort of experience and qualifications are these researchers likely to have? Many of the television companies publish guides to careers in television which detail the various roles in television production and the skills and background required.

DIFFERENT TYPES OF RESEARCH

Although there are many different types of research, they are generally divided into two different ways of doing research, one using primary data and the other using secondary data. We can also identify two main categories of research: quantitative and qualitative research.

KEY TERMS

QUANTITATIVE RESEARCH is usually based on numbers, statistics or tables and attempts to 'measure' some kind of phenomenon and produce 'hard' data. It often involves working with large groups of people.

QUALITATIVE RESEARCH often attempts to explain or understand something and may involve more discussion and analysis of people's attitudes and behaviour. It usually involves working with small numbers of people or 'focus groups'.

Carrying out primary research is where you conduct your own original research; perhaps by conducting interviews or doing your own content analysis. Secondary research is where you use research already carried out by other people, like the study discussed below by Cumberbatch or organisations like BARB (see p. 124) or the Glasgow University Media Group.

In terms of the different categories of research, quantitative research is usually larger-scale and may involve large amounts of data that are 'measured'. Its 'value' lies more in the large sample of data that is looked at rather than in the depth of the research. This type of research usually requires a lot of resources both in terms of time and access to the material being researched. Most students are likely to rely upon secondary sources for this type of data. BARB uses a panel of 4,485 homes to represent the viewing of the 23 million households in Britain. Every television set, video, cable and satellite decoder in each of the 4,485 homes is electronically monitored by a 'people meter'. The meters record when sets are switched on, to which channel and who is viewing. The system will download its information to the main computer overnight, so that advertising agencies and media buyers will have the data on their desks the following morning. Adjustments are then made for 'time-shifting' where video-recorders have been used. These metered households 'mirror' the demographic profile of the country's population. BARB can therefore make assumptions by extrapolation on the basis of their sample, i.e. that 18 million people watched last Tuesday's episode of *EastEnders*.

One of the attractions of using this kind of data is that it looks 'official' and authoritative and is usually easy to understand. However, it can also sometimes be rather limited. It may be interesting to know that 18 million people watched *EastEnders* last Tuesday but it would be more interesting to know why and how (e.g. what else the viewers might be doing at the same time as watching *EastEnders*); this type of quantitative research generally cannot answer those questions.

Qualitative research, on the other hand, probably could answer the questions 'why' and 'how' but only for a small number of that 18 million *EastEnders* audience. Qualitative research is where a smaller range of research is carried out but it is looked at in greater depth. Much of the work of people like Ien Ang and David Morley that we looked at in the section on Media Audiences attempts to answer the questions 'why' and 'how' and is therefore smaller in scope. Ien Ang's *Watching Dallas: Soap Opera and the Melodramatic Imagination* is a study based upon 42 people who replied to her advertisement in a magazine.

CARRYING OUT YOUR OWN PRIMARY RESEARCH

Questionnaires and surveys

One of the main methods of undertaking primary research is by asking people questions. This may be in the form of one-to-one interviews with a small number of people who have particularly relevant experience. They are often more 'in depth' than other interviews or surveys that may be shorter in terms of each piece of data produced but be answered by a wider range of people. Another popular method of asking people questions about the media is through surveys.

Figure 61 BARB Top 20 ratings from *Broadcast* magazine

Title	Day	Time	Viewers% (millions)	Change (week)	Broadcaster/ Producer	Last year
1 *Coronation Street*	Sun	1930	16.90	3.9	Granada	2
2 *Coronation Street*	Mon	1930	16.81	2.1	Granada	1
3 *Coronation Street*	Wed	1930	15.95	5.6	Granada	3
4 *Coronation Street*	Fri	1930	15.69	8.3	Granada	5
5 *EastEnders*	Mon	2000	14.20	5.8	BBC1	8
6 *EastEnders*	Tues	1930	14.18	3.9	BBC1	6
7 *EastEnders*	Thu	1935	13.76	5.1	BBC1	7
8 *EastEnders*	Sun	2000	12.90	0	BBC1	–
9 *Emmerdale*	Fri	1900	12.85	0	Yorkshire	–
10 *Emmerdale*	Wed	1900	12.25	1.1	Yorkshire	13
11 *Emmerdale*	Thu	1900	12.08	1.3	Yorkshire	12
12 *Emmerdale*	Tues	1900	12.05	2.2	Yorkshire	10
13 *Heartbeat*	Sun	2000	11.69	15.1	Yorkshire	4
14 *Casualty*	Sat	2010	11.36	7.9	BBC1	9
15 *Antiques Roadshow*	Sun	18.45	10.78	16.8	BBC1	24
16 *Emmerdale*	Mon	1900	10.77	0	Yorkshire	–
17 *London's Burning*	Sun	21.05	9.82	2.6	LWT	16
18 *Peak Practice*	Tue	2100	9.68	9.6	Carlton Central	–
19 *This is Your Life*	Mon	2030	9.50	9.4	BBC1 (Thames)	23
20 *Taggart*	Wed	2105	9.36	•	Scottish	–

Source: *Broadcast* 10.3.2000

These are usually carried out by asking a relatively large number of people to fill in a form or some sort of questionnaire. Surveys are a popular method for students to carry out research because they seem relatively easy and demand little in terms of resources. However, if they are not thought through carefully, surveys can often produce little of real use and end up being a waste of time and effort.

If you are going to use a questionnaire, you need to think carefully about the number and type of questions that you are going to include. (If you make the questionnaire too long, people will be reluctant to spend the time answering it or it will take you too long to collate the answers.) Asking the right type of questions is just as important. Closed questions are easier to collate but open questions may give you more information.

Open questions are those that start with 'what', 'where', 'why', 'when', 'how' or 'who' and encourage the interviewee to 'open up' and talk. Closed questions are those that require a very limited answer, often just yes or no. Another method for questionnaires is to use tick boxes where the responses are easy to collate and can be processed through software packages such as Microsoft's Excel.

The advantage of closed questions is that they are easier to quantify if you are carrying out a large number of interviews. The results can usually be easily transferred to visual images like pie-charts or bar-charts. Open questions are usually used in qualitative research, like David Morley's *Family Television* (1986), where a small number of people are being interviewed and the research is trying to gather more detailed information. Morley interviewed the members of 18 households about the manner in which they consumed television and the 'uses' they made of it (see p. 136).

Think about the logistics of undertaking a survey and also try to imagine yourself as a

ACTIVITY . . .

Design two small questionnaires dealing with the same topic. Each questionnaire should have about five or six questions, one with open questions and the other with closed questions. After you have done your research, list the advantages and disadvantages of the two questionnaires and decide which is more useful for your research.

respondent. If someone you didn't know came up to you in the street and asked you to fill in a questionnaire several pages long, how keen would you be? It is probably easier to ask people you know to fill in questionnaires but then there is the danger that you are only researching amongst a small and particular group and your sample does not have any value or reliability (see Morley below).

Researchers are often limited by lack of time and other resources and so cannot always carry out exercises on as large a scale as they would wish. Instead, like BARB (see p. 124), they collect information from a smaller group, or sample, in such a way that the information gained is representative of the larger group.

When using questionnaires, should you ask people to complete the questionnaires while you wait or should you let people take them away and hope that they will return them when you ask? If you want people to fill them in while you wait, this implies several things:

- the location is suitable for people to stop
- they have something to write with (you may need lots of pens)
- there is something for them to lean on (try writing without anything to lean on!)
- they will have the time and inclination to stop and complete the questionnaire.

It is also useful to pre-test your questionnaire or survey with a few people to check that none of your questions is ambiguous or confusing. Other people may also notice any bias that is inherent in your questions, i.e. 'Why do you think *The Royle Family* is so funny?' or 'In what ways does *Coronation Street* portray a negative representation of ethnic minorities?'

All these factors are part of the logistics of carrying out surveys and questionnaires. Perhaps more importantly you need to think about why you are doing this, the purpose of this particular piece of research and how it will help you test your hypothesis. Don't be tempted to undertake surveys and questionnaires just because they look easy or because they are a popular methodology with other students.

METHODOLOGY is the system or manner used to carry out research – the different ways in which 'data' can be captured.

INTERVIEWS

Interviews can play a large part in research and can be conducted as part of your primary research or as a secondary resource by using the interviews carried out by someone else, for instance Morley in *Family Television*. His methodology included conducting in-depth interviews, many with open-ended questions that allowed the individual members of the households to talk about their television consumption. Although much of this data was difficult to put into numerical form or to construct generalisations, it has been a very influential piece of research. It has helped our understanding of how individuals interact with the television programmes they are watching and the importance of the circumstances, or 'situated culture', in which most people consume the media.

Morley did not claim that his sample of 18 households was representative of the population as a whole. He recognised its limitations. If you are carrying out interviews, you also need to think of how representative your sample will be. To interview everyone in your Media Studies class will not be representative of the population as a whole, or even of all students, but only of those students who are studying the media in your locality and who may have a similar social background. This doesn't mean that your sample will be wasted because it may support other, more quantitative research. You do need, however, to recognise and acknowledge the limitations of your sample.

Although the amount of time you have to devote to your research is probably limited, it can be a useful check if you carry out more than one type of research. This will enable you to check the sets of results against each other. This should make your findings more reliable as well as possibly giving an extra dimension to your work. For example, Janice Radway in *Reading the Romance* (1984) used a variety of methodologies including structured questionnaires, open-ended group discussion, in-depth interviews and content analysis.

ORGANISING INTERVIEWS

Be prepared. Think about the type of interview you want to carry out and have a clear idea of its purpose. To draft a set of questions, it is helpful first to make a list of the points that need to be covered. Good questions are simple and direct. You should, however, be prepared to deviate from the prepared questions if other relevant issues come up.

Interviews are usually arranged well in advance, as most people are unwilling or unable to stop what they are doing and immediately answer questions in any meaningful or useful way. Interviewees sometimes ask to see the questions in advance, too, as they want time to prepare their answers or are nervous about being interviewed.

Wherever an interview takes place it should allow both you and the person being interviewed to relax, as it is usually when people are relaxed that they start to talk more openly and naturally. Body language is a good indication of how people are feeling. Part of your role as interviewer is to make sure that your interviewees are feeling comfortable.

People being interviewed often prefer to conduct the interview on familiar territory where they feel in control. If you are recording an interview, perhaps for future reference, try to use an environment that does not have any disturbing background noises, such as traffic noises or crowds of people (school or college corridors are NOT a good idea). Your recording equipment should be as unobtrusive as possible as it can sometimes have an intimidating effect on those being interviewed.

One of the difficulties in carrying out interviews is that often you are asking people to remember something, for instance what they listened to on the radio yesterday or last week, what adverts they saw at the cinema or who made the decision about last night's television viewing.

One of the tricks used by professional researchers is to include a series of prompts to help respondents remember particular programmes, products, etc. Perhaps have a copy of the television schedules to hand or a list of films as a means of jogging people's memory. Often professional researchers will also include a fictitious name to check the accuracy of people's responses. It is surprising how often people remember watching programmes that never existed or seeing adverts for products that were never shown.

ACTIVITY . . .

To test how accurately we can recall information, think about the last time you went to the cinema or the last magazine that you read. Can you recall the advertisements that were shown before the film started or that appeared in the magazine? Ask others to do the same exercise. How reliable to you think their (and your) memory is? Can you think of any ways in which you might be able to help people remember more accurately?

One of the ways around this problem is to ask your interviewees to keep a record or diary of their media consumption. (See section How to Study the Media in the Introduction,

p. 16.) This can, however, be quite burdensome for them to keep and quite time-consuming to read through and summarise unless it is very well designed.

Some people are unwilling to be open about their media consumption. They do not want to admit that they watch particular television programmes because they feel that the programmes are considered 'trashy'. They may be unwilling to admit to the number of soap operas they watch or that they read tabloid newspapers because they feel that they should be reading broadsheets. It is therefore very important that you do not appear to be judgemental. You may also need to reassure them that the results will remain anonymous.

FOCUS GROUPS

Professional organisations like advertising or marketing agencies will often use focus groups or panels. These are pre-selected groups of people who represent particular interests or habits or are a sample of larger groups. When new advertising campaigns or magazines are being launched, they often employ these methods to research the responses of their 'target' groups. If you want to run focus groups you need to think about how you are going to manage the group, prompt discussion and record what is said. You may wish to record the group's discussion using video or audio, but again this needs to be discreet otherwise it may inhibit some of the participants. You should, however, warn them that the meeting is going to be recorded and check that they are willing to co-operate and give their permission.

Academics sometimes use simulations or observations where they monitor people's behaviour. These, like focus groups, are quite time-consuming to set up and carry out, and if you do not have the time and resources to undertake this type of primary research yourself you might be able to use someone else's results as part of your secondary data.

CONTENT ANALYSIS

This is often a popular method of carrying out research into the content of media texts as it can be a relatively simple process. However, as significant or reliable results need large numbers to substantiate them, content analysis is often very time-consuming and sometimes does not provide the 'quality' of results that the effort involved suggests.

Content analysis involves the 'counting' of the number of times a particular phenomenon may appear in a selected range of media texts. For instance, Cumberbatch carried out a contents analysis for the Broadcasting Standards Council in 1990 looking at gender representation in television advertising. Part of their research involved 'counting' the number of times women appeared in adverts (twice as often as men), the number of adverts that had male voice-overs (80 per cent), and the different roles in which men and women were shown. Cumberbatch and his colleagues at Aston University, Birmingham, looked at 500 prime-time advertisements taken from a two-week period. Prime-time was defined by them as between 4 pm and 10 pm. They also looked at some additional pre-recorded material from an earlier period in the same year. (See also the reference to Gerbner in the Representation section, p. 69.)

One of the main problems with content analysis is in deciding the categories that you are going to 'count'. For instance in the Cumberbatch research one finding was that 64 per cent of the women appearing in television adverts were 'attractive', compared to only 22 per cent of men. Another finding was that 50 per cent of the women were aged between 21 and 39 compared to 30 per cent of men.

ACTIVITY . . .

Consider what difficulties a researcher might encounter in trying to use these categories. Can you suggest any other strategies that could be used to try to reach the same results?

One of the best-known examples of content analysis is the work carried out by the Glasgow University Media Group and published in books such as *Bad News, More Bad News, Really Bad News* and *War & Peace News*. They researched television news bulletins to see the manner in which various news items (such as the 1984 Miners' Strike) were presented, who spoke and the type of language used. Their data was then analysed by computer and they claimed to show how news reporting was 'biased' against the miners.

Content analysis can be an effective way of making comparisons between different media – for instance, the types of articles and news stories that appear in broadsheet and tabloid newspapers. It is also a useful methodology if you want to look at changing patterns over time; for example, Marjorie Ferguson's (1983) study of themes in popular women's magazines since the Second World War, *Forever Feminine: The Cult of Femininity*.

If you are using secondary sources, then content analysis can be quite useful, especially if as in the Ferguson or Cumberbatch cases someone has already carried out quite detailed quantitative work. However, you need to be aware that one of the main criticisms of content analysis is that, like the Hypodermic Needle theory (see p. 131), it concentrates too much on the text itself and does not take into account the audience's interaction with and interpretation of the text's meaning.

HOW TO UNDERTAKE YOUR OWN CONTENT ANALYSIS PROJECT

STEP ONE: The first stage of any research exercise is to clarify and define what it is you are trying to do, what it is you are trying to research, the basic patterns you are aiming to measure and why. At this stage you should be able to establish a hypothesis or argument to test in your research.

STEP TWO: Once you have decided what it is that you want to uncover, then that should determine the next stage of your research. This is to decide upon the range of media texts that you are going to look at. At this point it is important to be realistic in terms of the time and resources you have available.

If, like Cumberbatch, you are looking to do research that focuses on television advertising, then you need to think about how you are going to 'capture' your raw data – the television advertisements:

- What timespan will you cover? A 'typical' 24 hours (what is 'typical'?) or just peak-viewing time but across a range of days? Will you include weekends or focus on weekdays?
- Will you record the complete output, programmes as well as adverts? This will require a large amount of video-tape. You will also have many more hours of tape to look through.
- Will you instead just record the commercial breaks? In which case someone will need to be present to switch on and off the video-recorder as the times of these breaks cannot be set beforehand.
- Will you record all the television channels that carry advertising, or just the main terrestrial ones or some of the satellite/cable/digital channels as well? Your decision will have an impact on the technology that you will require to carry out these recordings.

STEP THREE: The next stage would be to decide upon the categories that you are going to 'count' when you have captured and looked through all this data. Your categories should be clear and easy for others to understand and identify. You should avoid the more subjective categories such as the 'attractive' example in the Cumberbatch exercise mentioned earlier.

As you can see, there are many decisions that you are required to make, each of which has an impact on your findings. You also need to be clear what your reasons are for the decisions that you reach, as they often reflect certain assumptions that you are making (perhaps unconsciously) about television consumption, advertising and its content.

STEP FOUR: This is where you actually carry out your research, recording and logging the material that you will be looking at.

STEP FIVE: Now you reach the most interesting stage of your content analysis, namely analysing the results. Has your hypothesis been supported? Are there any additional results that you had not anticipated? Does it support or contradict the findings of other similar research?

STEP SIX: This is the last stage of your content analysis. You should reflect upon the process that you have carried out, what you have learnt about this method of undertaking research, and make suggestions on how the exercise might be improved in the future.

ACTIVITY . . .

Content analysis as a methodology has many critics. What do you think are the problems with this type of research? Consider some of these suggestions and design your own contents analysis exercise.

Issues of representation are often good topics for content analysis and can cover subjects such as gender, age, class, race, sexuality etc. and, in terms of texts, you can focus on soap operas, television situation comedy, television dramas, children's comics, magazines, etc.

The study can be based on contemporary texts or can be a comparison between historical texts (assuming you can gain access to them – see the end of this section) and similar texts of today. Consider the difficulties that you may encounter and the extent to which these might detract from the value of your research.

USING SECONDARY DATA

Many commercial media organisations undertake their own research, usually for commercial reasons to identify market share, or size of audience, or to help inform scheduling decisions or the place and price of advertisements. Much of this research has a commercial value but sometimes, when it is out of date, companies may be willing to make it available to students.

Other organisations provide information regarding their work and often have some up-to-date facts and figures about the industry that may be useful. Sometimes, however, there is a tendency to use this material just because it comes from an 'official' source rather than because of its relevance to your research area. It is important therefore to make sure that any data you use are relevant and necessary and not included just to make your work more impressive.

Below we have listed some organisations that provide free information as well as websites that might be useful. There are, however, some drawbacks to using material from the Internet (see p. 23. You also need to be sure that you accurately reference any material that you may use for copyright reasons.

THE BIBLIOGRAPHY

A bibliography is where you list all the information sources that you have used in your research. You should provide all the details necessary for someone else to be able to trace and look up the original data. For books and articles from magazines, you should use the Harvard system, listing the author, date, title and publisher. Many books also give the place of publication. If you look at the Further Reading sections of this book you will see how the Harvard System is set out. It is useful to keep a record of the details of any books or articles that you look at as you go along, because it is sometimes difficult at the end to remember where a particular piece of data came from. (See the section on How to Study the Media in the Introduction.)

The rules for referencing non-print-based material are a little less clear. Again it is important to provide enough information for the original data to be traced. For data from the Internet you should include the URL and the date you accessed it to allow for any subsequent modifications. If you use video or television programmes you should, where possible, provide details of

- director (if appropriate)
- title of the film or programme
- broadcasting channel
- series title
- date of broadcast.

If you have undertaken your own primary research, then you will probably discuss the main findings and their implications in the body of your work. However, you need to include details of the methodology used, probably in appendices that are put at the end of your work. This is also where you might include copies of questionnaires, details and results of surveys, transcripts of interviews, etc.

Finally some key points:

- Be aware of the difficulty of being truly 'objective' and avoid trying to 'prove' a particular result that suits your own ideas.
- Make sure that you have a clear focus and hypothesis. Quantity is no substitute for quality.
- Be realistic and recognise and acknowledge the limitations of your research.
- Always explain to your respondents who you are and the purpose of your research.
- Explain what will happen to their responses, who will see the information and whether it will be anonymous or not. Ask their permission to use the material.
- Reflect on your methodology and the processes you have undertaken. There is always something new to learn.
- Always keep a record of your contacts and sources and make sure that you acknowledge your sources for secondary data.

FURTHER READING

Cumberbatch, G. (1990) *Television Advertising and Sex Role Stereotyping: A Content Analysis*, Broadcasting Standards Council.

Kirchner, D. (ed.) (1997) *The Researcher's Guide to British Film & Television Collections*, 5th edition, British Universities Film & Video Council.

Morley, D. (1986) *Family Television*, Comedia.

O'Sullivan, T., Dutton, B. and Rayner, P. (1998) 'Media Research and Investigation', in *Studying the Media*, 2nd edition, Arnold.

Stokes, J. (1999) 'Use it or lose it: sex, sexuality and sexual health in magazines for girls' in Stokes, J. and Reading, A. (eds) *The Media in Britain: Current Debates and Developments*, Macmillan.

Trowler, P. (1996) 'Approaches to Media Research', in Trowler, P., *Investigating Mass Media*, 2nd edition, Collins.

▼ PRODUCTION SKILLS

In this section we:

- explore the important area of the practical production
- guide you through the very important area of pre-production and planning
- suggest successful ways of going about the actual production process
- look at what is required in the post-production and evaluation section.

This section is necessarily general since everyone will have their own ideas as to the nature of their production, but most of what is suggested is relevant for all the media that you may wish to use.

This part of the course can be the most rewarding, the most fun, but also the most frustrating and occasionally the most disappointing.

Production work has a place in all current media courses for several reasons:

- The hands-on approach does teach a great deal about the realities of real-life media production.
- It allows you to grapple with the key concepts and methods of production within a real framework, rather than just a theoretical one.
- You can demonstrate what you have learnt about the media in a practical context.
- It also allows room for creativity and imagination.

Perhaps the most difficult aspect of the whole process is the first one.

PLANNING

This part of the process can be quite worrying to start with. You have to produce a piece of work which is going to be marked and looked at by external moderators. Perhaps you don't feel very confident with the equipment, you certainly aren't an actor and you have no idea what your production project will be.

This part of the process has to be considered as a holistic exercise. It may be that only certain media are available to you. This you must discuss with your teacher.

But three interlinked points require investigation and decision-making: the medium, the audience and the subject matter.

THE MEDIUM

First, find out which media you are allowed to work in. Then consider the following:

- Have you worked in any of these media before?
- Which do you feel most comfortable and confident with?
- Are you likely to work at the production only in lesson/school time or are you likely to work on the production outside school/college time?
- How much time do you have available to you?
- What sort of equipment is available to you?
- What media have you studied previously and do you feel that you have a working awareness of those media in terms of technique, genre, narrative, etc.?

THE AUDIENCE

Who is your target audience? It is no use saying that you will make a magazine about stock-car racing based on the fact that you go every week and really enjoy it. Market research may well suggest that there is insufficient demand for such a magazine, as fans of stock-car racing prefer watching it to reading a magazine about it.

Equally it is not necessarily a good idea to aim your product at a young teenage audience – it is likely to be the case that you are too close to that market and objective decision-making will become difficult. In many cases it is in fact far better to isolate a specific audience that you are *not* a part of, so that you can remain that much more objective. In this way, personal taste and opinion are less likely to get in the way of your decision-making.

Again this is linked with the medium you use and the subject matter (see below) BUT you must (a) attempt to identify a target audience and (b) then research their likes, dislikes, and media consumption habits. Ideally through your research you will discover an area that you feel is not well represented at present.

ACTIVITY...

Create a questionnaire which you can distribute widely across a spectrum of people. Consider carefully the type of questions you need to ask them about their media consumption. But also consider the personal information that you require to make the survey worth while. Remember, even if you are looking at a teenage audience, you will need to go further afield than your school or college if the survey is to be worth while.

One example of a media product aimed at a particular audience is the 'grey' magazines aimed specifically at the over-sixties. Such magazines can be difficult to find since they tend not to be on newsagents' shelves but are ordered specially – either by a newsagent for known customers (and therefore kept under the counter) or directly by the readers themselves on a subscription basis. However, if you were to look at these magazines, you would find that they make certain presumptions about the over-sixties which may well prompt you to think about the (possibly enormous) market of over-sixties who are not catered for by these magazines.

You may find it worth your while to interview your family and friends about their media consumption and ask them to suggest ways in which they feel they are not being catered for by existing media products.

THE SUBJECT MATTER

The subject material of your production is inevitably linked with its target audience – your subject matter must obviously appeal to its intended audience. It must also be possible within the constraints of the medium that you have decided to employ. For instance, you are unlikely to be able to make a video about a wartime submarine, although this would be possible to achieve in the form of a radio play.

You also have to be realistic about the time, money and energy that you have. Don't be over-ambitious – be realistic. For example, if you have decided to target 40-year-old sci-fi film enthusiasts, then it might be unrealistic to decide to make a fiction film, basically because you are unlikely to have the equipment and budget necessary to do so. But if you think around the problem, then you might

■ make a TV or radio magazine programme which is about sci-fi films
■ make a trailer/advertising campaign for a new sci-fi film
■ make a parody of a sci-fi film of the 1950s (though parody/pastiche is actually a sophisticated skill).

This is a good time to conduct a brainstorming session. Sit down with your group and jot down all the ideas that you have about a possible production. Allow yourself 15–20 minutes or so to do this. Then take a 15-minute break. Return and discuss carefully what you have written down and begin to examine the links between the various ideas.

INDIVIDUAL V. GROUP

One other point at this stage is important. In the real media world very few people work in total isolation. The reality is that most media productions are the result of teamwork

– someone may well make the primary decisions but essentially the product is made by a group of people, all with different well-defined roles within the organisation. This should be the way that you choose to work – in an ideal world within your classroom.

However, it may well be the case that you want to strike an individual path, for all sorts of reasons. Certainly other people can be unreliable and perhaps not as committed as you are. You may well have a particular interest in a medium, subject or audience that no one else shares. If you are not prepared to compromise, then perhaps you should go it alone – whilst remaining aware of the fact that this puts all the responsibility on you. There will be no one else to rely on. Equally there will be no one else to let you down.

This can be a very difficult decision and one you need to think about carefully.

At this point you have probably made all the choices that are possible. You now enter the second stage, which is actually producing the artefact or media product. The production process can be broken down into three stages:

1   pre-production
2   production
3   post-production.

PRE-PRODUCTION

Having made all the decisions about the nature of your product, you now enter the phase that is absolutely necessary to all media products. In the real world it is a rare media producer who is allowed completely free rein to go out and do whatever he/she sees fit at the time 'because it feels right'. Nowadays, whatever the product, an awful lot of work goes into the pre-production stage.

Researching similar media

Whatever the medium you are working in, it is almost inevitable that there are other products out there ploughing a similar path. You need to investigate your 'rivals' and 'competitors' to see what they are doing, investigate their subject material, research how well they seem to target their audience, and look at what works and what doesn't. Look particularly at how rival products are presented to the audience – study the opening sequences if visual, the front pages if print. What assumptions are being made about their audience? Do you want to alter these assumptions and if you do, then how are you going to do this?

For instance, it seems that children's TV presenters are required to be fairly 'wacky' and shout a lot whilst the camera never stops moving. Children's TV also seems to assume that the majority of children are interested only in boy bands and computer games and, it would appear, very little else. So what would you change if your area were children's TV? Again, you would need to watch a considerable amount of children's television before you could begin to form any conclusions – but remember that you should not be afraid to accept the things that work but rethink the things that seem to you not to work.

This is really the area of genre expectations (see the section on Genre, p. 000) and, whilst accepting the importance of these expectations, it is also important to confront and challenge these expectations (and be able to articulate the reasoning behind any decision you might make).

Researching the audience

We tend to assume that we know what's best for everyone and also that public taste is fairly uniform throughout the country. The truth is that even large-scale media productions can have varying success throughout different regions in the country. What works in London will not necessarily work in Taunton or Doncaster.

Equally, it is the case that not all teenage girls necessarily enjoy the same things – and the same is true of teenage boys. You could say that at present, for instance, the teenage magazine market tends to play safe by creating an identikit picture of a typical teenager and creating magazines based on that image. This works to an extent – sales figures are high – but there are still many teenagers nationwide who do not buy magazines because there is simply nothing that caters for their tastes. This again could be an interesting area for you to explore.

Having decided upon your medium, subject material and audience, you now have to go out and investigate the real nature of your target audience.

- What do they consume?
- What do they enjoy about it?
- Which parts do they most appreciate?
- But – most fundamentally – what more do they want?
- How could the product be improved?
- What else would they like to see?

This is very much what happens in the real media world. Media producers tend to build a profile of their consumers, and it can be a very detailed profile, based not just on sex, age and class but also encompassing such things as location, family circumstances, jobs, consumption patterns and preferences, and so on.

NOTEBOX

It is important to ensure that this research does not just take place in your class-room or indeed school. Whatever the nature of your target audience, you should spread your net as far and as wide as possible in an attempt to get a truly representative feel for the subject. This has pitfalls none the less, but as broad a survey as possible gives you more evidence upon which to format and create your eventual product.

Researching the subject matter

This might seem to be stating the obvious, but no one can just produce a media artefact without researching the subject matter in the first place. Whatever the nature of the production you are developing, it is absolutely essential that you have thought about and planned exactly what the subject matter and content will be. It is often the case that students use material that they have found and borrowed from other sources – for instance those who decide to create a girls' magazine often think it is enough simply to copy out articles that they have found in existing publications. This of course undercuts everything that we have discussed above. It suggests to the readers that you have not really thought about the nature of your audience or considered the results of all the research that you should have done.

This is even more the case when creating an audio-visual product. Your job is not simply to copy what is already out there, but to develop it and hopefully take it further.

There are secondary sources – by which we mean finding out information from books in the library, or perhaps from interesting websites on the Internet, but to make any production come alive you also need to investigate primary sources – interviewing people who are prepared to debate the issues that you may be investigating in your production, for example. And all this needs careful planning and advance preparation.

Organising

Now you have to get organised. Prepare yourself and your group so that everyone has a job to do. It is also very important that everyone else knows what that job involves. Equally it is vital that everyone knows when each of the different tasks is going to be done and the final date for completion of the project. This holds true for whatever medium you have decided to work in. All of this information needs to be itemised on paper and distributed throughout the group (as well as a copy being ready for submission at the end of the course).

Whatever the eventual product you have decided to create, there is still yet more planning to do. It is important that you do not start work without having a clear idea of what the finished product will look like. This involves serious consideration of the actual contents and the look of the final product.

For instance, a front cover of a magazine does not just happen. It involves taking into account all the research work that has gone on before and attempting to create a cover that will:

- appeal to the target audience
- give an idea about what is contained within the front cover
- demonstrate awareness of the generic rules of the sort of magazine it is
- have some immediate visual appeal – always remember that in theory you are competing with all the magazines that are already out there.

Similarly you will need to produce a mock-up of the magazine – as you would in real life – in which you are able to suggest what will actually be in it, and also suggest the order in which the editorial material, adverts and illustrations will actually appear. This is also your opportunity to start experimenting with the look/style/format of the magazine.

If you are making a video, then what you *don't* do is just go out and start filming. You will need to produce a script, and an accompanying series of shot-sheets so that you have a basic idea of what the final product will look like. You will also need to prepare careful plans of what will be shot, when, who in your group will be needed, when people will be available (especially if you are interviewing members of the public) and what will be needed (props, costumes, equipment, etc.).

While this may not necessarily all be true of a documentary, even then there are few documentary film-makers who simply go out with a camera and see what happens. They are much more likely to have decided in the first place whom they wish to interview, where, when, what they want to ask them, and also (if the truth be told) what sort of light they want to show them in.

NOTEBOX

This may well not be the most exciting part of the production process – and there will always be members of the group who just want to get on and do it. However, at the end of the day, this planning process will actually save you a great deal of time, and also prevent you from making a lot of errors and mistakes. It should mean that the final product is delivered on time – which of course in the real media world is incredibly important.

PRODUCTION

There are two very important primary stages to the production process: familiarisation and play. It is vital, first, to familiarise yourself with the technology available to you, to discover exactly what the equipment you are using is capable of doing. This may well also be a little depressing in the sense that most schools and colleges cannot necessarily afford the newest 'state of the art' technology. But this should not stand in your way. Far too many students have the idea that they need the very best of everything to complete the process and in fact nothing could be further from the truth.

You are not being judged on the technology that you have been using but on what you have managed to produce with the technology that is available to you. The beneficial aspect of this is that it will often force you into being far more creative and imaginative than you might have been if you were to rely on the technology to do everything for you.

This familiarisation process involves an element of 'play', as detailed in the Activity opposite.

Figure 62

Experiment with the software on your computer to see exactly what it is capable of. Walk around your school or college for an hour or two with the video camera and see what you can do with it – how good the picture quality is in a dark corridor for instance, and whether the auto-focus is a hindrance or a help. Find out what sound effects you can create on your tape recorder and how much extraneous sound the microphone picks up. Things are likely to happen that you might not have taken into consideration – for instance, can the end-of-lesson bell be heard when you record? Do other students tend to mug to the camera as they pass? Can your computer save the complicated graphic you have created?

When you feel comfortable with the equipment, when everyone has agreed on their tasks, when everyone knows what they are doing and when everyone feels confident and prepared . . . then you can begin!

You will have been given some kind of a deadline – do everything that you can to keep to this. In the best of all possible worlds you will have constructed a plan that is built around the deadlines set by your teacher/lecturer. Stick to it wherever possible. However, there can be little doubt that things will not always go strictly according to plan. Computers will crash. Video tapes will get eaten by the video-player. It will be raining on the day that you have organised to shoot outside. The music department will have double-booked the recording studio where you were going to record your live interview with the head or principal. These are the kind of things that can lead to total despondency.

However, if you have a well-organised plan, then it is not too difficult to look forward and work out exactly what you can do in the meantime. Because one thing is certain: there is always too much to do and not enough time to do it in. And if the item you were going to work on in any given day suddenly becomes impossible to do, then there should always be an alternative section or task that you can be working on.

Remember, too, to hold frequent 'progress report meetings'. These are important for several reasons. You will constantly need to assess how things are going, give everyone an opportunity to come up with new ideas or complaints, and also ensure that the entire production is still on track.

You may well have a plan but there is another important point to make at this stage. There is always the possibility that, no matter how good your plan, things will not necessarily work out as you thought they would. No matter how you see things in your head, in reality they might not be a success. There can be any number of reasons for this. Perhaps the sun was shining in the wrong direction. Maybe the colour printer did not have sufficient contrast, thereby making the shades of the same basic colour merge into one. Or an actor vital to the scene you have prepared to shoot did not turn up.

In cases like these you will have to be prepared to improvise, and maybe alter direction completely. Interestingly, this can sometimes be turned to your advantage; often what you least expected can be the best option. This flexibility is important. You have a plan, but something better turned up – when it does, seize the opportunity (but remember to note it down because it will be very relevant for your commentary).

Some other tips whilst you work on the production:

1   Keep everything. That front cover might not seem right at the time, but you may change your mind after you have tried and failed to improve on it. It will also be very useful as evidence when you explain the developmental process in your commentary. Equally all the video material you create may well come in useful when editing. Shoot, watch and log it all, every day if possible.
2   Bear in mind at all times that it is your ideas, and your attempts to get your ideas into concrete form, that matter. You are not professionals working full-time on the job. You will be rewarded for making a genuine attempt at something, even though it might seem to you to be a failure (as long as it is recorded in your log/commentary).
3   Never lose sight of the pre-production research that you did – and which should in any case have taken up much of your time. You will almost certainly be working within a genre – keep in mind at all times the conventions of that genre and its likely audience. Your audience needs to be entertained and challenged, otherwise your product has failed.
4   Even though you might be striving for originality, the chances of achieving it are fairly slight. For instance, if you are working within a particular magazine genre and want to produce a product that is totally original (and has the potential to be a

fantastic financial success), you should always bear in mind that there are people employed in the media world who are paid thousands of pounds a year to try to dream up similar ideas. And they rarely succeed either. It is a good idea to be as ambitious as possible, but the ambition needs to be tempered with a dose of reality. This is a cruel way of suggesting that, even though your end product might not be all you had hoped, it will probably have a great deal of merit – and why give all your best ideas to an examiner – for nothing? Save the really good ones until you are working!

5   Keep a log/diary. You will forget what happened six weeks ago. The practicalities of media production are important. It is not simply about ideas but also technique and coping with external pressures to get the whole thing finished. This process needs to be articulated in your commentary. If corners are cut because of budgetary or time constraints, then you will need to articulate how you coped and how it affected what you achieved.

POST-PRODUCTION

All media products need to be marketed and advertised. They do not sell themselves. Many candidates simply produce an artefact and leave it at that.

It is very important that you consider the presentation of your product very carefully. There is little point in working very hard on your video production and then delivering the finished product in a shabby unmarked video case. The same is often true of a radio production. Similarly, do not present a magazine that is unkempt, badly bound or a second-generation copy which is hard to read.

First appearances count for a great deal – and not only in the high street. If the product has been well packaged and looks clean and smart, then it is much more likely to be considered a success. Therefore, if you have made a video, package it in a new plastic cover and create a proper video cover that fits the genre of the piece, and gives suitable information about the product on the back for those who need to know. Bear in mind that the video should look as if it could compete with all the other videos on the shelf in the local video hire shop.

Equally, if your product is print-based, then it needs to look good so that people browsing in a newsagent will be tempted to pick it up. At all times bear in mind the competition on the newsagents' shelves and think carefully about the audience that you are trying to attract.

You will have spent a long time considering the look of your front page. But the product as a whole needs to be kept pristine. Think very carefully about the different forms of binding available to you. Consider laminating each page and creating a rather firmer front wrap-around cover so that it always stays in one piece. (Remember that you are not being marked for the type of binding that you employ.) Indeed, some candidates in the past have dispensed completely with the pretence of binding their product and have simply placed each page within a plastic folder – and explained why they have done so in their rationale. This ensures that your product will be marked looking its best.

Figure 63

Figure 64

MEDIA STUDIES: THE ESSENTIAL INTRODUCTION

The commentary/rationale

The practical production means very little unless it is accompanied by a commentary. This is where you have the opportunity to write, usually about 1,000 words or so, explaining the rationale behind the product, how you went about it and how you would evaluate the finished product.

Everybody who works on a production team will have to produce their own commentary. It is your chance to articulate how your product illuminates your understanding of the key concepts of the Media Studies syllabus that you are following. As a guide it is probably a very good idea to divide your piece of writing into three distinct parts:

1 **Intention** This section is very similar to the idea of a brief. You should explain what it is that you have set out to do and the ideas behind it. Explain why you have chosen the particular product and the subject material of that particular product, as well as suggesting the target audience that you are aiming for and how you intend to attract them. You should refer to the key concepts of the course and it is here that you should reveal your engagement with those very key concepts and how your practical production puts that engagement into concrete form. Media theory into media practice!

2 **Process** In this section you should explain the actual technical process of getting your media product made. There is a danger here of going into far too much detail. With this in mind you should watch the word count very carefully. What is *not* needed is a day-by-day, blow-by-blow account of the minutiae of the production process – rather it is an opportunity to discuss the technical and other problems you may have encountered and how you overcame them. There will have been technical hitches. Explain how and why they occurred and how you dealt with them. Do not dwell on how one particular character kept on letting you down because this often ends up sounding like sour grapes. As your teachers and lecturers should be monitoring your production at all times, it's likely that they will know who is doing what and, more importantly, who is doing very little.

3 **Outcome** In this part of the commentary you should do to your production what you have been doing to other media products since you started the course. In other words you should try, as objectively as possible, to evaluate the effectiveness of your product, in terms of its use of the chosen media, its subject matter and its suggested target audience. Try to be as honest as you can. Do not be overcritical, but at the same time try not to be too bland. Marks are not given for the following phrases: '. . . and I really enjoyed making it . . . I don't think it could be improved on . . . all in all I think it's pretty good' .

In all three parts of the rationale it is important to avoid description and to concentrate on showing how you have got to grips with media concepts through the practical process. In other words you need to be as critical and analytical of your own production as you have been with every other media product you have studied over the course. It is also an opportunity for you to reflect on your own learning and the relevance of what you think you have learnt in the past.

It will not be a perfect production – although it may well be very close to perfection – but the important thing is that the production will be assessed as positively as is possible. With this in mind, anyone looking at the production and rationale will respond to a healthy dose of self-criticism in a flexible and encouraging way.

Do not simply leave this part of the process to the last minute. It is a piece of work that has to be shaped and considered in exactly the same way as the product itself and can earn you a substantial rise in your marks. Keep to the word length, type the essay, spell-check what you have written, and again ensure that it is well presented and relevant to the production that you have submitted.

FURTHER WORK . . .

1   Create a text, such as a short film sequence, the opening of a TV programme, or a trail for a radio play, that disrupts narrative conventions in order to achieve a particular effect on the audience.

2   Plan a media product that challenges existing stereotypes; for example, an advertisement that inverts existing gender roles.

3   Create a media production that might be used to contribute to a campaign persuading people that exceeding the speed limit is dangerous and anti-social.

4   Imagine you are going to shoot a documentary about an event in your school or college. It might be a performance or an important sporting event. What preparations will you want to make before you prepare to shoot? How might these influence the level of 'realism' in the end product?

▼ PREPARING FOR EXAMS

Chances are you have worked hard all year on your Media Studies course. Now it is time for the exams. Remember that exams are your opportunity to show off what you have learned and to convert this knowledge into a good grade. You will find that in general Media Studies exams are not about finding out what you don't know. They are more likely to be an opportunity for you show off precisely what you *do* know and to demonstrate how well you have grasped the concepts that underpin a study of the media. If you approach your exams with this in mind, you are more likely to do well than if you go into the exam room in a state of fear and loathing. Try to see the exam as your opportunity to let the world know just what you can do.

NOTEBOX

As we pointed out in the section on how to study the media, there are very few, if any, 'right' answers in this discipline. Media Studies is about the skills of analysis and evaluation. You must be willing to accept that there are few set rules or set patterns. In fact much of the intellectual reward in studying the media lies in the ambiguity of the issues it raises. The debate about the need to regulate the media is a good example. For you to say that there is too much regulation of the media is neither right nor wrong. Indeed it is unlikely that any position on such a complex issue can be adopted successfully or convincingly. What examiners are looking for is your ability to show you have understood the complexity of the debate. You should do this by rehearsing the key issues that surround it and supporting these with appropriate examples.

DRAWING UP A REVISION PLAN

A revision plan is the essential first step towards preparing yourself for your Media Studies exam. You may find the following steps a useful way to guide you in drawing up such a plan:

1   Make sure you know what you need to revise. Either check with the specification or syllabus yourself, or ask your teacher what you need to do. In some cases you may find that there is a choice of topic areas and you may have to decide how many of these you are going to prepare for the exam.

2   Make a list of the topics you have decided you need to cover. Check where you can best find the information you need on these topics. Start with your own notes and then look at how textbooks, such as this one, may be able to help you.

3   Draw up a revision timetable devoting a suitable amount of time to each topic. Be realistic about how many hours you can devote to this. There will almost certainly be other subjects making demands on your time, as well as all of those diversions you will have to succumb to.

4   Put together a list of up-to-date examples that you can draw upon to illustrate your answers. If you have made good notes throughout your course, you should have a good range of texts such as films, television and radio programmes, newspaper and magazine articles you can call upon. It is also worth thinking in advance about how you may be able to use these in the exam. Remember, too, to keep an eye on such sources as the *Media Guardian* for up-to-date information on key media issues and debates.

5   Remember that revision you do at the very last minute may be of little use. Revising is like preparing yourself for a sporting event. A sustained programme of preparation will always be more effective than a last-minute panic.

UNSEEN PAPERS

Most exam boards set a paper which requires you to write about a media text you will see for the first time in the exam itself. This is often called the unseen paper. Typically the exam will consist of a video or sound extract that will be played to you once you are in the exam room. Alternatively you may be asked to look at a print-based text, such as a magazine article. Usually you are asked to respond to the text in around an hour and a half to two hours. The type of text, video, sound and print may vary, as will the precise instructions telling you what to do. The principles for approaching this type of exercise, however, remain very similar. In fact it is likely you will have had a go at some practice papers in class to help you get the hang of it.

NOTEBOX

A good way of practising for the unseen paper is to look at texts you have chosen yourself. Magazine covers, radio advertisements, extracts from television programmes and cinema trails are all good examples. Then try to get down some notes as quickly as you can on what specific aspects of the text you would want to point out if you were writing an analysis. This way you will help prepare yourself mentally for the task of unseen analysis in the exam itself.

The current trend in unseen papers is to provide fairly detailed information advising you what you should look for in your commentary on the text. (See specimen paper in Appendix.) This guidance provides a useful checklist of points to cover. It is important to bear in mind that it may not be a good idea to work mechanically through the list trying to get something down under each heading. Each text that you will be asked to consider is unique. As such it needs an individual response. Your ability to identify the unique qualities of the text and base your commentary on these is the real test of your ability in such a paper. You should not, for example, spend time on an issue such as narrative if you feel that this is a relatively unimportant aspect of the text. Rather focus on those elements that you feel are significant and be prepared to highlight these in your analysis. The checklist is, however, a useful mechanism for ensuring that you have not disregarded a key element of the analysis which is important.

Organising your response is an important aspect of this question. A brilliantly perceptive textual analysis is of little use if it is confused and difficult to follow. The guidance or checklist may come in useful here as a way of suggesting to you headings under which to organise your response. However you decide to organise what you have to say, make sure that it is both logical and user-friendly for the examiner. The easier it is for someone to digest what you have to say, the more likely you are to be rewarded for it.

It is important that you also spend some time thinking before you start to write your response. This is true for all exams, but it is especially important for an unseen paper. This is probably the first time you will have seen the text you are to deal with. You need, therefore, to spend time getting familiar with it and preparing yourself to develop your idea on the text. If the exam rubric permits, by all means start scribbling down some notes to help remind you of the important points. Whatever you do, though, do not try to start writing your analysis straight away. Give yourself time to see the text as a whole before you look at the individual parts.

You should always check that you know what the question is asking. You may have practised this exercise many times before, but there may be subtle changes between the version you practised and the examination paper you are sitting. So read the questions carefully and avoid making assumptions.

Timing is an important aspect of all exams as we explain below. It is likely that you will have more to say than the time allows in a paper like this. You will almost certainly come out of the exam room thinking of many other points you wished you had made. The essence of good exam timing is to prioritise the important points and deal with them first. Similarly it is important that you avoid getting bogged down on one particular aspect and find yourself with insufficient time to develop other key points. A rough plan with key headings and notes of the points you want to make will help you both to structure your response and to optimise the use of the time allowed.

Analysing texts is a test of your ability to apply key Media Studies concepts. It follows that if you can use the technical terminology of the discipline with accuracy and authority you will produce a convincing analysis. Understanding key terms such as connotation, anchorage, intertextuality or ideology is important. Using them appropriately to describe how the text functions is even more important.

The mistake that many students make in this sort of paper is that they focus too much on simply describing the text itself. You can safely assume that the examiner has already seen the text. Your job is to *analyse*. This means you should be able to explain how the text works, by exposing some of the underlying thinking that has gone into its construction.

It is the complexities of the text that you should attempt to reveal; simply describing what is in front of you goes little way to doing this.

NOTEBOX

Try to avoid thinking of the formal written exam as something separate from the production work you have done on your course. Media Studies is very much about seeing the links between theory and production. The confident use of production terminology will help you a lot in this unseen paper. In looking at moving image texts, remember you can describe shot sizes such as close-up, types of edits (cut, dissolve) as well as camera movement (track, pan). In print texts you can use the terminology you will have picked up in DTP, such as font, point size, crop and scale, to explain how a text has been put together. Combining these with appropriate theoretical language will allow you to write a confident and authoritative commentary.

ESSAY PAPERS

The other type of paper you are most likely to encounter is the essay paper. In this you are expected to write a number of essays, often two or three in a given period of time.

It is always a good idea to make yourself familiar with the type of paper you are sitting in advance of the exam. It is common for a paper to be split into sections, each reflecting an area of the specification you have studied. For example, there may be a section on newspapers, another on documentary and a third on cinema. If you are sitting such a paper, two things are important. One is to make sure just what questions you are supposed to attempt. Look out for an instruction on the paper telling you what to do. It may say, for example: 'Attempt one question from any two sections'. Clearly you will not do well in the exam if you disregard such an instruction.

The second important issue is about preparing yourself for an exam of this sort. If you know that you are to answer two questions on two different topics from a choice of four, how are you going to prepare? Some students will only prepare for the questions in two sections, while others may prepare three or even four topics to give themselves the widest choice on the day. There are arguments for and against both approaches, and your teacher may be the best person to advise you on a strategy. Do, however, be absolutely certain that you follow the instructions on the paper and answer the right number of questions.

Much of the advice that we can offer about dealing with essay papers is relevant to most other subjects. However, the problem of repeating advice you may already have been given is much outweighed by the advantages you will get in the exam by hearing it a second time.

When you turn over your paper at the beginning of the exam, read through it thoroughly and carefully. Don't jump to rash conclusions and rush headlong into decisions about which questions you are going to attempt. It is a well-known fact that often an 'easy' question in the end will prove more difficult and vice versa. Make sure also that you read each question in great detail. Don't assume that, because you feel familiar with a few words or a quotation, this is the best question for you. Conversely, if you read a question that has a quotation that you don't recognise or is from someone you have never heard of, don't assume that you cannot do the question. Spend some time looking at key words and use these to determine what the question is really asking. Some students find that underlining these key words helps keep them focused on the main points of their answer.

Identify what you consider to be the key words in the following question that was set by AQA in January 2001. Explain why you think these are the words that are most important:

Promotional and covert advertising techniques have become increasingly widespread. Account for this using specific examples.

Once you have decided what the question is asking you to do, it is important that you then try to answer this question precisely. Do not decide that the question is close to an answer you have already prepared and write that down instead. By all means have a response prepared, but make sure you adapt it to the real needs of the question in front of you.

Once you have decided which questions you are going to attempt, you need to consider the order in which you are going to tackle them. Experience of marking exam papers suggests that the last answer that candidates attempt is often their weakest. There are a number of possible explanations for this, but the most obvious is to do with time management. Many students simply run out of time and are forced to rush the last answer. It follows that careful planning and apportioning of an equal amount of time to each question should help you ensure an even performance over the whole paper.

One strategy you might like to consider is to spend time planning all the questions you are to answer as soon as you have chosen them. This entails mapping out your response to each in note form before you actually start writing the first one. This will mean that you can then use your notes as the basis for each response and allocate the remaining time equally between the questions. It also means that, if other points occur to you as you are working on another question, it is simple to note it down ready for use later on.

Rough notes are an invaluable help in producing a good essay response. One approach that many students find effective is to use a sheet of paper and write down in note form all the relevant points that come into their head. Once this has been done, it is a good idea to put together points that have an obvious link between them. Then you can look at the notes to impose a structure on what you are going to write. It is surprising how often you will find that there will be six to eight key points that you want to make. If you number these in order of importance this can form a useful paragraph-by-paragraph route through your essay.

ACTIVITY

Using one of the 'Further Work' questions at the end of a chapter, try noting down and numbering the points you would want to make as your response.

Your style of writing is an important element of how well your essay is received. Rambling, unstructured or disorganised responses full of waffle do not get good marks in examinations. Examiners are not easy people to fool. The best approach is a simple and straightforward style of writing. Try to avoid seeming pretentious, for example by trying to use words that you do not properly understand but think sound convincing.

A good essay answer will also start in an interesting way. Do not think that the first paragraph has to be a mere re-hash of the question. If you can think of a bright attractive introduction, perhaps a quotation or even something controversial, then do not be afraid to use it. Similarly try to end on a high note. Do not just let your essay trail off at the end, but look for an assertive ending that will help sum up what has gone before.

A particularly important point you need to bear in mind is the importance of supporting your arguments. This can be done specifically in two ways. The first is by drawing upon published authorities to give weight to the point you are making.

Similarly, you should refer to examples of media texts which you think support your point of view. For example, you may allude to a particular film or magazine cover as evidence of changing attitudes to a particular minority group. The best examples are generally those you have found yourself, rather than texts that the whole class has studied and is likely to refer to *en masse* in the same exam.

Finally, it is to be hoped that you will have developed a great deal of enthusiasm for your Media Studies course. Do not be afraid to let this shine through in the exam. Examiners enjoy reading scripts that demonstrate genuine engagement and commitment on the part of students and they always try to reward this.

▼ APPENDIX

EXAM PAPER 1

Consider the exam paper on the opposite page. It was set for the A/S Level examination by AQA in January 2001. Candidates were allowed one and a half hours to complete the two questions required. The paper is typical of an essay-based examination set by all the boards at AS/A Level.

Let us consider some of the issues you would need to take into account if you were in the exam room about to sit this paper. First you would need to think about timing. Assuming that you allow yourself five minutes' thinking time at the beginning and five minutes to check your work at the end, that means 80 minutes to work on the questions or 40 minutes for each.

In preparing yourself for the exam, you should have explored at least two of the topic areas identified for each of the questions. It makes sense, therefore, to focus your attention on these. Of course, if you have prepared more than two areas, then you need to consider all possibilities. This is not, however, a good time to decide that you can answer a question on an area that you have not explored, even if it does look an attractive option. If you have not studied an area, you may not be aware of the particular issues that the examiner will be expecting you to discuss.

Note that on this paper each topic area has two options. You need to read *each* of these carefully. It is common under the pressure of an exam to jump in and decide to write on one option without first considering the other fully. Spend a little time deciding which is the better choice for you. It is probably worth noting down a few ideas for both and then choosing the one that you feel most confident about.

Let us look in more detail at question 1 on the topic of Film and Broadcast Fiction. To some extent the nature of your preparatory work on this topic might decide which option to tackle. As you can see, question (a) calls for knowledge of both film and television, whereas option (b) requires you to have looked at just one of these forms. Both tasks require you to make a detailed response, but in slightly different ways. Option (a) asks specifically for textual analysis of two texts, one film and one piece of fictional television. You are invited to use this to demonstrate your broader awareness of how media texts are put together. In this question you need to be confident that you have prepared a good and detailed account of the two texts. Note in the question you are asked to provide a 'reading'. Reading does not mean description; it means analysis and interpretation. If you find yourself spending a large amount of time on plot summary, you are not doing a very good job.

Answer **two** questions, from different topic areas.

All questions carry 30 marks.

1 **Film and Broadcast Fiction**

EITHER (a) Provide a reading of **one** film and **one** broadcast fictional text showing how they help you to understand the ways in which media texts are constructed.

OR (b) Describe the ways in which different film **or** television fictional narratives appeal to their audiences. Refer to specific texts in your answer.

2 **Documentary**

EITHER (a) Account for the similarities and differences between **two** documentaries made in different decades. At least **one** of the documentaries must have been made before 1990.

OR (b) Outline the arguments about the reliability of documentaries as ways of representing reality. Illustrate with reference to a range of documentary material.

3 **Advertising and Marketing**

EITHER (a) Describe and analyse the ways in which a recent advertising **or** marketing campaign targeted its audience.

OR (b) Promotional and covert advertising techniques have become increasingly widespread. Account for this using specific examples.

4 **British Newspapers**

EITHER (a) Compare **two** British newspapers accounting for the similarities and differences between them.

OR (b) Are criticisms of the British tabloid press fair?
Refer to specific stories to support your arguments.

Source: Assessment and Qualifications Alliance (AQA), General Certificate of Education, January 2001, Advanced Subsidiary Examination. With kind permission.

Choosing appropriate texts is important for this question. You will no doubt have spent time in class looking at texts your teacher has introduced. Many other members of the class are likely to use these. It may well be in your interests to choose your own texts rather than on relying on those you have considered in class. This way you should bring a freshness and personal engagement to your response in a way that would be lacking if you rely heavily on the ideas of the teacher and the rest of the class. Do not worry too much about choosing text that you think an examiner will consider 'appropriate'. What is important is to provide evidence of your ability to engage with the texts in the way we have suggested. Do, however, make sure that your chosen text meets the requirements of being a *fictional* text.

Finally do not forget that this question is inviting you to demonstrate your awareness of broader media theory. Your reading of the two texts should give you a platform from which to show how they help you to understand the ways in which media texts are constructed. This means that you need to spend some time talking about concepts such as genre and audience expectations – they are used as a guiding principle in the construction of such texts.

Option (b) looks on the surface a much wider question; it does not limit you to the detailed analysis of just two fictional texts. Note, however, that it does limit you to one media form 'film **or** television'. Note also that it is a question about narrative, or more specifically about how fictional narratives appeal to their audiences. An answer that simply lists different narrative devices without making this important link to audience appeal is unlikely to do well. For example, you could consider how audiences might enjoy trying to solve the narrative enigmas or choosing allegiances in conflicts in soap operas.

Do not forget that all-important last sentence in this question, 'Refer to specific texts in your answer.' Just as in option (a), there will be examples you have discussed in class that may be relevant to this question. A good response to this task will offer a range of fictional texts to support your arguments. Take this opportunity to use some examples of your own. Again this will demonstrate your own personal critical engagement in preparing for the exam.

So it is up to you to decide which of the questions you feel better-equipped to tackle. Now you need to apply this kind of thinking process to the other topic area you have prepared.

ACTIVITY . . .

Working in pairs, choose another topic area and give careful consideration to each of the alternative questions. You do not need detailed knowledge of the topic area to do this. Working together, write down what you consider to be the key points you need to take into account in choosing your question. Then individually provide a brief essay plan for the question you prefer.

When you have finished, compare your essay plan with your partner's. Identify and discuss similarities and differences.

EXAM PAPER 2: READING THE MEDIA

You will find that this process – Reading the Media – is common to all Media Studies examinations, although it might also be called something else such as 'Modern Media Forms'.

Yet, whatever the title of the examination, the process will invariably be the same. All Media Studies specifications are based upon a range of Key Concepts which you should be introduced to very early on in the course. These Key Concepts are listed for you in the Reading the Media examination published by AQA in January 2001 (see opposite).

When confronted by an examination which asks you to read a text it is important that you always utilise the Key Concepts.

Look at the text carefully – at first take in the text as a whole and then try to break it down into its constituent parts. What is the main purpose of the text? How does it achieve this purpose? What is actually going on in the text? How does it communicate with its audience? Who is this audience?

Spend some time making notes under each of the Key Concepts – don't rush this process because it is actually the most important part. You will find that the time given over to a Reading question is usually a little bit more generous than the more conventional essay papers and you are unlikely to be rushed.

Ensure you cover all of the Key Concepts to the best of your ability.

Do not spend time carefully describing the text. The examiner will have a copy of the text and will know it well. You will be given no marks for a description /denotation. All you will be doing is wasting your time.

It is the analysis that will gain you marks. Your analysis will need to refer to the text as closely as possible. Try to avoid generalisations. Comments such as 'all advertisements tend to be sexist' are not helpful. However, reference to other advertisements that might be sexist in the correct context will gain you marks.

Do not be afraid to use your imagination. You may well 'see' things in the text that had not occurred to the examiners. As long as you can back up any statement you make with evidence from the text then feel confident enough to put it down in writing.

It might sound rather silly but enjoy yourself – reading the media is about giving examination candidates the opportunity to express themselves, show engagement and develop a sense of critical autonomy.

Answer the **one** compulsory question below.

The question carries 60 marks.

- You have 15 minutes to read and make notes on the question and the accompanying advertisement for the JVC TH-A10 DVD Digital Camera System.

- You will then have 1 hour to write a continuous analysis of the extract.

- You will be rewarded for making detailed references to the text.

- You should place major emphasis upon the Key Concepts of Media Language, Representation and Media Audiences. You may also wish to comment upon Values and Ideology and Media Institutions.

You may find the following useful in thinking about your analysis:

MEDIA LANGUAGE
Content: main theme and purpose
Layout and design
Use of language
Use of photographs/illustrations

REPRESENTATION
Gender
Age
Class

MEDIA AUDIENCES
Target audience
Likely readership and audience positioning
'Lifestyle'

In addition you may like to comment upon

VALUES AND IDEOLOGY
Values implicit in the representations offered
Assumptions being made about the audience
Values of the text as a whole

MEDIA INSTITUTIONS
Media technologies

END OF QUESTION

Source: Assessment and Qualifications Alliance (AQA), General Certificate of Education, January 2001, Advanced Subsidiary Examination. With kind permission.

▼ RESOURCES

SECONDARY DATA SOURCES:

Advertising Association
Abford House
15 Wilton Road
London SW1V 1NJ ☏ 020 7828 2771

Advertising Standards Authority (ASA)
2 Torrington Place
London WC1E 7HW
☏ 020 7580 5555

BBC
Television Centre
Wood Lane
London W12 7RJ ☏ 020 7743 8000

British Board of Film Classification (BBFC)
3 Soho Square
London W1V 5DE ☏ 020 7440 1570

Broadcasting Standards Commission (BSC)
7 The Sanctuary
London SW1P 3JS ☏ 020 7233 0544

Channel 4 Television
124 Horseferry Road
London SW1P 2TX ☏ 020 7396 4444

Community Media Association
5 Paternoster Square
Sheffield S1 2BX ☏ 0114 279 5219

Film Education
Alhambra House
27–31 Charing Cross Road
London WC2H 0AU ☏ 020 7976 2291

Independent Television Commission (ITC)
31 Foley Street
London W1P 7LB ☏ 020 7255 3000

The Institute of Practitioners in Advertising (IPA)
44 Belgrave Square
London SW1X 8QS ☏ 020 7235 7020

Market Research Society
15 Northburgh Street
London EC1V 0AH ☏ 020 7490 4911

Northern Ireland Film Commission
21 Ormeau Ave
Belfast BT2 8HD ☏ 028 9023 2444

The Publishers Association
1 Kingsway
London WC2 6XF ☏ 020 7565 7474

Press Complaints Commission (PCC)
1 Salisbury Square
London EC4Y 8AE
☏ 020 7353 1248

Radio Authority
Holbrook House
Great Queen Street
London WC2B 5DG
☎ 020 7430 2724

Scottish Screen
249 West George Street
Glasgow G2 4QE
☎ 0141 302 1700

Voice of the Listener Broadcast Consumer
101 King's Drive
Gravesend
Kent DA12 5BQ ☎ 01474 352835

South Wales Film Commission
The Media Centre
Culverhouse Cross
Cardiff CF5 6XJ ☎ 029 2059 0240

USEFUL PUBLICATIONS

These may be available in school, college or university libraries or in central reference libraries in large towns. Some are expensive to buy; others, like the weekly trade papers, are available for little cost from newsagents in major towns and cities.

British Rate & Data (BRAD)
Publishes a range of reference material on all forms of media advertising. Expensive to buy.

Broadcast
Leading weekly trade journal for the broadcast industry. Includes a weekly BARB top 100 television programmes.

Campaign
Leading weekly trade journal for the advertising industry.

Cultural Trends
Annual publication from the Policy Studies Institute which provides information on video, broadcasting and cinema consumption.

Free Press
Magazine produced by the Campaign for Press and Broadcasting Freedom, 8 Cynthia Street, London N1 9JF.

Guardian Media Guide
Annual guide that contains a large

amount of information and contact details.

Marketing Week
Leading trade magazine for the marketing industry.

Media Week
Leading trade magazine for media buyers.

New Media Age
Specialist magazine for 'new' digital media.

Radio Magazine
Trade magazine for the (mainly) commercial sector.

Screen International
Trade magazine for film (and video) production and distribution industry.

Sight & Sound
Monthly film magazine from the BFI that contains features and reviews.

Social Trends
Annual publication from the Government Statistical Service which provides demographic information, plus sections on home leisure and social activities.

Stage, Screen & Radio
Journal of the media workers union BECTU.

UK Press Gazette
Trade paper for journalists in UK broadcasting and press industries.

Willings Press Guide, Reed Information Services.
Similar to *BRAD* and again expensive to buy.

WEBSITES

Most major media organisations now have their own websites that contain information that varies in its usefulness. Often of more use are the links they provide to other sites that you may not be aware of. Many magazines, television programmes or films will also have their own dedicated websites or newsgroups.

www.telegraph.co.uk
www.dailyexpress.co.uk
www.ft.com
www.guardian.co.uk
www.independent.co.uk
www.the.european.com
www.itc.co.uk
www.itn.co.uk
www.carltontv.co.uk
www.granadatv.co.uk
www.htv.co.uk
www.channel4.co.uk
www.channel5.co.uk
www.sky.co.uk
www.barb.co.uk
www.rajar.co.uk

Below are some possibly less well-known sites:

Media Zoo   www.mediazoo.co.uk
Contains lots of up-to-date and varied information, ideas, discussions about British media.

Media UK   www.mediauk.com/directory
Details the media scene with links to

websites of all the main TV and radio stations, magazines and newspapers.

British Film Institute   www.bfi.org.uk
Contains details of the services the BFI provides.

Centaur Communications
www.mad.co.uk
Site for publishers of many titles including *Marketing Weekly*, some useful trade discussion, information and links.

Internet Movie Database
www.uk.imdb.com
Lots of information and search engines.

Media Channel   www.mediachannel.org
A USA-based site with many links worldwide although can be rather too US-focused.

Internet Newspaper Directory
www.discover.co.uk/NET/NEWS/news.html
A worldwide guide and access to newspapers.

Radio Advertising Bureau
www.rab.co.uk
Official site for the commercial radio industry with lots of information regarding who owns whom etc. Some information regarding ratings is only available via subscription.

Radio Days www.otr.com/main.html
Site devoted to old time radio, includes historical clips and information.

The Radio Magazine
www.theradiomagazine.co.uk
Official site for the trade publication. Lots of information but some of it is only available via subscription.

The Radio Site
www.i-way.co.uk/~stunova
Site set up by a radio enthusiast contains links to stations and organisations around the world.

Stock Photo Agency
www.tssphoto.com
A photo agency site that contains lots of resources of interest to photographers plus links to other photographic sites.

Benetton www.benetton.com
Has a large site that includes photographs of all their United Colors of Benetton advertisements, plus explanations of the ideas behind them and a comments page where the public can express their opinions.

The Bookseller www.thebookseller.com
The 'organ' of the book publishing industry; contains information on new publications, best-seller lists and other trade information as well as details of career and training opportunities.

ARCHIVES

It can be quite difficult to get access to historical texts. They are often only available by appointment, are not free of charge and may require you to produce some kind of evidence to prove that you are a 'bona fide' student. They will often give priority to degree or postgraduate students. It is therefore important to check before going along.

British Film Institute (BFI)
21 Stephen Street
London W1P 1PL
☎ 020 7255 1444

Newspaper Library
British Library
Colindale Avenue
London NW9 5HE
☎ 020 7412 7353

East Anglian Film Archive
University of East Anglia
Norwich
NR4 7TJ ☎ 01603 456161

Museum of the Moving Image
South Bank,
London SE1 8XT
☎ 020 7928 3535
(Currently closed until 2003.)

National Museum of Photography, Film
& Television (NMPFT)
Bradford BD1 1NQ
☏ 01274 202030

National Sound Archive
British Library
96 Euston Road
London NW1 2DB ☏ 020 7412 7436

North West Film Archive
Manchester Metropolitan University
Minshull House
47–49 Chorlton Street
Manchester M1 3EU
☏ 0161 247 3097

North West Sound Archive
Old Steward's Office
The Castle
Clitheroe
Lancs BB7 1AZ ☏ 01200 427897

Scottish Screen Archive
1 Bowmont Gardens
Glasgow G12 9LR ☏ 0141 337 7413

South East Film & Video Archive
University of Brighton
Grand Parade
Brighton BN2 2JY ☏ 01273 643213

Wales Film & Television Archive
Unit 1
Science Park
Cefn Llan,
Aberystwyth
Ceredigion SY23 3AH
☏ 01970 626007

Wessex Film & Sound Archive
Hampshire Record Office
Sussex Street
Winchester SO23 8TH
☏ 01962 847742

▼ GLOSSARY

Action code A narrative device by which a resolution is produced through action, e.g. a shoot-out.

Actuality Recordings of images and sounds of events made on location as they actually happen for inclusion in news reports or documentaries.

ADSL (Asymmetric Digital Subscriber Line) A telephone network that turns an ordinary telephone copper wire into a high-speed connection for Internet, broadcasting and video-on-demand services.

Anchorage The fixing or limiting of a particular set of meanings to an image, e.g. the use of a caption beneath a photograph.

Anti-narrative Describes a text which seeks deliberately to disrupt narrative flow in order to achieve a particular effect, such as the repetition of images or the disruption of a chronological sequence of events.

Breaking news A news story, the details of which are unfolding as the story is being reported.

Bricolage The way in which signs or artefacts are borrowed from different styles or genres to create something new.

Broadsheet A large rectangular newspaper, such as the *Daily Telegraph* or *The Times*. Broadsheets are visually associated with serious journalism reporting important events at home and abroad. They are targeted at an upmarket, professional readership.

Closed questions These demand a very limited answer, often just yes or no.

Codes Rules or conventions by which signs are put together to create meaning.

Connotation The meaning of a sign that is arrived at through the cultural experiences a reader brings to it.

Content analysis A method of collecting, collating and analysing large amounts of information about the content of media products, e.g. television advertisements, in order to draw conclusions about such issues as representation of gender roles.

Convergence The coming together of different communication technologies such as the telephone, the computer and television.

Denotation   What an image actually shows and which is immediately apparent as opposed to the assumptions an individual reader may make about it.

Dissolve   Film term for the transition between two images where one 'dissolves' into the next.

Docu-soap   A hybrid genre in which elements of documentary and soap opera are combined to create a series about the lives of real people.

Encoding   A process by which the media construct messages.

End credits   At the end of a film or television production, a detailed list of all the people who contributed to the production, from producers and directors to actors and technical, administrative and support crews.

Enigma   A narrative device that teases the audience by presenting a puzzle or riddle to be solved.

Feature   In newspapers, this is generally an article that concerns itself with a topical issue, while not having any hard news content.

Genre   The classifying of media texts into groups that have similar characteristics.

Hard news   News that is important and happening at the time it is reported. A rescue attempt on a ferry, the death or a major national figure or a rise in the mortgage interest rate could all be classified as hard news.

Hegemony   The concept used by Marxist critic Gramsci to describe how people are influenced into accepting the dominance of a power elite who impose their will and world-view. He maintains that this elite is able to rule because the rest of the population allow it to do so. It can be argued, therefore, that the ideological role of the media is to persuade us that it is in our best interests to accept the dominance of the elite.

Horizontal integration   This involves the acquisition of competitors in the same section of the industry. It might be possible for one company to seek to control all of the market – a monopoly position – but most capitalist countries have laws to try to stop this happening.

Hypodermic needle theory   This suggests that the media 'inject' ideas into a passive audience, like giving a patient a drug.

Hypothesis   An assumption or question about something that the research will investigate and hopefully either prove or disprove.

Icon   A sign that works by resemblance.

Iconography   Those particular signs that we associate with particular genres, such as physical attributes and dress of actors, the settings and 'tools of the trade' (cars, guns, etc.).

Ideology   A system of beliefs which determines how power relations are organised within society.

Independents   Companies (usually relatively small ones) which maintain a status outside the normal big business remit and therefore tend to focus on minority interest products.

Index   A sign that works by a relationship to the object or concept it refers to, e.g. smoke is an index of fire.

Interpellation   The process by which a media text summons an audience in much the same way as a town crier in the past would ring a bell and shout to summon an audience for an important announcement.

Intertextuality   The way in which texts refer to other media texts that producers assume audiences will recognise.

Linear narrative   A plot that moves forward in a straight line without flashbacks or digressions.

Media imperialism   The idea that powerful and wealthy countries can exercise economic, cultural and social control over others through control of media industries.

Media saturation   A term used to describe the extent to which our experience of the world is dominated by the media, not only at an individual level but also nationally and globally.

Mediation   The process by which a media text represents an idea, issue or event to us. This is a useful word as it suggests the way in which things undergo change in the process of being acted upon by the media.

Methodology   The system or manner used to carry out research, the different ways in which 'data' can be captured.

Mode of address   The way in which a particular text will address or speak to its audience.

Moral panic   A mass response to a group, a person or an attitude that becomes defined as a threat to society.

Multiplex   A cinema that contains several screens all under one roof – usually with one projection booth servicing all screens. The number of screens can vary; the new Warner Village in Birmingham contains 30 screens.

Multi-tracking   The process whereby different instruments and voices are recorded separately and then mixed together in a recording studio.

Narrative   The way in which a story is told in both fictional and non-fictional media texts.

Narrowcasting   The opposite of broadcasting, where texts are aimed at very small, special interest social groups.

Niche marketing   A small target audience with specific interests.

Open questions   Those that start with 'what', 'where', 'why', 'when', 'how' or 'who'. These encourage the interviewee to 'open up' and talk freely.

Parallel action   A narrative device in which two scenes are observed as happening at the same time by cutting between them.

Polysemic   The way in which a text has a variety of meanings and the audience is an important component in determining that meaning.

Postmodernism   This refers to the social, political and cultural attitudes and images of the late twentieth century.

Primary media   Where we pay close attention to the media text, for example, in the close reading of a magazine or newspaper or in the cinema where we concentrate on the film in front of us.

Process model   A linear model of communication (sender–channel–message–receiver) in which the meaning of the message is thought to be 'fixed' by the producer.

PSB (Public Service Broadcasting)   Introduced in the UK in the 1920s by Lord Reith, later Director General of the BBC, with a remit to 'inform, educate and entertain'. The yearly licence fee was payable first to cover radio sets and then, after the Second World War, to include televisions, too. This form of financing meant that the service was not reliant on outside commercial backing and could therefore, in principle, remain unbiased. PSB is designed to ensure a balanced coverage of different types of programme.

Qualitative research   This attempts to explain or understand something and may involve more discussion and analysis of people's attitudes and behaviour. It usually involves working with small numbers of people or 'focus groups'.

Quantitative research   This is based on numbers, statistics or tables, and it attempts to 'measure' some kind of phenomena and produce 'hard' data. It often involves working with large groups of people.

Realism   Representation by the media of situations or ideas in a way that they seem real.

Semiotics   The study of signs and sign systems.

Sign   According to Fiske and Hartley (1985), the sign consists of two components: the signifier and the signified. The signifier is a physical object, e.g. a sound, printed word, or advertisement. The signified is a mental concept or meaning conveyed by the signifier.

Simulacra   Simulation or copies that are replacing the 'real' artefacts.

Situated culture   A term used to describe how our 'situation' (i.e. daily routines and patterns, social relationships with family and peer groups) can influence our engagement with and interpretation of media texts.

Soundbite   A snappy and memorable quote that can easily be assimilated into a broadcast news story (e.g. Tony Blair's 'Education, education, education').

Structuralism   This approach argues that identifying underlying structures is vital in undertaking analysis. In linguistics, for example, it can be argued that all languages have a similar underlying grammatical structure, which we are born with the capacity to learn. Similarly, certain social structures, such as the family unit, may be common to many cultures.

Symbol   A sign that represents an object or concept solely by the agreement of the people who use it.

Tabloid   A compact newspaper, half the size of a broadsheet, designed to appeal to a mass audience. Tabloids, particularly at the lower end of the market, are associated with

sensationalising trivial events rather than with comprehensive coverage or national and international news.

Uses and Gratifications theory   The idea that media audiences make active use of what the media offer. The audience has a set of needs which the media in one form or another meet.

Vertical integration   This involves the ownership of every stage of the production process (production + distribution + exhibition) thereby ensuring complete control of a media product.

▼ BIBLIOGRAPHY

Allen, S. (2000) *News Culture*, Open University Press.

Ang, I. (1985) *Watching Dallas – Soap Opera and the Melodramatic Imagination*, Methuen.

—— (1991) *Desperately Seeking the Audience*, Routledge.

Armes, R. (1988) *On Video*, Oxford University Press.

Baehr, H. and Dyer, G. (eds) (1987) *Boxed In: Women and Television*, Pandora.

Barker, M. (1989) *Comics, Ideology, Power and the Critics*, Manchester University Press.

Barker, M. and Petley, J. (eds) (1997) *Ill-Effects – The Media/Violence Debate*, Routledge.

Barnard, S. (2000) *Studying Radio*, Arnold.

Bell, A., Joyce, M. and Rivers, D. (1999) *Advanced Level Media*, Hodder & Stoughton.

Berger, J. (1972) *Ways of Seeing*, Penguin.

Blumler, J. and Katz, E. (eds) *The Uses of Mass Communications: Current Perspectives on Gratification Research*, Sage.

Bordwell, D. and Thompson, K. (1979) *Film Art: An Introduction*, McGraw-Hill.

Boyd, A. (1994) *Broadcast Journalism. Techniques of Radio and TV News*, Focal Press.

Branston, G. and Stafford, R. (1999) *The Media Student's Book*, 2nd edition, Routledge.

Buckingham, D. (1987) *Public Secrets: EastEnders and its Audience*, BFI Publishing.

Cohen, S. (1972) *Folk Devils and Moral Panics: The Creation of Mods and Rockers*, MacGibbon & Kee.

Corner, J. (ed.) (1991) *Popular Television in Britain*, BFI Publishing.

Crisell, A. (1994) *Understanding Radio*, Routledge.

—— (1997) *An Introductory History of British Broadcasting*, Routledge.

Cumberbatch, G. (1990) *Television Advertising and Sex Role Stereotyping: A Content Analysis*, Broadcasting Standards Council.

Curran, J. and Seaton, J. (1997) *Power without Responsibility: The Press and Broadcasting in Britain*, Routledge.

Deacon, D. *et al.* (1999) *Researching Communications: A Practical Guide to Methods in Media and Cultural Analysis*, Arnold.

Dutton, B. (1995) *Media Studies: An Introduction*, Longman.

Dyer, R. (1977) 'Entertainment and utopia', *Movie*, vol. 24.

—— (1982) *Advertising as Communication*, Methuen.

Dyja, E. (ed.) (1999) *Film and Television Handbook 2000*, BFI Publishing.

Evans, H. (1986) *Pictures on a Page*, Heinemann.

Ferguson, M. (1983) *Forever Feminine: Women's Magazines and the Cult of Femininity*, Heinemann.

Fiske, J. (1987) *Television Culture*, Routledge.

—— (1990) *Introduction to Communication Studies*, Methuen.

Fiske, J. and Hartley, J. (1978) *Reading Television*, Methuen.

Frith, S. and Goodwin, A. (eds) (1990) *On Record*, Routledge.

Galtung, J. and Ruge, M. (1973) 'Structuring and selecting news' in S. Cohen and Young (eds) *The Manufacture of News: Deviance, Social Problems and the Mass Media*, Constable.

Geraghty, C. (1991) *Women and Soap-Opera*, Polity Press.

Glasgow University Media Group (1985) *War and Peace News*, Open University Press.

Goodwin, A. and Whannel, G. (eds) (1990) *Understanding Television*, Routledge.

Gray, A. (1992) *Video Playtime*, Routledge.

Halloran, J. (1970) *The Effects of Television*, Panther.

Hartley, J. (1982) *Understanding News*, Methuen.

Hebdige, D. (1988) *Hiding in the Light: On Images and Things*, Routledge.

Hobson, D. (1982) *Crossroads: The Drama of a Soap Opera*, Methuen.

Hollows, J. and Jancovich, M. (1996) *Approaches to Popular Film*, Manchester University Press.

Katz, E., Blumler, J. and Gurevitch, M. (1974) 'Utilisation of mass communication by the individual' in Blumler, J. and Katz, E. (eds) *The Uses of Mass Communications: Current Perspectives on Gratifications Research*, Sage.

Kirchner, D. (ed.) (1997) *The Researcher's Guide to British Film & Television Collections*, 5th edition, British Universities Film & Video Council.

Livingstone, S. (1998) *Making Sense of Television*, Routledge.

McLuhan, M. (1964) *Understanding Media*, Routledge & Kegan Paul.

McLuhan, M. and Fiore, Q. (1997) [1967] *The Medium Is the Massage*, Wired Books.

McMahon, B. and Quinn, R. (1986) *Real Images*, Macmillan.

—— (1988) *Exploring Images*, Macmillan.

McRobbie, A. (1983) 'Teenage Girls, *Jackie* and the ideology of adolescent femininity' in Waites B. *et al. Popular Culture: Past and Present*, Croom Helm.

—— (1994) 'More! New sexualities in girls' and women's magazines' in Curran, J., Morley, D. and Walkerdine V. (eds) *Cultural Studies and Communications*, Arnold.

Messenger Davis, M. (1989) *Television Is Good for Kids*, Hilary Shipman.

Mitchell, C. (2000) *Women and Radio*, Routledge.

Monaco, J. (1977) *How to Read a Film*, Oxford University Press.

Morley, D. (1980) *The Nationwide Audience*, BFI Publishing.

—— (1986) *Family Television*, Comedia.

Mulvey, L. (1975) 'Visual pleasure and narrative cinema', *Screen*, vol. 16, no. 3.

Myers, G. (1985) *Understains: The Sense and Seduction of Advertising*, Comedia.

O'Sullivan, T. *et al.* (1994) *Key Concepts in Communication and Cultural Studies*, Routledge.

—— (1998) *Studying the Media*, Arnold.

O'Sullivan, T. and Jewkes, Y. (eds) (1997) *The Media Studies Reader*, Arnold.

Packard, V. (1979) *The Hidden Persuaders*, Penguin. First published 1957 by Longman.

Paget, D. (1998) *No Other Way to Tell It. Dramadoc/Docudrama on Television*, Manchester University Press.

Peak, S. and Fisher, P. (eds) (Annual) *Guardian Media Guide*, Fourth Estate.

Perkins, T. (1979) 'Rethinking stereotypes' in Barratt, M., Corrigan, P., Kuhn, A. and Wolff, V. (eds) *Ideology and Cultural Production*, Croom Helm.

Price, S. (1997) *The Complete A–Z Media and Communication Handbook*, Hodder & Stoughton.

Radway, J. (1984) *Reading the Romance: Women, Patriarchy and Popular Literature*, Verso.

Schlensinger, P. (1987) *Putting Reality Together: BBC News*, Methuen.

Selby, K. and Cowdery, R. (1995) *How to Study Television*, Macmillan.

Shingler, M. and Wieringa, C. (1998) *On Air: Methods and Meanings in Radio*, Arnold.

Stacey, J. (1994) *Star Gazing: Hollywood Cinema and Female Spectatorship*, Routledge.

Stokes, J. (1999) 'Use it or lose it: sex, sexuality and sexual health in magazines for girls' in Stokes, J. and Reading, A. (eds) *The Media in Britain: Current Debates and Developments*, Macmillan.

Storey, J. (1993) *An Introductory Guide to Cultural Theory and Popular Culture*, Harvester Wheatsheaf.

Strinati, D. (1995) *An Introduction to Theories of Popular Culture*, Routledge.

Strinati, D. and Wagg, S. (eds) (1992) *Come On Down: Popular Media Culture in Post War Britain*, Routledge.

Taylor, K. (2000) 'Girl Power! How an audience perceives the teenage girl through various media forms'. Unpublished dissertation, Cheltenham & Gloucester College of Higher Education.

Taylor, L. and Willis, A. (1999) *Media Studies*, Blackwell.

Tilley, A. (1991) 'Narrative' in D. Lusted (ed.) *The Media Studies Book: A Guide for Teachers*, Blackwell.

Trowler, P. (1996) *Investigating Mass Media*, 2nd edition, Collins.

Tunstall, J. (1983) *The Media in Britain*, Constable.

Watson, J. and Hill, A. (1996) *A Dictionary of Communication and Media Studies*, Arnold.

Watts, H. (1982) *On Camera*, Aavo.

Williams, K. (1997) *Get Me a Murder a Day: A History of Mass Communications in Britain*, Arnold.

Williams, R. (1974) *Television, Technology and Cultural Form*, Routledge.

Williamson, J. (1978) *Decoding Advertisements: Ideology and Meaning in Advertisements*, Boyars.

Winship, J. (1987) *Inside Women's Magazines*, Pandora.

MEDIA STUDIES: THE ESSENTIAL INTRODUCTION

▼ INDEX

MEDIA STUDIES: THE ESSENTIAL INTRODUCTION

MEDIA STUDIES: THE ESSENTIAL INTRODUCTION

This Sporting Life, 88
tie-ins, 158
Time-Life, 155
Time Out, 180–1, 213
Time-Warner, 9, 11, 202
Times, The, 2, 26, 62, 79, 225
Titanic, 5, 179, 209–10
title sequence: Coronation Street, 100–2; Neighbours, 103–5; role, 97; Taxi Driver, 105–7
TiVo, 13, 197
Today, 256
Todorov, Tzvetan, 46
Top Gear, 124
Top of the Pops, 115, 158
Top Santé, 156
Top Shop, 151, 152
trailers, 52, 76
Travel, 111
Travolta, John, 16
Tribe, 30, 31, 32, 33, 35, 37, 38, 39, 40
TriStar, 175
TV Hits, 158
Twentieth Century Fox, 179
Twin Peaks, 15

UCI, see United Cinemas International
United Cinemas International (UCI), 178
Universal Vivendi, 202, 203
Uses and Gratification Theory, 133–4, 148
Utopian solution, 140

Vanessa, 132
Vanity Fair, 155, 239
vertical integration, 178–80
vested interests, 183
Viacom, 172
video, 112, 114, 135, 263; music, 72, 267; nasties, 142; television series, 79
Video Nation, 139
Video Recording Act (1984), 142, 189
Vietnam War, 105
Virgin, 218; Radio, 11
Vivendi, 202, 203
Viz, 155
Vogue, 155

voice-over, 51
vulnerability, 10

Walt Disney Corporation, 9, 16, 182; Disney Channel, 111, 182; Disneyland, 182; Epcot Center, 182; Euro-Disney, 182
WAP telephones, see telephones
War of the Worlds, The, 57, 132
Warehouse, 152
Warner Brothers, 171, 175, 178
Watson, Paul, 139
Weakest Link, The, 79
Wedding in the Family, A, 139
Welles, Orson, 132
Wells, H. G., 132
West Side Story, 239, 240
What's My Line, 139
What's on TV, 148
Who Wants to Be a Millionaire?, 5
Wilder, Billy, 51
Williams, Raymond, 135
Wiltshire Times, The, 123, 124
Wireless Application Protocol (WAP) telephones, see telephones
Woman, 153
Woman's Own, 153, 157
Woman's Realm, 148
Woman's Weekly, 153
women, 69, 70, 84, 134, 140
Working Man's Friend, The, 62
Working Title, 211
World Cup, 111, 120
world time, 14

X Files, 78–9, 158
X-FM, 254

Yahoo, 24
Young Ones, The, 59
Youth culture, 68
You've Been Framed, 139
Yugoslavia, 17

Zee TV, 192
Zombie Flesh Eaters, 142